C000200002

REGISTER of
CLOSED
RAILWAYS
1948–1991

Geoffrey Hurst

1st Edition

ISBN 0-947796-18-5

Published by:Milepost Publications, 39 Kilton Glade, WORKSOP, Notts.

Printed by:BDC Printing Services Ltd., Slack Lane, DERBY DE3 3FL (Inside)
          :Ryton Typing Services, Ryton Street, WORKSOP, Notts. (Covers)

Introduction

This book lists in chronological order, the known closure dates of British Railways passenger and goods lines from 1st January 1948 to 31st December 1991, as well as the dates of withdrawal of regular and most seasonal passenger services. Temporary closures are not dealt with in this book, and neither are the closure dates of Passenger and Goods Stations, which is covered by - "C.R.Clinker's Register of Closed Passenger Stations and Goods Depots 1830-1977", published by Avon-Anglia.

As this is the first edition, the compiler and publishers have made every effort to locate typesetting errors, however if you find any errors or omissions we will be glad to hear from you. It is hoped to update and correct this book with a supplement six months after publication, for details please write with a stamped addressed envelope to the publishers. The address is given on the title page.

It was hoped to include closures in Ireland and Northern Ireland over the same period, however due to lack of space this section has been ommitted.

This book is divided into three parts, 1. The Closure Dates, 2. Notes (extra information) and 3. Index.

The first part lists the withdrawals of passenger services as well as total closures to either passenger or goods.

Each page has 5 columns and are explained as follows -:

Column 1 *Date*

This book follows the Clinker principle, that the date given is *normally* the first Monday when services ceased to operate. In the case of passenger services the last day of operation may have been a Friday (rare), a Saturday or a Sunday. Closure to goods is normally given as a Monday, but exceptions do occur. Goods usually last ran on either the Friday or Saturday morning before closure.

In some cases the actual date is not known, however a footnote next to the date gives the following extra information.

[1] The day on which the *Last Train* ran or is known to have operated. For a passenger service with P*, the last train most likely ran on a Saturday.

[2] *Regular Traffic Ceased* this note is used when traffic ceased to run regularly, but line was known not to have closed on that day, but at a latter unknown date.

[3] *Official Closure* A line may have lost its booked passenger service, but was not closed. After the 1962 Transport Act any line which is about to lose its passenger service should have a Section 56(7) closure notice. Followed by a local TUCC public enquiry, who then submits a report to the Minister of Transport for his/her decision. However in two recent cases - Wensum and Wortley curves, both lost its booked passenger service and without the appropriate notice. Great Yarmouth Council took BR to court and lost, yet Bradford Council won and BR was forced into a public enquiry. After the TUCC enquiry, the Minister of Transport approved the closure of Wortley curve for 16th May 1988 and this is the official closure date, even though the last train ran three years earlier.

Goods lines can close anytime, however if it is an official date, it usually indicates traffic had ceased and the line had been out of use for sometime.

[4] *Line Severed On* The line or points physically cut on this day. This is usually at the weekend.

[5] *Taken Out of Use* The day when the points were clamped out of use and could not be used for traffic. Usually traffic had ceased sometime before.

[6] *Permanent Closure* A line may have taken out of use because of a landslide or a flood, but the line was subsequently closed on this day.

[7] *Track Removed* The date of closure is not known and this date was when the line was removed.

[8] *Out of Use by ...* The date when the line was noted as not being used.

[9] *Colliery Closed On* The day or month shows when the colliery closed. Traffic may have ceased upon closure, but in most cases it will have continued for a short period using up stockpiles. In South Wales the colliery stockpile could take a couple of years to empty.

[10] *Mothballed* The line closed on this day, but was left insitu for possible future use, e.g. Millerhill Jn - Bilston Glen Colliery which closed on 05.06.1989, but subsequently reopened in May 1991 to remove coal to Cockenzie Power Station. Or for use in future reopening to passenger services e.g. Bestwood Park Jn - Linby Colliery as part of the proposed Nottingham - Mansfield - Worksop scheme.

Column 2 *Line*

In this column the section of line closed to all traffic or just passenger traffic are listed e.g.:-

KINGHAM - CHELTENHAM SPA (Malvern Road)[Lansdown Jn]
Bourton on the Water - Lansdown Jn

Passenger services between passenger stations are always shown in capitals, the odd curve is in lower case. The example shows that passenger services were withdrawn between KINGHAM and CHELTENHAM SPA (Malvern Road), and passenger services ceased totally between Kingham and [Lansdown Jn]. Any location enclosed by [ ] shows that this section was closed to passenger traffic. The next line shows that ALL traffic had ceased between Bourton on the Water and Lansdown Jn. Lower case letters are used for goods lines.

In the case of multiple closures on one day, the closures are listed in order of region :- London Midland; Western; Southern; Eastern; North Eastern and Scottish. Anglia is normally placed before the Eastern Region lines.

BA	British Aerospace
BC	British Coal
CEGB	Central Electricity Generating Board
E.	East
ECC	English China Clay
EGB	Eastern Gas Board
EWS	Empty Wagon Siding
FLT	Freightliner Terminal
GF	Ground Frame
H.L.	High Level
ICI	Imperial Chemical Industries
Jn	Junction
LC	Level Crossing
L.L.	Low Level
LWS	Loaded Wagon Siding
MOA	Ministry of Agriculture
MOD	Ministry of Defence

MPD	Motive Power Depot
N.	North
NCB	National Coal Board
OT	Oil Terminal
OCDP	Open Cast Disposal Point
PDS	Public Delivery Siding
PS	Power Station
ROF	Royal Ordnance Factory
RNAD	Royal Navy Armaments Depot
S.	South
SB	Signal Box
S.F.	Shunting Frame
Sid.	Siding
SWGB	South Western Gas Board
USNS	United States Naval Stores
Yd	Yard
W.	West

Column 3 *Region (Company)*

Each line was administered by one or more regions, and every region has a code and are listed below.
In 1967 the North Eastern Region was merged with the Eastern Region. The Anglia region was formed from the old Liverpool Street and Norwich Divisions of the Eastern Region.

A	Anglia
E	Eastern
LM	London Midland
NE	North Eastern
S	Southern
Sc	Scottish
W	Western

Followed in brackets by the Pre Grouping company or if after 1922, the constructing company e.g. LMS (London Midland and Scottish Railway). The company codes are listed on the inside front and inside rear cover.

Column 4 *Type of Traffic*

The type of traffic to which the line is closed is shown by the following letters :-

P	Regular Passenger services
P*	Dated Passenger services
W(Un)	Workmans services normally unadvertised
G	Goods
E	Engineers Department
Ecs	Empty Coaching Stock
R	Parcels Traffic
T	Technical Department (Derby)
M	Military Traffic
(All)	Closed to All traffic

Column 5 *Reference Number*

Each line has a unique reference number from 0101-3516 and if it is followed by an *, a footnote in Part 2 and will list extra information on reopenings or other saliant facts.

Part 2 - *Notes*

In this part the dates of railtours (sorry the name has been missed out as space is at a premium), reopening dates to passenger and goods and other bits of information.

Part 3 - *Index*

The 14 page Index shows most locations listed in the first part. However where you have a city e.g. Birmingham all references to Birmingham New Street, Snow Hill and Central Goods are compiled together.

Acknowledgements

I would like the following people for the help and information they have supplied, without whom this book would have been impossible. :- British Rail, British Coal, National Railway Museum Library, Birmingham City Library, Nottinghamshire Libraries at Nottingham Central and Worksop. Peter Fox; Nicki Williamson; Glyn Waite; David Carter; David Gray; Andrew Greenwood; Peter Hall and Paul Griffin. And to the photographers :- J.L.Stevenson (courtesy of H.Stevenson); P.J.Lynch; Steve Turner; Brian Hilton; R.J.Buckley: R.C.Riley; and John Edgington.

Bibliography

The information in this book has been compiled from the following sources :- Railway Observers 1948 - 1983; Branch Line Newsletters/News 1955 - 1991; Railway Magazine; Modern Railways; Rail; Clinker's Register of Closed Stations and Goods Depots 1838 - 1977; Forgotten Railways Volume 1,2 and 9; Passengers No More; A Guide to Closed Railways 1948 - 1975; The Midland Railway around Notts Vol.1; Great Central East of Sheffield Vol.1: A Chronology of the Midland Railway and Todays Railways Review of the Year Volumes 1,2,3,and 4.

Date	Line	Region (Company)	Type of Traffic	Reference Number
00.02.1948 [3]	Mantle Lane East - Swannington (Foot of Incline)	LM(Mid)	G(All)	0101
31.05.1948	WOODFORD & HINTON - BYFIELD [Woodford West Jn]	E/LM(GCR/SMJ)	P	0102
00.07.1948	Sheffield No.1 - Wicker Goods	E/LM(GCR/Mid)	G(All)	0103
13.08.1948	Ilderton - Wooler	NE(NER)	G(All)	0104 *
13.08.1948	Greenlaw - Duns	Sc(NBR)	G(All)	0105
21.08.1948	Machynlleth Low Level - Aberllefeni	W(Corris)	G(All)	0106
21.08.1948	Escairgeiliog - Era Welsh Slate Quarries	W(Corris)	G(All)	0107
01.12.1948	North Crofty Jn - North Crofty Siding	W(GWR)	G(All)	0108
01.01.1949 [3]	Ellon - Boddam	Sc(GNoSR)	G(All)	0109
26.02.1949 [3]	LIVERPOOL (Lime St.) [Spellow (Bootle Jn)] - LIVERPOOL (Alexandra Dock)	LM(LNW)	P	0110
04.04.1949	Castlehill Jn (Chapel Sidings) - Carluke Goods	Sc(NBR)	G(All)	0111
10.04.1949	Bennerley Jn - Ilkeston West Jn	LM(Mid)	G(All)	0112
16.05.1949	Clynderwen Jn - Puncheston	W(GWR)	G(All)	0113
23.05.1949 [3]	STRATFORD UPON AVON - BROOM	LM(SMJ)	P	0114
02.07.1949 [6]	ST BOSWELL [Ravenswood Jn] - DUNS	Sc(NBR)	P	0115 *
04.07.1949	Cairn Valley Jn - Moniaive	Sc(GSW)	G(All)	0116
02.08.1949	Awre Jn - Blakeney Goods	W(GWR)	G(All)	0117
25.07.1949 [2]	Laymoor Jn - Bilson North Jn	W(SWJt)	G(All)	0118
01.09.1949	Arbuckle Arden Siding - Slamannan	Sc(NBR)	G(All)	0119
22.09.1949	Old Ynysybwl Halt - Mynachdy Colliery Siding	W(Taff)	G(All)	0120
26.09.1949	SUTTON JN - SUTTON IN ASHFIELD (General)	LM(Mid)	P	0121
27.10.1949 [2]	Eastry - Richborough Castle Siding	S(EKLR)	G(All)	0122
00.11.1949	Crawley Bank Top - Ashes Quarry	NE(NER)	G(All)	0123
07.11.1949	FENCHURCH STREET [Burdett Road Jn] - STRATFORD [Bow Jn]	E(GER)	P	0124
15.11.1949	Auchincruive Collieries - Mossblown Jn	Sc(GSW)	G(All)	0125
15.11.1949	Monkton Jn - Jn of new spur from Prestwick	Sc(GSW)	G(All)	0126
11.12.1949	New Lount Colliery EWS - Ashby (Holywell Mill)	LM(Mid)	G(All)	0127 *
01.01.1950 [3]	Eastry - Richborough Castle Siding	S(EKLR)	G(All)	0128
02.01.1950	Dorstone - Hay	W(GWR)	G(All)	0129
06.02.1950	STRANRAER (Town) - PORTPATRICK	Sc(P&WJt)	P	0130
06.02.1950	Colfin - Portpatrick	Sc(P&WJt)	G(All)	0131
06.03.1950	Blackhall Jn - Shotts East	Sc(NBR)	G(All)	0132
27.03.1950	MOLD [Tryddyn Jn] - BRYMBO	LM(W&MJt)	P	0133
27.03.1950	Coed Talon (Star Quarry Siding) - Ffrith (Bwlchgwyn Siding)	LM(W&MJt)	G(All)	0134
31.03.1950	Clay Cross & Egstow - Ashover	Ashover	G(All)	0135
03.04.1950	Holland Arms - Red Wharf Bay & Benllech	LM(LNW)	G(All)	0136
03.04.1950	BEDLINGTON - MORPETH	NE(NER)	P	0137
03.04.1950	HOLEHOUSE - OCHILTREE [Belston Jn]	Sc(GSW)	P	0138
03.04.1950	Rankinston (Littlemill Colliery) - Holehouse Jn	Sc(GSW)	G(All)	0139
31.05.1950	Lugton East Jn - Giffen	Sc(Cal)	G(All)	0140
05.06.1950	PICKERING - SEAMER	NE(NER)	P	0141
05.06.1950	Thornton Dale - Seamer Jn	NE(NER)	G(All)	0142
05.06.1950	DRIFFIELD - MALTON	NE(NER)	P	0143
05.06.1950	FALLSIDE [Bothwell Jn] - BOTHWELL (LMS)	Sc(Cal)	P(All)	0144
05.06.1950	LADYBANK - MAWCAWSE	Sc(NBR)	P	0145
05.06.1950	SYMINGTON - PEEBLES	Sc(Cal)	P	0146
03.07.1950	Merrybent - Merrybank Quarries	NE(NER)	G(All)	0147
03.07.1950	AUCHINLECK - CRONBERRY	Sc(GSW)	P	0148
25.07.1950 [2]	Eastry - Wingham Canterbury Road	S(EKLR)	G(All)	0149 *

Date	Line	Region (Company)	Type of Traffic	Reference Number
12.08.1950 [5]	Celtic Halt - Pontyrhyll Jn	W(PTR)	G(All)	0150
01.09.1950	Dunmore Jn - South Alloa	Sc(Cal)	G(All)	0151
25.09.1950	SWANSEA (St.Thomas) - BRYNAMMAN (East)	W(Mid)	P	0152
25.09.1950	Swansea Harbour Branch Sidings - Swansea St.Thomas	W(Mid)	G(All)	0153
25.09.1950	Glais Jn - Clydach on Tawe South (Mond Nickel)	W(Mid)	G(All)	0154
25.09.1950	KNARESBOROUGH [Jn] - PILMOOR	NE(NER)	P	0155
25.09.1950	Brafferton (RAF Siding) - Pilmoor	NE(NER)	G(All)	0156
00.10.1950	Albert Dock Jn - Gallions	PLA	G(All)	0157
16.10.1950	Hartwoodhill Siding - Fortisset Mains Siding	Sc(NBR)	G(All)	0158
30.10.1950	Darwen (Shaw's Siding) - Hoddlesden	LM(L&Y)	G(All)	0159
00.11.1950	Plymouth Friary A - Sutton Harbour North Quay	S(LSW)	G(All)	0160
01.11.1950	Wrington - Blagdon	W(GWR)	G(All)	0161
01.11.1950	Buchlyvie - Mye Siding	Sc(NBR)	G(All)	0162
01.11.1950	Dolphinton Jn - Dolphinton	Sc(Cal)	G(All)	0163
01.11.1950	Gartness Jn - Dryman	Sc(NBR)	G(All)	0164
13.11.1950	Pilling - Knott End	LM(GKER)	G(All)	0165
20.11.1950	Hexham - Allendale	NE(NER)	G(All)	0166
04.12.1950	QUEENBOROUGH - LEYSDOWN	S(SEC)	P(All)	0167
18.12.1950	Middlestown Jn - Dewsbury Savile Town	LM(Mid)	G(All)	0168
31.12.1950 [5]	Laymoor Jn - Cinderford Jn	W(SWJt)	G(All)	0169
31.12.1950 [5]	Serridge Jn - Drybrook Road	W(SWJt)	G(All)	0170
00.00.1951 [7]	Shirebrook Jn - Langwith East Jn	E(Mid)	G(All)	0171 *
15.01.1951	OSWESTRY [Llynclys Jn] - LLANGYNOG	W(Cam)	P	0172
03.02.1951	BEAUFORT - EBBW VALE HL	W(LNW)	P	0173
05.02.1951	KINGTON - NEW RADNOR	W(GWR)	P	0174
05.02.1951	SHREWSBURY [Cruckmeole Jn] - MINSTERLEY	W(S&WJt)	P	0175
05.02.1951	Morningside Jn - Newmains	Sc(Cal)	G(All)	0176
12.02.1951	LAMPETER [Aberayron Jn] - ABERAYRON	W(GWR)	P	0177
12.02.1951	MERTHYR [Rhydycar Jn] - QUAKERS YARD H.L.	W(QYMJt)	P	0178
12.02.1951	Merthyr Vale Jn - Merthyr Vale Colliery	W(QYMJt)	G(All)	0179
12.02.1951	NEWBURGH [Glenburnie Jn] - ST FORT	Sc(NBR)	P	0180
15.02.1951	Limpley Stoke - Camerton	W(GWR)	G(All)	0181 *
01.03.1951	Bearley North Jn - Alcester	W(GWR)	G(All)	0182
01.03.1951	Eythorne - Eastry	S(EKLR)	G(All)	0183
01.03.1951 [2]	Eastry - Wingham Canterbury Road	S(EKLR)	G(All)	0184 *
05.03.1951	Bromshall Jn - Stafford Common Air Ministry (16MU) Sids.	LM(GNR)	G(All)	0185 *
13.03.1951	Pillowell Siding - Acorn Patch GF	W(SWJt)	G(All)	0186
26.03.1951	Fodderty Jn - Strathpeffer	Sc(High)	G(All)	0187
00.04.1951	Gatehead Fairlie Branch Jn - Caprington Collieries	Sc(GSW)	G(All)	0188
02.04.1951	HARROGATE [Ripley Valley Jn] - PATELEY BRIDGE	NE(NER)	P	0189
02.04.1951	JORDANHILL [West] - WHITEINCH (Victoria Park)	Sc(NBR)	P	0190
02.04.1951	MARYHILL [Kelvin Valley East Jn] - KILSYTH	Sc(NBR)	P	0191
14.04.1951 [1]	Stepney East - Limehouse Jn	E(GER)	G(All)	0192 *
17.04.1951	Kipps Incline Foot - Thrushbush Quarry	Sc(NBR)	G(All)	0193
28.04.1951	Weatherhill - Stanhope Kilns Depot	NE(NER)	G(All)	0194
07.05.1951	KELVEDON - TOLLESBURY	E(GER)	P	0195
07.05.1951	EDINBURGH (Princes Street) [Craigleith] - BARNTON	Sc(Cal)	P	0196
07.05.1951	Davidson's Mains Depot - Barnton	Sc(Cal)	G(All)	0197
00.06.1951	Tonteg Jn - Pontypridd Pwllgwaun	W(Barry)	G(All)	0198
03.06.1951	Sutton Oak Fleet Lane - Havannah Colliery	LM(LNW)	G(All)	0199
04.06.1951	BANBURY - CHIPPING NORTON	W(GWR)	P	0200
04.06.1951	TITLEY - PRESTEIGN	W(GWR)	P	0201
07.06.1951	Gask Jn - Lethans No.2 Colliery	Sc(NBR)	G(All)	0202

Date	Line	Region (Company)	Type of Traffic	Reference Number
11.06.1951	GRAIN CROSSING Halt - PORT VICTORIA	S(SEC)	P(All)	0203 *
18.06.1951	ST HELENS (Shaw Street) [Sutton Oak Jn] - WIDNES [St Helens Jn]	LM(LNW)	P	0204
18.06.1951	ST HELENS (Shaw Street) [Gerards Bridge Jn] - RAINFORD JN	LM(LNW)	P	0205
18.06.1951	WELWYN GARDEN CITY - HERTFORD NORTH	E(GNR)	P	0206
18.06.1951	BOURNE [West Jn] - ESSENDINE	E(GNR)	P(All)	0207
26.06.1951	Pannal Jn - Starbeck (Stonefall Sidings)	NE(NER)	G(All)	0208
01.07.1951	Pwllyrhebog - Cambrian Colliery	W(Taff)	G(All)	0209
01.07.1951 3	Cemmes Road - Dinas Mawddwy	W(Cam)	G(All)	0210 *
02.07.1951	BLISWORTH [Towcester] - BANBURY (Merton Street) [Cockley Brake]	LM(SMJ/LNW)	P	0211
02.07.1951	FELIXSTOWE (Beach) - FELIXSTOWE (Pier)	E(GER)	P	0212
02.07.1951	ALYTH JN - ALYTH	Sc(Cal)	P	0213
01.08.1951	Daybrook Jn GF - Thorneywood	E(GNR)	G(All)	0214
06.08.1951	Forncett - Wymondham	E(GER)	G(All)	0215
06.08.1951	Banavie Jn GF - Banavie Pier	Sc(NBR)	G(All)	0216 *
06.08.1951	KIRKINTILLOCH [Kelvin Valley West Jn] - KILSYTH	Sc(NBR)	P	0217
01.09.1951	Heanor Goods Jn - Heanor North	LM(Mid)	G(All)	0218
03.09.1951	STOKE JN - GRAIN CROSSING Halt	S(SEC)	P	0219
04.09.1951	Hallcraig Jn - Hallcraig Brickworks	Sc(Cal)	G(All)	0220
10.09.1951	Bigrigg Branch Token Hut - Bigrigg Mine (Clint's Pit)	LM(WCEJt)	G(All)	0221
10.09.1951	KINGTON - NEW RADNOR	W(GWR)	P	0222
10.09.1951	LAMPETER [Aberayron Jn] - ABERAYRON	W(GWR)	P	0223
10.09.1951	LITTLE SOMERFORD - MALMESBURY	W(GWR)	P	0224
10.09.1951	TITLEY - PRESTEIGN	W(GWR)	P	0225
10.09.1951	PLYMOUTH (Friary) - TURNCHAPEL	S(LSW)	P	0226
10.09.1951	Saltburn West Jn - BROTTON	NE(NER)	P	0227
10.09.1951	WAKEFIELD (Kirkgate) [Crofton West Jn] - EDLINGTON	NE(L&Y/DVR)	P	0228
10.09.1951	AYR [Annbank Jn] - MUIRKIRK [Cronberry]	Sc(GSWR)	P	0229
10.09.1951	AUCHENGRAY [Wilsontown South Jn] - WILSONTOWN	Sc(Cal)	P	0230
10.09.1951	BLAIRHILL & GARTSHERRIE [Sunnyside] - BOTHWELL	Sc(NBR)	P	0231
10.09.1951	ESKBANK [Esk Valley Jn] - POLTON	Sc(NBR)	P	0232
10.09.1951	GALASHIELS - SELKIRK	Sc(NBR)	P	0233
10.09.1951	RESTON - DUNS	Sc(NBR)	P	0234
10.09.1951	ROSEWELL & HAWTHORNDEN - PENICUIK	Sc(NBR)	P	0235
00.10.1951 5	Canterbury A Jn - Canterbury B Jn	S(SR)	G(All)	0236 *
01.10.1951	Oxford North Jn - OXFORD (Rewley Road)	LM(LNW)	P	0237
01.10.1951	SUTTON JN - SUTTON IN ASHFIELD (General)	LM(Mid)	W(All)	0238
01.10.1951	HATFIELD - St ALBANS (London Road)	E(GNR)	P	0239
01.10.1951	West Halton - Whitton	E(GCR)	G(All)	0240
01.10.1951	Grosmont Deviation Jn - Esk Valley	NE(NER)	G(All)	0241
01.10.1951	COMRIE - BALQUHIDDER	Sc(Cal)	P	0242
01.10.1951	HAMILTON [Ferniegair Jn] - BROCKETSBRAE	Sc(Cal)	P	0243
01.10.1951	KIRKINTILLOCH - ABERFOYLE	Sc(NBR)	P	0244
01.10.1951	INVERAMSEY - MACDUFF	Sc(GNoSR)	P	0245
01.10.1951	MONTROSE [Broomfield Jn] - INVERBERVIE	Sc(NBR)	P	0246
01.10.1951	MUIR OF ORD - FORTROSE	Sc(High)	P	0247
01.10.1951	PERTH - CRIEFF	Sc(Cal)	P	0248
29.10.1951	Towcester - Cockley Brake Jn	LM(SMJ)	G(All)	0249
29.10.1951	GLASTONBURY & STREET - WELLS (Priory Road)	W(S&DJt)	P(All)	0250
29.10.1951	HIGHBRIDGE - BURNHAM ON SEA	S(S&DJt)	P	0251
29.10.1951	Tudwick Road Siding - Tollesbury	E(GER)	G(All)	0252
29.10.1951	BATLEY - BEESTON	E(GNR)	P	0253
29.10.1951	CHATHILL - SEAHOUSES	NE(NSLt)	P(All)	0254
29.10.1951	DURHAM [Reilly Mill Jn] - WATERHOUSES	NE(NER)	P	0255
00.11.1951 5	Winchester Jn - Worthy Down	W(GWR)	G(All)	0256 *
05.11.1951	LOUTH [Wragby Jn] - BARDNEY	E(GNR)	P	0257

Date	Line	Region (Company)	Type of Traffic	Reference Number
20.11.1951	Cocking - Midhurst	S(LBSC)	G(All)	0258 *
26.11.1951	LLANTRISANT [Cowbridge Jn] - COWBRIDGE	W(Taff)	P	0259
01.12.1951	BANGOR - BETHSEDA	LM(LNW)	P	0260
03.12.1951	SANDLING JN - HYTHE	S(SER)	P(All)	0261
03.12.1951	CHESTERFIELD (Market Place) - SHIREBROOK (North)	E(GCR)	P	0262
03.12.1951	Markham Jn - Shirebrook North	E(GCR)	G(All)	0263
09.12.1951 [3]	Serridge Jn - Cinderford Jn	W(SWJt)	G(All)	0264 *
10.12.1951	Almond Jn - Craigend Colliery Siding	Sc(NBR)	G(All)	0265
31.12.1951	Dolyhir - New Radnor	W(GWR)	G(All)	0266
31.12.1951	CRAVEN ARMS [Marsh Farm Jn] - MUCH WENLOCK	W(GWR)	P	0267
31.12.1951	Marsh Farm Jn - Longville	W(GWR)	G(All)	0268
31.12.1951	UFFINGTON - FARINGDON	W(GWR)	P	0269
00.00.1952?	Greenodd Jn - Levens Jn	LM(Furn)	G(All)	0270
00.01.1952 [7]	Dungeness Jn GF - Dungeness	S(SER)	G(All)	0271 *
01.01.1952	Shepherds - Treamble	W(GWR)	G(All)	0272 *
21.01.1952	Butts Lane Jn - Hillhouse Jn	LM(L&Y)	G(All)	0273
06.02.1952	WELLINGTON - COALPORT (East)	W(LNW)	P	0274
03.03.1952	LOWTON ST MARYS - ST HELENS (Central)	LM(GCR)	P	0275
03.03.1952	WATFORD (High Street) [Croxley Green Jn] - RICKMANSWORTH (Church Street)	LM(LNW)	P	0276
03.03.1952	BISHOPS STORTFORD - BRAINTREE	E(GER)	P	0277
03.03.1952	WEYMOUTH [Jn] - EASTON	S(PWJt)	P	0278
03.03.1952	CORYTON - CORRINGHAM	CorrRly	P(All)	0279
15.03.1952	SCOTSGAP - REEDSMOUTH	NE(NBR)	P	0280
30.03.1952	Ardler Jn - Nethermill Jn	Sc(Cal)	G(All)	0281
31.03.1952	LLANTRISANT [Mwyndy Jn] - PONTYPRIDD [Tonteg Jn]	W(GW/Taff)	P	0282
31.03.1952	FERRYHILL [Coxhoe Jn] - SPENNYMOOR	NE(NER)	P	0283
31.03.1952	STOCKTON ON TEES [Norton South Jn] - FERRYHILL	NE(NER)	P	0284
31.03.1952	Dykehead Branch Jn - Dykehead	Sc(NBR)	G(All)	0285
07.04.1952	BLISWORTH - STRATFORD UPON AVON (Old Town)	LM(SMJ)	P	0286
07.04.1952	EDINBURGH (Waverley) [Abbeyhill Jn] - LEITH (Central)	Sc(NBR)	P	0287
10.04.1952	Whaley Bridge Shallcross Branch Jn - Canal Basin (Bingswood Works Siding)	LM(LNW)	G(All)	0288
05.05.1952	BURY (Bolton Street) [Tottington Jn] - HOLCOMBE BROOK	LM(L&Y)	P	0289
19.05.1952	DUMFRIES - LOCKERBIE	Sc(Cal)	P	0290
06.06.1952	HEACHAM - WELLS ON SEA	E(GER)	P	0291
07.06.1952	WEST HARTLEPOOL [Hart Jn] - FERRYHILL [Coxhoe Jn]	NE(NER)	P	0292
16.06.1952	Coryton Halt - Nantgawr New Spur Jn	W(Card)	G(All)	0293 *
30.06.1952	Launceston 1943 Spur Jn - LAUNCESTON (North)	W(GWR)	P	0294
30.06.1952	PANT - DOWLAIS (Central)	W(B&M)	P	0295
30.06.1952	SALISBURY [Amesbury Jn] - BULFORD	S(LSW)	P	0296
30.06.1952	GRATELEY - NEWTON TONY	S(LSW)	P	0297
30.06.1952	Amesbury Jn - Newton Tony Jn	S(LSW)	G(All)	0298
01.07.1952	Llanrhaiadr Mochnant - Llangynog	W(Cam)	G(All)	0299
01.07.1952	Aberllefeni - Ratgoed	Corris	G(All)	0300 *
07.07.1952	AINTREE (Central) - SOUTHPORT (Lord St)	LM(CLC)	P	0301
07.07.1952	Altcar & Hillhouse - Southport (Lord St)	LM(CLC)	G(All)	0302
21.07.1952	BROOKWOOD - BISLEY CAMP	S(LSW)	P*(All)	0303
28.07.1952	PONTYPRIDD [Clydach Court Jn] - OLD YNYSYBWL Halt	W(Taff)	P	0304
28.07.1952	ABERCYNON [Stormstown Jn] - OLD YNYSYBWL Halt	W(Taff)	P	0305
28.07.1952	Clydach Court Jn - Windsor Passing Siding	W(Taff)	G(All)	0306
28.07.1952	Windsor Passing Siding - Old Ynysybwl Halt	W(Taff)	G(All)	0307
28.07.1952	HAUGHLEY - LAXFIELD	E(MSL)	P(All)	0308
04.08.1952	BRIDGE OF DUN - BRECHIN	Sc(Cal)	P	0309
04.08.1952	BRECHIN - FORFAR	Sc(Cal)	P	0310

Date	Line	Region (Company)	Type of Traffic	Reference Number
04.08.1952	DUBTON JN - MONTROSE	Sc(Cal/NBR)	P	0311
04.08.1952	FORFAR - KIRRIEMUIR	Sc(Cal)	P	0312
04.08.1952 [3]	Anchor Pit Jn - Wyke Jn	LM(L&Y)	G(All)	0313
15.09.1952	BROMYARD - LEOMINSTER	W(GWR)	P(All)	0314 *
15.09.1952	PENCADER [Jn] - NEWCASTLE EMLYN	W(GWR)	P	0315
15.09.1952	MERSTONE - VENTNOR (West)	S(IWCR)	P(All)	0316
15.09.1952	Brinsley Jn - Great Northern Jn	E(GNR)	G(All)	0317
15.09.1952	COUNTY SCHOOL - WROXHAM	E(GNR)	P	0318
15.09.1952	MORPETH - ROTHBURY	NE(NBR)	P	0319
15.09.1952	BOTHWELL - HAMILTON	Sc(NBR)	P	0320
15.09.1952	Bothwell - Blantyre Jn	Sc(NBR)	G(All)	0321 *
15.09.1952	Peacock Cross (Allanshaw) - Hamilton	Sc(NBR)	G(All)	0322
24.09.1952	Calverton Branch Jn - Papplewick Jn	E(RE)	G(All)	0323 *
06.10.1952	HOLMES - ROTHERHAM (Westgate)	LM(Mid)	P	0324
06.10.1952	Holmes Jn (Booth's Sidings) - Rotherham Westgate	LM(Mid)	G(All)	0325
28.10.1952	Wells on Sea - Wells Harbour	E(GER)	G(All)	0326
01.12.1952	Aspatria - Mealsgate	LM(MCR)	G(All)	0327
01.12.1952	EDLINGTON JN - BRIDGWATER (North)	S(S&DJt)	P	0328
01.12.1952	UPTON ON SEVERN - GREAT MALVERN	LM(Mid/GWR)	P	0329
01.12.1952	Upton on Severn - Malvern (New Midland Sidings)	LM(Mid)	G(All)	0330
01.12.1952	UPWEY - ABBOTSBURY	W(GWR)	P(All)	0331
01.12.1952	Canterbury West - Whitstable Harbour	S(SEC)	G(All)	0332 *
01.12.1952	Port of Menteith - Mye Siding	Sc(NBR)	G(All)	0333
03.12.1952	WICKHAM MARKET - FRAMLINGHAM	E(GER)	P	0334
03.12.1952	KIRKBY STEPHEN (East) - TEBAY	NE(NER)	P	0335
01.01.1953 [2]	Upper Lydbrook - Lydbrook Jn	W(SWJt)	G(All)	0336
05.01.1953	SUNDERLAND [Ryhope Grange Jn] - PITTINGTON	NE(NER)	P	0337
00.02.1953	Whimsey Goods - Drybrook Quarries Siding	W(GWR)	G(All)	0338
02.02.1953	CHEDDINGTON - AYLESBURY (High Street)	LM(LNW)	P	0339
02.02.1953	Abbeydore - Dorstone	W(GWR)	G(All)	0340
02.02.1953	GILLING - PICKERING [Mill Lane]	NE(NER)	P	0341
02.02.1953	Kirby Moorside - Pickering Mill Lane	NE(NER)	G(All)	0342
02.02.1953	YORK [Pilmoor South Jn] - GILLING	NE(NER)	P	0343
12.02.1953	Ripponden & Barkisland - Rishworth	LM(L&Y)	G(All)	0344
21.02.1953	Workington (Derwent Jn) - Prince of Wales Dock	LM(LNW)	G(All)	0345
02.03.1953	Canterbury West - Whitstable Harbour	S(SEC)	G(All)	0346
02.03.1953	Alnwick - Ilderton	NE(NER)	G(All)	0347
30.03.1953	Giffen - Lissens Goods	Sc(Cal)	G(All)	0348
31.03.1953	Burnham Market - Wells on Sea	E(GER)	G(All)	0349
01.04.1953	Woodham Ferrers - Maldon West	E(GER)	G(All)	0350
07.04.1953	Patricroft Jn - Clifton Hall No.1	LM(LNW)	G(All)	0351
07.04.1953	MUNDESLEY ON SEA - CROMER BEACH [Roughton Road Jn]	E(NSJt)	P(All)	0352
20.05.1953 [2]	Canterbury A Jn - Canterbury B Jn	S(SR)	G(All)	0353
01.06.1953	Widnes (Moor Lane) - Broughton Copper Works Sidings	LM(GC&MidJt)	G(All)	0354
01.06.1953	Elsenham - Thaxted	E(GER)	G(All)	0355
08.06.1953	FAREHAM - GOSPORT	S(LBSC)	P	0356
16.06.1953 [1]	Drybrook Road - Acorn Patch WD Sidings	W(SWJt)	G(All)	0357
16.06.1953 [1]	Bilson South Jn - Drybrook Road	W(SWJt)	G(All)	0358
29.06.1953	BISHOP AUCKLAND [Wear Valley Jn] - WEARHEAD	NE(NER)	P	0359
06.07.1953	Beeston Jn - Tingley	E(GNR)	G(All)	0360
06.07.1953	Woodkirk - Batley	E(GNR)	G(All)	0361
03.08.1953	FARNINGHAM ROAD [Fawkham Jn] - GRAVESEND WEST	S(SEC)	P	0362
31.08.1953	CHICHESTER [Fishbourne Crossing] - MIDHURST	S(LBSC)	P	0363

Date	Line	Region (Company)	Type of Traffic	Reference Number
31.08.1953	Lavant - Cocking	S(LBSC)	G(All)	0364
21.09.1953	BRADLEY FOLD [Jn] - RADCLIFFE (Central)	LM(L&Y)	P	0365
21.09.1953	BRADING - BEMBRIDGE	S(IWR)	P(All)	0366
21.09.1953	NEWPORT - FRESHWATER	S(FYN)	P(All)	0367
21.09.1953	BURRY PORT - CWMMAWR	W(BPGV)	P	0368
21.09.1953	RHYMNEY - RHYMNEY BRIDGE	W(NRJt)	P(All)	0369 *
21.09.1953	LAWRENCE HILL - BRISTOL (St Philips)	W(Mid)	P	0370
21.09.1953	YARMOUTH (Beach) [Lowestoft Line Jn] - GORLESTON NORTH	E(NSJt)	P	0371
21.09.1953	Southfield Jn - Alton Heights Jn	Sc(Cal)	G(All)	0372
21.09.1953	High Blantyre - Strathaven North Goods	Sc(Cal)	G(All)	0373
21.09.1953	Whiteshawgate Jn - Strathaven Central	Sc(Cal)	G(All)	0374
00.10.1953 [7]	Jamage Jn - Jamage Colliery	W(NRJt)	G(All)	0375
12.10.1953 [8]	Kingham East Jn - Kingham West Jn	W(GWR)	G(All)	0376 *
23.11.1953	Lighthouse - Whitburn Colliery	SSM	G(All)	0377
07.12.1953	BARNSLEY (Exchange) [New Oaks Jn] - SHEFFIELD (Victoria) [Tinsley Station Jn]	E(GCR)	P	0378
07.12.1953	GRANTHAM [Bottesford East Jn] - LEICESTER (Belgrave Road)	E(GN&LNWJt)	P	0379
07.12.1953	NOTTINGHAM (Victoria) [Bottesford West] - MARKET HARBOROUGH [Welham Jn]	E(GN&LNWJt)	P	0380
07.12.1953	NEWARK (Northgate) - MARKET HARBOROUGH [Bottesford South Jn]	E(GNR)	P	0381
04.01.1954	PORTISHEAD (New) - PORTISHEAD (Old)	W(GWR)	P(All)	0382
04.01.1954	HEADCORN - ROBERTSBRIDGE	S(KESL)	P	0383
04.01.1954	Headcorn - Tenterden Town	S(KESL)	G(All)	0384
11.01.1954	Broomside - Durham Elvet	NE(NER)	G(All)	0385
01.02.1954	Basford Jn - Kimberley West	LM(Mid)	G(All)	0386
01.02.1954	BOLTON (Great Moor Street) - KENYON JN [Pennington South Jn]	LM(LNW)	P	0387
01.02.1954	BOLTON (Great Moor Street) - WORSLEY [Rose Green Jn]	LM(LNW)	P	0388
01.02.1954	CLAPHAM (Yorks) - LOW GILL	LM(Mid/LNW)	P	0389
01.02.1954	Watnall Jn GF - Watnall Colliery	LM(Mid)	G(All)	0390
01.02.1954	NEWCASTLE UPON TYNE [Scotswood Jn] - BLACKHILL	NE(NER)	P	0391
01.03.1954	KIDLINGTON - BLENHEIM & WOODSTOCK	W(GWR)	P(All)	0392
23.03.1954	Looe Goods - Looe Quarry Sidings	W(GWR)	G(All)	0393
26.04.1954	NORTHALLERTON [Castle Hills South Jn] - HAWES	NE(NER)	P	0394
03.05.1954	Cleator Moor Jn - Birks Bridge Jn	LM(WCEJt)	G(All)	0395
03.05.1954 [2]	Marron Jn - Rowrah	LM(WCEJt)	G(All)	0396
03.05.1954	LOCHLUICHART deviation	Sc(High)	P(All)	0397
09.05.1954	Margam Forge - Oakwood GF	W(PTR)	G(All)	0398
31.05.1954	Marehay Jn - Ripley Old Yard	LM(Mid)	G(All)	0399
31.05.1954	Moorhouse & South Elmsall - Hickleton & Thurnscoe	NE(HBR)	G(All)	0400
07.06.1954	Broughton - Peebles West	Sc(Cal)	G(All)	0401
14.06.1954	DUNFORD BRIDGE - WOODHEAD (old tunnels)	E(GCR)	P(All)	0402
14.06.1954	BATTERSBY - PICTON	NE(NER)	P	0403
14.06.1954	BILLINGHAM ON TEES - HAVERTON HILL	NE(NER)	P	0404
23.06.1954	Blaenavon (Furnace Siding) - Brynmawr No.1	W(LNW)	G(All)	0405
05.07.1954	CHESTERFIELD (Midland) [Tapton Jn] - ELMTON & CRESWELL	LM(Mid)	P	0406
05.07.1954	FINSBURY PARK - ALEXANDRA PALACE	E(GNR)	P	0407
05.07.1954	Muswell Hill - Alexandra Palace	E(GNR)	G(All)	0408
02.08.1954	Old Harpur (SMRE Siding) - Ladmanlow	LM(LNW)	G(All)	0409
02.08.1954	Ponteland - Darras Hall	NE(NER)	G(All)	0410
01.09.1954	Maldon East & Heybridge - Maldon West	E(GER)	G(All)	0411 *
06.09.1954	HOLYWELL JN - HOLYWELL TOWN	LM(LNW)	P	0412
06.09.1954	Crescent Siding - Holywell Town	LM(LNW)	G(All)	0413
06.09.1954	FARNINGHAM ROAD [Fawkham Jn] - GRAVESEND (West)	S(SEC)	P	0414
06.09.1954	Meilkeriggs Jn - Meilkeriggs Goods	Sc(Cal)	G(All)	0415
13.09.1954	WOODHALL JN - HORNCASTLE	E(GNR)	P	0416

Date	Line	Region (Company)	Type of Traffic	Reference Number
13.09.1954	Rockingham Colliery EWS - Birdwell & Pilley Wharf	LM(Mid)	G(All)	0417
13.09.1954	Alton Heights Jn - Poniel Jn	Sc(Cal)	G(All)	0418
20.09.1954	LONDON BRIDGE [Nunhead] - CRYSTAL PALACE H.L.	S(SEC)	P	0419
20.09.1954	Newstead Lane Jn - Runton West Jn	E(NSJt)	P	0420
20.09.1954	NORWICH (Thorpe) [Cromer Jn] - CROMER (High)	E(GER)	P	0421
04.10.1954	Edington Jn - Bridgwater North (Board's Siding)	S(S&DJt)	G(All)	0422 *
04.10.1954	Rosyth Naval Base Jn - North Queensferry Goods	Sc(NBR)	G(All)	0423
11.10.1954	Facit - Bacup Engine Shed	LM(L&Y)	G(All)	0424
25.10.1954	Gardden Lodge (Ruabon Brick & Terracotta) - Aberderfyn Goods	W(GWR)	G(All)	0425
01.11.1954	BUXTON (No.1) - UTTOXTER [Rocester]	LM(LNW)	P	0426
01.11.1954 [7]	Quakers Yard H.L. - Lucy Thomas Colliery	W(QYMJt)	G(All)	0427
22.11.1954 [2]	Dowlais No.1 (Ivor Jn) - Penywern Jn	LM(LNW)	G(All)	0428
30.11.1954	Gatewen Colliery Siding - Plas Power	LM(GCR)	G(All)	0429
06.12.1954	BEATTOCK - MOFFAT	Sc(Cal)	P	0430
06.12.1954	Rigghead Coup - Greengairs Goods	Sc(NBR)	G(All)	0431
16.12.1954	Leek Brook Jn - Cheddleton NSM Hospital	NSMHRly	G(All)	0432
00.01.1955 [7]	Tongham - Farnham Jn	S(LSW)	G(All)	0433
08.01.1955	THORNTON JN - METHIL	Sc(NBR)	P	0434
10.01.1955	DUNDEE (West) [Ninewells Jn] - ALYTH JN	Sc(Cal)	P	0435
10.01.1955	COUPAR ANGUS - BLAIRGOWRIE	Sc(Cal)	P	0436
10.01.1955	DUNDEE (East) [Broughty Jn] - FORFAR [North Jn]	Sc(Cal)	P	0437
10.01.1955	THORNTON JN - METHIL	Sc(NBR)	P	0438
07.02.1955	Petersfield - Midhurst Goods	S(LSW)	G(All)	0439
07.02.1955	ALTON [Butts Jn] - FAREHAM [Knowle Jn]	S(LSW)	P	0440
07.02.1955	Droxford - Farringdon	S(LSW)	G(All)	0441
07.02.1955	Reepham (Norfolk) - Foulsham	E(GER)	G(All)	0442 *
07.02.1955	LEOMINSTER [Kington Jn] - KINGTON	W(GWR)	P	0443
10.02.1955 [5]	Swansea Harbour Branch Sidings - Swansea North Docks	W(Mid)	G(All)	0444
20.02.1955 [4]	Middlewood South Jn - Middlewood Low Level Jn	LM(LNW)	G(All)	0445
21.02.1955	Kirtlebridge - Annan Shawhill	Sc(Cal)	G(All)	0446
28.02.1955	Heads of Ayr - Girvan (Grangeston Siding)	Sc(GSW)	G(All)	0447
28.02.1955	Solway Jn - Shawhill Jn	Sc(Cal)	G(All)	0448
28.02.1955	Shawhill Jn - Annan (Shawhill)	Sc(Cal)	G(All)	0449
26.03.1955	Holyhead Carriage Sidings - Admiralty Pier	LM(LNW)	G(All)	0450
31.03.1955	Bathgate East Jn - West Calder (Easter Inch Moss Litter Works)	Sc(NBR)	G(All)	0451
01.04.1955	Denny (Anchor Paper Works) - Ingliston Goods	Sc(Cal)	G(All)	0452
02.05.1955	OLDHAM (Clegg Street) - DELPH [Delph Jn]	LM(LNW)	P	0453
23.05.1955	BRADFORD (Exchange) [St Dunstans Jn] - KEIGHLEY [Keighley GN Jn]	NE(GNR)	P	0454
23.05.1955	BRADFORD (Exchange) [Queensbury] - HALIFAX	NE(H&OJt)	P	0455
23.05.1955	NEWCASTLE (Central) [Ouston Jn] - BLACKHILL	NE(NER)	P	0456
30.05.1955	Castlehill Jn - Chapel Brick Works	Sc(NBR)	G(All)	0457
13.06.1955 [3]	PONTYPOOL ROAD [Little Mill Jn] - MONMOUTH (Troy)	W(GWR)	G(All)	0458 *
13.06.1955 [3]	Usk - Monmouth Troy	W(GWR)	G(All)	0459 *
13.06.1955 [3]	Crowhurst Jn North - Crowhurst Jn South	S(C&OJt)	P	0460
13.06.1955 [3]	EAST GRINSTEAD L.L. - HORSTED KEYNES	S(LBSC)	P	0461 *
13.06.1955 [3]	LEWES [Culver Jn] - HORSTED KEYNES	S(LBSC)	P	0462 *
04.07.1955	SHETTLESTON - BOTHWELL	Sc(NBR)	P	0463
01.08.1955	HULL (Paragon) [Walton Street Jn] - SOUTH HOWDEN	NE(H&B)	P	0464
19.09.1955	RHYL [Foryd Jn] - DENBIGH [Mold & Denbigh Jn]	LM(LNW)	P	0465
19.09.1955	LUDGERSHALL - TIDWORTH	S(MSWJ)	P	0466 *
19.09.1955	LINCOLN (Central) [Pyewipe Jn] - SHIREBROOK (North)	E(GN/GCR)	P	0467
19.09.1955	LADYBANK - PERTH [Bridge of Earn]	Sc(NBR)	P	0468
09.10.1955	Chatterley Jn - Talk O'the Hill (High Carr Tileries)	LM(NSR)	G(All)	0469

Date	Line	Region (Company)	Type of Traffic	Reference Number
31.10.1955	Shepshed (Charnwood Granite Co's Siding) - Loughborough Derby Road	LM(LNW)	G(All)	0470
07.11.1955	Bramwith old alignment	E(WRGJt)	P(All)	0471 *
28.11.1955	Ludgershall - Tidworth	S(MSWJ)	G(All)	0472
00.12.1955 [8]	Bishophouse Jn - Sunbeck Jn	NE(NER)	G(All)	0473
05.12.1955	ARBROATH [St Vigeans Jn] - FORFAR [Guthrie Jn]	Sc(Cal)	P	0474
05.12.1955	St Vigeans Jn - Letham Mill Siding	Sc(Cal)	G(All)	0475
00.00.1956	Roose - Yarlside Mine	LM(Furn)	G(All)	0476
02.01.1956	NOTTINGHAM (Victoria) [Kirkby South Jn] - EDWINSTOWE	LM(GCR)	P	0477
09.01.1956	EDINBURGH (Waverley) [Bathgate Jn] - GLASGOW (Queen Street L.L.) [Airdrie]	Sc(NBR)	P	0478 *
09.01.1956	LEUCHARS JN - TAYPORT	Sc(NBR)	P	0479
09.01.1956	Leuchers Old - Tayport (Morton's Siding)	Sc(NBR)	G(All)	0480
16.01.1956	SLOUGH [Farnham Road] - SLOUGH TRADING ESTATE	W(GWR)	W(All)	0481
30.01.1956	Mierystock Siding GF - Upper Lydbrook	W(SWJt)	G(All)	0482 *
01.02.1956	Epworth - Haxey Jn	E(IAJt)	G(All)	0483
06.02.1956	NEWPORT - SANDOWN	S(IWCR)	P(All)	0484
01.03.1956	Mannieshall Siding - Salsburgh	Sc(Cal)	G(All)	0485
01.03.1956	Banknock Siding - Dennyloanhead Siding	Sc(K&BJt)	G(All)	0486
05.03.1956	YELVERTON - PRINCETOWN	W(GWR)	P(All)	0487
19.03.1956 [4]	Newbury Park - Seven Kings West	E(GER)	G(All)	0488
26.03.1956	Shaw Cross Colliery - Runtlings Lane Jn	E(GNR)	G(All)	0489
07.05.1956	SILVERDALE - MARKET DRAYTON	LM(NSR)	P	0490
07.05.1956	STOKE ON TRENT [Stoke Jn] - LEEK [Leek Brook Jn]	LM(NSR)	P	0491
07.05.1956	BO'NESS JN H.L. - BO'NESS	Sc(NBR)	P	0492
01.05.1956	Abermule - Kerry	W(Cam)	G(All)	0493
04.05.1956	Poplar Jn - Poplar Dock (Riverside)	LM(Mid)	G(All)	0494
28.05.1956	Fullerton Jn - Longparish	S(LSW)	G(All)	0495
28.05.1956	Cullingworth - Ingrow East	NE(GNR)	G(All)	0496
28.05.1956	Holmfield - Queensbury West	NE(GNR)	G(All)	0497
28.05.1956	Queensbury South - Queensbury East	NE(GNR)	G(All)	0498
04.06.1956	Trehafod Jn - Pontypridd (Maesycoed Goods)	W(Barry)	G(All)	0499
11.06.1956	SWANSEA (High Street) [Hafod Jn] - FELIN FRAN	W(GWR)	P	0500
11.06.1956	FELIN FRAN [Lonlas Jn] - NEATH [Skewen East]	W(GWR)	P	0501
11.06.1956	CROOK - TOW LAW	NE(NER)	P	0502
14.06.1956	Cranley Gardens - Muswell Hill	E(GNR)	G(All)	0503
24.06.1956 [5]	Kelvin Valley East Jn - Torrance	Sc(NBR)	G(All)	0504
01.07.1956	Grimsby Corporation Bridge - Cleveland Bridge	E(G&I)	P(All)	0505
18.07.1956	Robin Hood - Beeston Pit	NE(EWYU)	G(All)	0506
28.07.1956	Sleaford East Jn - Billingborough & Horbling	E(GNR)	G(All)	0507 *
31.07.1956	Wimberry Jn - Serridge Jn	W(SWJt)	G(All)	0508
31.07.1956	Serridge Jn - Mierystock Sidings	W(SWJt)	G(All)	0509
01.08.1956	Commonhead - Arbuckle Arden Siding	Sc(NBR)	G(All)	0510
17.09.1956	MACHEN - PONTYPRIDD [Caerphilly East Jn]	W(B&M)	P	0511
17.09.1956	MACHEN [Caerphilly West Branch Jn] - PONTYPRIDD [Penrhos Jn]	W(Rhy)	P	0512
17.09.1956	MACHEN [Penrhos Jn] - PONTYPRIDD [PC&N Jn]	W(ADR)	P	0513
17.09.1956	NOTTINGHAM (Victoria) [Kirkby South Jn] - SUTTON IN ASHFIELD (Town)	E(GNR)	P	0514
17.09.1956	Wragby Jn - Donington on Bain	E(GNR)	G(All)	0515
15.10.1956	HEXHAM [Border Counties Jn] - RICCARTON JN	NE(NBR)	P	0516
28.10.1956 [5]	Uxbridge High St. North GF - Uxbridge High Street	W(GWR)	G(All)	0517
05.11.1956	RAINFORD JN - ORMSKIRK	LM(L&Y)	P	0518
05.11.1956	Welshpool - Llanfair Caereinion	W(WLLR)	G(All)	0519 *
31.12.1956	DINGLE - SEAFORTH & LITHERLAND	LOR	P(All)	0520

Date	Line	Region (Company)	Type of Traffic	Reference Number
00.00.1957?	Blackmill - Hendreforgen	W(GWR)	G(All)	0521
01.01.1957	Cleobury Mortimer - Ditton Priors	W(CMDPLR)	G(All)	0522 *
29.01.1957	Ladybank (Heatherinch Siding) - Auchtermuchty	Sc(NBR)	G(All)	0523
01.02.1957	Tewkesbury (Engine Shed) - Tewkesbury Quay	W(Mid)	G(All)	0524
01.02.1957	Worcester Foregate Street - Worcester Racecourse	W(GWR)	G(All)	0525
25.02.1957	BRADFORD (Forster Sq.) [Menston Jn] - HARROGATE [Milnerwood Jn]	NE(OIJt)	P	0526
25.02.1957	BRADFORD (Forster Sq) [Arthington West Jn] - HARROGATE [Arthington North Jn]	NE(NER)	P	0527
04.03.1957	Arkwright Colliery Sidings - Chesterfield Market Place	E(GCR)	G(All)	0528
04.03.1957	Stamford [Jn with Mid] - STAMFORD (East)	E(GNR)	P	0529
07.04.1957	Shields Bank - Scotland Street Jn	Sc(Cal)	G(All)	0530
29.04.1957	LEICESTER (Belgrave Road) - JOHN O'GAUNT	E(GNR)	W(Un)	0531
05.05.1957 [5]	Grafton East - Grafton South Jn	W(MSWJ)	G(All)	0532
18.05.1957	EAST NORTON - MARKET HARBOROUGH [Welham Jn]	LM(GN&LNWJt)	W(Un)	0533
18.05.1957	Park Jn - Cranley Gardens	E(GNR)	G(All)	0534
24.05.1957	Ashchurch East Jn - Ashchurch West Jn	W(Mid)	G(All)	0535
01.06.1957	Cwmbach - Cwmbach Colliery	W(Taff)	G(All)	0536
03.06.1957	Abbeydore - Moss MOS Depot GF	W(GWR)	G(All)	0537
01.07.1957	PRINCES RISBORO - WATLINGTON	W(GWR)	P	0538
01.07.1957	GRIMSARGH - WHITTINGHAM	WhittRly	P(All)	0539
11.08.1957	Holywell Jn - Crescent Siding	LM(LNW)	G(All)	0540
20.08.1957	Warboys - Ramsey East (Messrs Cordell's PrS)	E(GN&GEJt)	G(All)	0541
02.09.1957	Gowerton No.2 - Llanmorlais	W(LNW)	G(All)	0542
16.09.1957	CHESTER (General) [Tattenhall Jn] - WHITCHURCH	LM(LNW)	P	0543
16.09.1957	BENTLEY - BORDON	S(LSWR)	P	0544
30.09.1957	NORTH WALSHAM (Town) - Antingham Road Jn	E(MGN)	P	0545
01.10.1957 [3]	TRENTHAM [Jn] - TRENTHAM GARDENS	LM(NSR)	P*(All)	0546 *
17.11.1957 [1]	EPPING - ONGAR	E(GER)	P(All)	0547
30.11.1957	Tufts Jn - Pillowell Siding	W(SWJt)	G(All)	0548
02.12.1957	BLACKBURN [Great Harwood Jn] - ROSE GROVE [Padiham Jn]	LM(L&Y)	P	0549
30.12.1957	Alne - Easingwold	Easingwd	G(All)	0550
30.12.1957	Burghead - Hopeman	Sc(High)	G(All)	0551
00.00.1958	Gloucester West - Over Jn	W(GWR)	P(All)	0552 *
00.00.1958	Hatherley Jn - Gloucester Loop	W(GWR)	G(All)	0553
06.01.1958	ABERGAVENNY JN - MERTHYR [Morlais Tunnel Jn]	W(LNW)	P(All)	0554
06.01.1958	Abergavenny (Brecon Road) - Golivan	W(LNW)	G(All)	0555
06.01.1958	Beaufort Brickworks Siding - Brynmawr No.2	W(LNW)	G(All)	0556
06.01.1958	Brynmawr No.1 - Abergavenny (Brecon Road No.2)	W(LNW)	G(All)	0557
06.01.1958	Nantybwch - Morlais Jn	W(LNW)	G(All)	0558
01.03.1958	Tinsley Park Colliery Jn - Tinsley Park Colliery	E(GCR)	G(All)	0559
03.03.1958	Falkirk High - Camelon Goods	Sc(NBR)	G(All)	0560
17.03.1958	HORSTED KEYNES - EAST GRINSTEAD	S(LBSC)	P(All)	0561 *
17.03.1958	LEWES [Culver Jn] - HORSTED KEYNES	S(LBSC)	P(All)	0562 *
17.03.1958	Edzell Jn - Careston	Sc(Cal)	G(All)	0563
00.04.1958 [7]	Whifflet East Jn (R.B.Tennant's Foundary Siding) - Bothwell Jn	Sc(NBR)	G(All)	0564
13.04.1958	Wigan (Belle Green Lane Crossing) - Kirklees Hall Jn	LM(LNW)	G(All)	0565 *
01.05.1958	Carling Howe - Kilton Viaduct reversing siding	NE(NER)	G(All)	0566
01.05.1958	Kilton Viaduct reversing siding - Kilton Beck reversing siding	NE(NER)	G(All)	0567
01.05.1958	Kilton Beck reversing siding - Skinningrove Coal Depot	NE(NER)	G(All)	0568
05.05.1958	Antingham Road Jn - North Walsham (Town)	E(NSJt)	G(All)	0569
05.05.1958	LOFTUS - WHITBY (West Cliff)	NE(NER)	P(All)	0570
05.05.1958	Auchterhouse - Newtyle	Sc(Cal)	G(All)	0571
09.06.1958	Exeter Alphington Road GF - Christow	W(GWR)	G(All)	0572 *
09.06.1958	Kington - Dolyhir	W(GWR)	G(All)	0573

Date	Line	Region (Company)	Type of Traffic	Reference Number
09.06.1958	LLANTRISANT [Llantrisant East Jn] - PEN–Y–GRAIG	W(GWR)	P	0574
09.06.1958	BARNSLEY (Court House) [Barnsley West Jn] - CUDWORTH [South Jn]	NE(Mid)	P	0575
09.06.1958	Cudworth West Jn - Cudworth South Jn	NE(Mid)	G(All)	0576
09.06.1958	Oaks Colliery Sidings - Monk Bretton	NE(Mid)	G(All)	0577
19.06.1958	Broughton Crossing - Brymbo	LM(GCR)	G(All)	0578
19.06.1958 [\]	Brymbo - Brymbo (Fishponds Sidings)	LM(GCR)	G(All)	0579
27.06.1958	Swynnerton Jn - COLD MEECE	LM(LMS)	W(Un)	0580
30.06.1958 [3]	Ravenstone Wood - Towcester	LM(SMJ)	G(All)	0581 *
30.06.1958 [2]	Blackbyres Jn - Paisley East Goods	Sc(Cal)	G(All)	0582
07.07.1958	MANCHESTER (Central) - GUIDE BRIDGE	LM(CLC/GCR)	P(Locals)	0583
11.08.1958	Gollanfield Jn - Fort George	Sc(High)	G(All)	0584
11.08.1958	Prestonpans - Tranent Siding	Sc(NBR)	G(All)	0585
17.08.1958	Upper Abbey Mills Jn - Abbey Mills Jn	E(LTS)	G(All)	0586
18.08.1958	PANTYFFYNNON - BRYNAMMAN (West)	W(GWR)	P	0587
18.08.1958	Garnant - Brynamman (West)	W(GWR)	G(All)	0588
00.09.1958	Smethwick Jn - Galton Jn	LM(LNW)	G(All)	0589
00.09.1958 [2]	Hook Norton - Great Rollright Siding	W(GWR)	G(All)	0590
01.09.1958	OLD HILL - LONGBRIDGE	LM(HJt)	W(Un)	0591 *
01.09.1958	Bellingham - Riccarton Jn	NE(NBR)	G(All)	0592
01.09.1958	Border Counties Jn - Reedsmouth	NE(NBR)	G(All)	0593
01.09.1958	Sowerby Bridge - Ripponden & Barkisland	NE(L&Y)	G(All)	0594
15.09.1958	Dalton Jn Park - South Jn	LM(Furn)	P*	0595
15.09.1958	WEEDON [Marton Jn] - LEAMINGTON SPA (Avenue)	LM(LNW)	P	0596
15.09.1958 [1]	Cuckoo Jn - Welland Bank	E(MGN)	P*	0597
15.09.1958	GRAFTON & BURBAGE [Grafton South Jn] - MARLBOROUGH L.L.	W(MSWJ)	P(All)	0598
15.09.1958	Mount Gould Jn - Cattewater Jn	W(LSW)	G	0599
15.09.1958	PLYMOUTH (North Road) [Lipson Jn] - PLYMOUTH (Friary)	W(LSW)	P	0600
15.09.1958	DONCASTER - YORK	E/NE(GNR/NER)	P(Locals)	0601
15.09.1958	Little Ilford No.1 - EAST HAM [Loop North]	E(LTS)	P(All)	0602
15.09.1958	WAKEFIELD (Westgate) [Lofthouse S. Jn] - CASTLEFORD (Central) [Lofthouse E. Jn]	NE(MJt)	P	0603
15.09.1958	YORK - DARLINGTON	NE(NER)	P(Locals)	0604
22.09.1958 [1]	North Walsham Main - Jn with new spur	E(BRB)	P(All)	0605
01.10.1958	Fountainhall - Lauder	Sc(NBR)	G(All)	0606
06.10.1958	FOXFIELD - CONISTON	LM(Furn)	P	0607
06.10.1958	Bluntisham - Sutton	E(GER)	G(All)	0608
06.10.1958	DONCASTER - GRANTHAM	E(GNR)	P(Locals)	0609
20.10.1958	Aire Jn - Bullcroft Jn	NE(GC&HBJt)	G(All)	0610
20.10.1958	Malton Scarborough Road - Driffield West	NE(NER)	G(All)	0611
03.11.1958	NEWNHAM [Bullo Pill] - CINDERFORD	W(GWR)	P	0612 *
03.11.1958	TOTNES [Ashburton Jn] - ASHBURTON	W(GWR)	P	0613
15.11.1958	Swynnerton Jn - Cold Meece	LM(LMS)	G(All)	0614
01.12.1958	Tonmawr Jn - Blaenavon (Glam)	W(PTR)	G(All)	0615
01.12.1958	Firsby - Spilsby	E(GNR)	G(All)	0616
03.12.1958	Grange Lane - Grange Colliery	E(GCR)	G(All)	0617
01.12.1958	Wragby - Donnington on Bain	E(GNR)	G(All)	0618
01.12.1958 [2]	Gowdall Jn - Carlton Towers	NE(HBR)	G(All)	0619
01.12.1958	Picton - Stokesley	NE(NER)	G(All)	0620
08.12.1958	Forfar North Jn - Kingsmuir	Sc(Cal)	G(All)	0621
01.01.1959	Camps - Viaduct No.7	Sc(NBR)	G(All)	0622
01.01.1959	Colliston - Letham Mill Siding	Sc(Cal)	G(All)	0623
01.01.1959	Pumpherston Oil Works - Camps	Sc(NBR)	G(All)	0624
05.01.1959	Barnsley West Jn - Oaks Colliery Sidings	E(Mid)	G(All)	0625
05.01.1959	CHEPSTOW [Wye Valley Jn] - MONMOUTH (Troy)	W(GWR)	P	0626

Date	Line	Region (Company)	Type of Traffic	Reference Number
05.01.1959	MONMOUTH (Troy) - ROSS ON WYE	W(GWR)	P(All)	0627
05.01.1959	Monmouth (Mill Hill) - Lydbrook Jn	W(GWR)	G(All)	0628
05.01.1959	DUNDEE (East) - Camperdown Jn	Sc(D&AJt)	P	0629
19.01.1959	Bilsthorpe - Eakring Road Siding	E(MNJt)	G(All)	0630
31.01.1959	Maldon East & Heybridge - Maldon West	E(GER)	G(All)	0631
02.02.1959	Hollinswood Sidings - Stirchley	W(GWR)	G(All)	0632
02.02.1959	KILMACOLM - GREENOCK (Princes Pier)	Sc(GSW)	P	0633
02.02.1959	NEWTON ABBOT [East] - MORETONHAMPSTEAD	W(GWR)	P	0634
02.03.1959	LEICESTER (London Road) [Saxby Jn] - SPALDING [No.1 SB]	E(MGN)	P	0635
02.03.1959	South Witham - Bourne	E(MGN)	G(All)	0636
02.03.1959	Cuckoo Jn - Welland Bank (Spalding Avoider)	E(MGN)	G(All)	0637
02.03.1959	SPALDING [No.1 SB] - SOUTH LYNN	E(MGN)	P	0638
02.03.1959	Sutton Bridge - South Lynn (Single Line Jn)	E(MGN)	G(All)	0639
02.03.1959	SOUTH LYNN - KINGS LYNN [Harbour Jn]	E(MGN)	P	0640
02.03.1959	SOUTH LYNN - YARMOUTH (Beach)	E(MGN)	P	0641
02.03.1959	East Rudham - Melton Constable	E(MGN)	G(All)	0642
02.03.1959	Melton Constable - North Walsham Town	E(MGN)	G(All)	0643
02.03.1959	North Walsham Town 1958 Spur Jn - Yarmouth Beach	E(MGN)	G(All)	0644
02.03.1959	Yarmouth Yard - Yarmouth Ormond Road	E(MGN)	G(All)	0645
02.03.1959	MELTON CONSTABLE - NORWICH (City)	E(MGN)	P	0646
02.03.1959	PETERBOROUGH (North) [Wisbech Jn] - SUTTON BRIDGE	E(MGN)	P	0647
02.03.1959	Horse Shoe Lane Crossing - Sutton Bridge Jn	E(MGN)	G(All)	0648
16.03.1959	GARSDALE - HAWES	LM(Mid)	P(All)	0649
20.03.1959	Bridgend Jn - Waterside Jn	Sc(NBR)	G(All)	0650
06.04.1959	Foryd Jn - Foryd Pier	LM(LNW)	G(All)	0651
06.04.1959	Hensall Jn - Gowdall Jn	NE(HBR)	G(All)	0652
06.04.1959	Wrangbrook Jn - Little Weighton	NE(HBR)	G(All)	0653 *
16.04.1959	Stranraer Town - Colfin	Sc(P&WJt)	G(All)	0654
30.04.1959	Cairnryan Jn - Cairnryan Port (Pile Construction Yard)	WD	G(All)	0655
01.05.1959	Bothwell Jn - Hamilton Palace Colliery	Sc(Cal)	G(All)	0656
04.05.1959	GUIDE BRIDGE [Crowthorne Jn] - OLDHAM (Clegg Street)	LM(OAGB)	P	0657
04.05.1959	STOCKPORT (Edgeley) [OAGB Jn] - OLDHAM (Clegg Street)	LM(LNW/OAGB)	P	0658
04.05.1959	Old Oaks Jn - Oakwell Jn	E(GCR)	G(All)	0659
04.05.1959	Potterhill - Gleniffer Depot	Sc(GSW)	G(All)	0660
30.05.1959	Tillietudlem - Blackwood Jn	Sc(Cal)	G(All)	0661
31.05.1959	Crewe Works [Erecting Shop Yard] - Merrills Bridge Wharf	LM(LNW)	G(All)	0662
15.06.1959	KETTERING [Jn] - HUNTINGDON (East)	LM(Mid)	P	0663
15.06.1959	Kimbolton - Huntingdon East	LM(Mid)	G(All)	0664
15.06.1959	ROLLESTON JN - SOUTHWELL	LM(Mid)	P	0665
15.06.1959	RUGBY (Midland) [No.7 SB] - LEAMINGTON SPA (Avenue)	LM(LNW)	P	0666
15.06.1959	WELLINGBOROUGH (Midland) [Irchester Jn] - HIGHAM FERRIERS	LM(Mid)	P	0667
15.06.1959	CHOLSEY & MOULSFORD - WALLINGFORD	W(GWR)	P	0668
15.06.1959	ESSENDINE - STAMFORD (Town) [East Jn]	E(GNR)	P(All)	0669
15.06.1959	HUNTINGDON EAST [St Ives] - CAMBRIDGE	E(GN&GEJt)	P	0670
15.06.1959	Godmanchester - St Ives	E(GN&GEJt)	G(All)	0671
15.06.1959	PETERBOROUGH - GRANTHAM	E(GNR)	P(Locals)	0672
15.06.1959	SHEFFIELD (Victoria) - PENISTONE	E(GCR)	P(Locals)	0673
22.06.1959	Grafton South Jn - Marlborough LL	W(MSWJn)	G(All)	0674
27.06.1959 [4]	Cwmdu St Johns Colliery Jn - Celtic Halt	W(PTR)	G(All)	0675
29.06.1959	BARNSLEY (Court House) [Quarry Jn] - DONCASTER [Mexborough No.2]	E(GCR)	P(Locals)	0676
29.06.1959	PENISTONE [Barnsley Jn] - BARNSLEY (Court House)	E(GCR)	P(Locals)	0677
29.06.1959	Thornton Jn - Thornton Old Goods	Sc(NBR)	G(All)	0678
01.07.1959	Roslin Colliery Sidings GF - Penicuik Gasworks	Sc(NBR)	G(All)	0679 *
13.07.1959	GLOUCESTER (Central) [Over Jn] - LEDBURY	W(GWR)	P	0680
13.07.1959	Dymock - Ledbury	W(GWR)	G(All)	0681

Date	Line	Region (Company)	Type of Traffic	Reference Number
01.08.1959	Peebles Jn - Peebles West	Sc(NBR/Cal)	G(All)	0682
03.08.1959	Elbowend Jn - Netherton Siding	Sc(NBR)	G(All)	0683
03.08.1959	Newfields Jn - Newfields reversing siding	LM(NSR)	G(All)	0684
03.08.1959	Newfields reversing siding - Greengate Sidings	LM(NSR)	G(All)	0685
31.08.1959	Hemel Hempstead (Midland Road) - Boxmoor Gasworks	LM(Mid)	G(All)	0686 *
03.09.1959	Park Jn - East Mendalgief Jn	W(ADR)	G(All)	0687
11.09.1959 [2]	Norwood Spur Jn - Norwood Jn	S(LBSC)	G(All)	0688
14.09.1959 [4]	Tilbury Jn - Bromley Jn	LM(NLR)	G(All)	0689
14.09.1959	WEYMOUTH [Jn] - MELCOMBE REGIS	S(W&PJt)	P*	0690
14.09.1959	SKEGNESS [Rectory Jn] - BIRMINGHAM (NEW St.) [Colwick North Jn]	E(GNR)	P*	0691
14.09.1959	SKEGNESS [Egglinton Jn] - BIRMINGHAM (New Street) [Dove Jn]	LM(GNR)	P*	0692
14.09.1959	Greetland - Stainland & Holywell Green	NE(L&Y)	G(All)	0693
14.09.1959	MELMERBY [North] - THIRSK	NE(NER)	P	0694
14.09.1959	Melmerby North - Thirsk Town Jn	NE(NER)	G(All)	0695
14.09.1959	YOKER [Clydebank Jn] - CLYDEBANK (East)	Sc(NBR)	P(All)	0696
15.09.1959	MARYHILL (Central) - Knightswood South Jn	Sc(NBR)	W(Un)	0697
15.09.1959	Whiteinch North Jn - Whiteinch West Jn	Sc(NBR)	W(Un)	0698
19.09.1959 [3]	Corfe Mullen - Carter's Siding	S(S&DJt)	G(All)	0699
05.10.1959	Jamestown - Drymen	Sc(NBR)	G(All)	0700
05.10.1959	Stirling North - Port of Menteith	Sc(NBR)	G(All)	0701
05.10.1959	Balmore - Torrance	Sc(NBR)	G(All)	0702
05.10.1959	Lennox Castle Hospital Siding - Aberfoyle	Sc(NBR)	G(All)	0703
12.10.1959	Swansea - Mumbles Pier	SIT	P(All)	0704
02.11.1959	Stockingford - Ansley Hall Colliery	LM(Mid)	G(All)	0705
02.11.1959	BRISTOL (Temple Meads) [North Somerset Jn] - FROME	W(GWR)	P	0706
02.11.1959	Windsor Passing Siding - Ynysybwl	W(Taff)	G(All)	0707
02.11.1959	Nantybwch - Beaufort Brickworks Siding	W(LNW)	G(All)	0708
02.11.1959	Nantybwch - Ebbw Vale H.L.	W(LNW)	G(All)	0709
02.11.1959	Ebbw Vale Jn - Ebbw Vale Steelworks	W(LNW)	G(All)	0710
02.11.1959	BECCLES [North Jn] - YARMOUTH (South Town)	E(GER)	P	0711
02.11.1959	Beccles North Jn - Aldeby	E(GER)	G(All)	0712
02.11.1959	Fleet Jn - St Olaves	E(GER)	G(All)	0713
02.11.1959 [4]	St Olaves - Yarmouth (South Town)	E(GER)	G(All)	0714 *
02.11.1959	RETFORD [Clarborough Jn] - LINCOLN (Central) [Sykes Jn]	E(GCR)	P(All)	0715 *
02.11.1959	Shirebrook Welbeck Colliery Jn - Welbeck Colliery	E(LMS)	G(All)	0716
02.11.1959	HUDDERSFIELD [Brockholes] - HOLMFIRTH	NE(L&Y)	P	0717
02.11.1959	STOBCROSS - MARYHILL [Jn]	Sc(Cal)	P	0718
02.11.1959	Woodleys Jn - Bridgend Jn	Sc(NBR)	G(All)	0719
07.12.1959	Dumbuck - Dumbuck Siding	Sc(NBR)	G(All)	0720
00.00.1960	Pontllanfraith H.L. - Bird–in–Hand West	W(LNW/GWR	G(All)	0721
00.00.1960	Pontcysyllte (Monsanto Sidings) - Acrefair L.L (Hughes & Lancaster's Sidg)	W(GWR)	G(All)	0722
00.00.1960	Tow Law - Sunniside Depots	NE(NER)	G(All)	0723
04.01.1960	BIDSTON [Seacombe Goods Jn] - SEACOMBE & EGREMONT	LM(Wirral)	P(All)	0724
04.01.1960	CHORLEY [No.4] - BLACKBURN [Cherry Tree Jn]	LM(L&Y)	P	0725
04.01.1960	CHORLEY [Adlington Jn] - WIGAN (North Western) [Boar's Head Jn]	LM(L&Y)	P	0726
04.01.1960	Crow Nest Jn - Hindley & Blackrod Branch Jn	LM(L&Y)	P	0727
04.01.1960	CREWE [Sandbach Jn] - NORTHWICH	LM(LNW)	P	0728
04.01.1960	NORTHAMPTON (Castle) - [No.5] MARKET HARBOROUGH [No.1]	LM(LNW)	P	0729
04.01.1960	NORTHAMPTON (Castle) [Duston Jn North] - BLISWORTH	LM(LNW)	P(Locals)	0730
04.01.1960	NORTHFIELD [Halesowen Jn] - LONGBRIDGE	LM(HJt)	W(Un)	0731
04.01.1960	BALA - BLAENAU FFESTINOG (Central)	W(GWR)	P	0732
04.01.1960	NEWBURY - LAMBOURN	W(GWR)	P	0733
04.01.1960	Welford Park - Lambourn	W(GWR)	G(All)	0734

Date	Line	Region (Company)	Type of Traffic	Reference Number
04.01.1960	Kinnerley - Criggion Quarry	W(S&M)	G(All)	0735 *
04.01.1960	Dalserf - Tillietudlem	Sc(Cal)	G(All)	0736
06.01.1960	SWANSEA (Rutland St) - SOUTHEND	SIT	P(All)	0737
31.01.1960	Kennishead - Spiersbridge	Sc(GB&KJt)	G(All)	0738
01.02.1960	Uxbridge Road Jn - Latimer Road Jn	LM(HCJR)	G(All)	0739
01.02.1960 [2]	Tonygroes East GF - Port Talbot Central	W(PTR)	G(All)	0740
01.02.1960	Bardney (John Morrell Siding) - Wragby	E(GNR)	G(All)	0741
01.02.1960	Yarmouth South Town - St Olaves	E(GER)	G(All)	0742
01.02.1960	Harleston - Bungay	E(GER)	G(All)	0743
29.02.1960 [1]	Berkeley South Jn - Berkeley Loop Jn	W(GWR)	P*	0744
29.02.1960	Hookagate Depot - Nesscliffe & Pentre	W(S&M)	G(All)	0745 *
29.02.1960	Kinnerley - Nesscliff Camp	W(S&M)	WG(All)	0746 *
29.02.1960	Kinnerley - Llanymnech	W(S&M)	G(All)	0747 *
29.02.1960	Plymstock (APCM Siding) - Yealmpton	W(GWR)	G(All)	0748
29.02.1960	Rye Harbour GF - Rye Harbour	S(SEC)	G(All)	0749
07.03.1960	NEWBURY [Enborne Jn] - SOUTHAMPTON [Shawford Jn]	W(GWR)	P	0750
07.03.1960	Honeybourne W.Loop - Honeybourne N.Loop	W(GWR)	P	0751
07.03.1960	Snatchwood Sidings - Blaenavon L.L	W(GWR)	G(All)	0752
07.03.1960	Snape Jn - Snape Goods	E(GER)	G(All)	0753
07.03.1960	Cromer Jn - Cromer High	E(GER)	G(All)	0754
07.03.1960	GRANGE - Grange North	Sc(GNoSR)	P(All)	0755
11.03.1960	Hookagate - Shrewsbury Abbey Jn with new spur	W(S&M)	G(All)	0756 *
01.04.1960	Hemel Hempstead & Boxmoor - Boxmoor EGB Sidings	LM(BRB)	G(All)	0757
03.04.1960	Sherburn Colliery North - Hetton North	NE(NER)	G(All)	0758
04.04.1960 [1]	BASFORD (North) - NETHERFIELD & COLWICK	E(GNR)	P	0759 *
04.04.1960	Gedling Colliery Sidings - Daybrook	E(GNR)	G(All)	0760
10.04.1960	Kings Ferry Bridge old line	S(SEC)	P(All)	0761
18.04.1960	Glenburnie Jn - Lindores	Sc(NBR)	G(All)	0762
19.04.1960	BARNSLEY (Court House) - Jn with new spur near Quarry Jn	E(Mid)	P(All)	0763
19.04.1960	Barnsley West Jn - Quarry Jn	E(GCR)	G(All)	0764
25.04.1960	Bowling New Jn - Dumbarton East Jn	Sc(NBR)	P(All)	0765
00.05.1960 [8]	Southport Jn - Altcar & Hillhouse	LM(CLC)	G(All)	0766
02.05.1960	Tottington - Holcombe Brook	LM(L&Y)	G(All)	0767
02.05.1960	Moreton in Marsh - Shipston on Stour	W(GWR)	G(All)	0768
02.05.1960	PANT - DOWLAIS (Central)	W(B&M)	P	0769
02.05.1960	Poole B - Poole Quay	S(LSW)	G(All)	0770
02.05.1960	GUISBOROUGH [Hutton Jn] - LOFTUS [Brotton Jn]	NE(NER)	P	0771
02.05.1960	Lambley - Lambley Colliery	NE(NER)	G(All)	0772
02.05.1960	Selby West Jn - Cawood	NE(NER)	G(All)	0773
02.05.1960	Saltoun - Humbie	Sc(NBR)	G(All)	0774
02.05.1960	Winton Mine - Macmerry	Sc(NBR)	G(All)	0775
09.05.1960	Rhydycar Jn - Lucy Thomas Colliery	W(QYMJt)	G(All)	0776
11.05.1960	PARKESTON QUAY (West) - PARKESTON QUAY	E(GER)	P	0777
16.05.1960	Kirklee Jn - Bellshaugh Jn	Sc(Cal)	G(All)	0778
30.05.1960	Dewsbury West Jn - Headfield Jn	NE(L&Y)	G(All)	0779
30.05.1960	Falkirk Camelon Goods - Rough Castle Tar Works	Sc(NBR)	G(All)	0780
01.06.1960	Camps Jn - Camps	Sc(Cal)	G(All)	0781
01.06.1960	Craigleith - Davidson's Mains	Sc(Cal)	G(All)	0782
01.06.1960	Strathaven Jn - High Blantyre	Sc(Cal)	G(All)	0783
13.06.1960	Broom North Jn - Stratford-upon-Avon Old Town	LM(SMJ)	G(All)	0784
13.06.1960	Broom East Jn - Broom West Jn	LM(LMS)	G(All)	0785
13.06.1960	Molyneux Jn - Clifton Hall Sidings	LM(LNW)	G(All)	0786
13.06.1960	North Stafford Jn - Marston Jn	LM(NSR)	P	0787
13.06.1960	SEATON - UPPINGHAM	LM(LNW)	P	0788
13.06.1960	Barnstaple East Loop GF - Barnstaple (Victoria Road)	W(GWR)	G(All)	0789

Date	Line	Region (Company)	Type of Traffic	Reference Number
13.06.1960	Barnstaple South Loop - BARNSTAPLE (Victoria Rd)	W(GWR)	P	0790
13.06.1960	CYMMER AFAN [Gelli GF] - ABERGWYNFI	W(GWR)	P	0791
13.06.1960	Cymmer Afan - near Blaengwynfi (RSB alignment)	W(RSB)	P(All)	0792
13.06.1960	NEWPORT (High St.) [Risca] - NANTYBWCH	W(GW/LNW)	P	0793
13.06.1960	Sirhowy - Nantybwch	W(LNW)	G(All)	0794
13.06.1960	Royston Jn - Thornhill Jn	NE(Mid)	P	0795
13.06.1960	Clyde Bridge Jn - Rutherglen West Jn	Sc(Cal)	P	0796
13.06.1960	INVERNESS - WICK	Sc(High)	P(Locals)	0797
13.06.1960	Larkfield Jn - Shield No.1	Sc(Cal)	P	0798
13.06.1960	Muir of Ord - Fortrose	Sc(High)	G(All)	0799
13.06.1960	THE MOUND - DORNOCH	Sc(High)	P(All)	0800
27.06.1960	Thetford West Jn - Bury St Edmunds Jn	E(GER)	G(All)	0801
27.06.1960	Halifax North Bridge Goods - Holmfield	NE(HOJt)	G(All)	0802
27.06.1960	Holmfield - Halifax St Pauls	NE(HHLJt)	G(All)	0803
27.06.1960	Kidwelly Jn - Mynydd–y–Garreg	W(GV)	G(All)	0804
09.08.1960	Longtown Bush Level Crossing - Gretna (Blackbank Litter Siding)	Sc(NBR)	G(All)	0805
14.08.1960	Stobcross Jn - Kelvin Bridge	Sc(Cal)	G(All)	0806
28.08.1960	London Road No.1 - MANCHESTER (Mayfield)	LM(LNW)	P	0807
00.09.1960 [8]	Walsall Wood - Jn with NCB (Chacewater)	LM(Mid)	G(All)	0808
05.09.1960	Bonnington East - Warriston Jn	Sc(Cal)	G(All)	0809
12.09.1960	Melton Constable - Themelthorpe Jn with new connection	E(MGN)	G(All)	0810
03.10.1960	Stairfoot North Jn - Houghton Main Colliery	NE(GCR)	G(All)	0811
03.10.1960	Grimethorpe Jn - Grimethorpe Colliery (GCR)	NE(GCR)	G(All)	0812
03.10.1960	Storrs Mill Jn - Grimethorpe GC Jn	NE(Mid)	G(All)	0813
03.10.1960	Inverteil Jn - Auchtertool	Sc(NBR)	G(All)	0814
24.10.1960	Roe Green Jn - Little Hulton Jn	LM(LNW)	G(All)	0815
26.10.1960	SHARPNESS - LYDNEY (Town)	W(SWJt)	P	0816
26.10.1960	Sharpness North GF - Otters Pool Jn	W(SWJt)	G(All)	0817 *
26.10.1960	Otters Pool Jn - Lydney Engine Shed	W(SWJt)	G(All)	0818
05.11.1960	PARTICK HILL [Jn] - HYNDLAND	Sc(NBR)	P	0819
07.11.1960	GATEACRE - AINTREE (Central)	LM(CLC)	P	0820
07.11.1960	Halewood East Jn - Halewood North Jn	LM(CLC)	P	0821
07.11.1960	NORTH RODE - LEEK	LM(NSR)	P	0822
07.11.1960 [3]	Marron Jn - Rowrah	LM(WCEJt)	G(All)	0823
07.11.1960	Bitterley - Clee Hill Dhustone Quarry	W(S&HJt)	G(All)	0824 *
07.11.1960	Fraserburgh - St.Combs	Sc(GNoSR)	G	0825
18.11.1960	Lydney Upper Dock Jn - Lydney Lower Dock Coal Tips	W(SWJt)	G(All)	0826
21.11.1960	Speech House Road - Cannop Colliery Sidings	W(SWJt)	G(All)	0827 *
21.11.1960	Serridge Jn - Mierystock Sidings	W(SWJt)	G(All)	0828 *
21.11.1960	Wimberry Jn - Serridge Jn	W(SWJt)	G(All)	0829 *
00.12.1960	Leadburn - Macbiehill	Sc(NBR)	G(All)	0830 *
05.12.1960	Lawley & Stirchley - Coalport East	LM(LNW)	G(All)	0831
05.12.1960	LOUTH [Mablethorpe Jn] - MABLETHORPE	E(GNR)	P(All)	0832
31.12.1960	Leighswood Sidings - Aldridge Brickworks	LM(LNW)	G(All)	0833
02.01.1961	BUCKINGHAM - BANBURY (Merton Street)	LM(LNW)	P	0834
02.01.1961	Chinnor Cement Works Siding - Watlington	W(GWR)	G(All)	0835
02.01.1961	Ash Jn - Tongham Gasworks	S(LSW)	G(All)	0836
02.01.1961	St John's Chapel - Wearhead	NE(NER)	G(All)	0837
08.01.1961	Bearley North Jn - Bearley East Jn	W(GWR)	G(All)	0838
30.01.1961	Bala - Blaenau Ffestinog Central	W(GWR)	G(All)	0839 *
30.01.1961	Maesycwmmer Jn - Fleur–di–Lis	W(GWR)	W(Un)	0840
05.02.1961 [5]	Radstock North B - Middle Pit Colliery Sidings	W(S&DJt)	G(All)	0841
06.02.1961	Headfield Jn - Dewsbury Market Place	NE(L&Y)	G(All)	0842

Date	Line	Region (Company)	Type of Traffic	Reference Number
20.02.1961 [2]	Churchbridge Sidings - Wyrley and Church Bridge Goods	LM(LNW)	G(All)	0843
06.03.1961	Cartsburn Jn - Inchgreen	Sc(GSW)	G(All)	0844 *
27.03.1961	Peterborough Wisbech Jn - Dogsthorpe Siding	E(MGN)	G(All)	0845
31.03.1961	Robin Hood - Thorpe	NE(EWYU)	G(All)	0846
03.04.1961	Blackwood Jn - Blackwood (Old)	Sc(Cal)	G(All)	0847
10.04.1961	BURY ST EDMUNDS - LONG MELFORD	E(GER)	P	0848
10.04.1961	Lavenham - Long Melford	E(GER)	G(All)	0849
24.04.1961	Llanhilleth Middle - Crumlin Jn	W(GWR)	W(Un)	0850
24.04.1961	Little Mill Jn - GLASCOED ROF	W(GWR)	W(Un)	0851
00.05.1961	Dynevor Jn - Carlonnel Jn	W(RSB)	G(All)	0852
01.05.1961 [3]	Trusham - Christow	W(GWR)	G(All)	0853 *
01.05.1961	Cymmer Corrwg - Abercregan Siding	W(SWM)	G(All)	0854
01.05.1961	Falkirk old alignment - across Summerford Viaduct	Sc(NBR)	P(All)	0855
19.05.1961 [4]	Norwood Tar Distillers Siding - Kiveton Park Colliery	E(Mid)	G(All)	0856
29.05.1961	Winterton & Thealby - West Halton	E(GCR)	G(All)	0857
31.05.1961	Griff Jn - Stanleys Siding	LM(LNW)	G(All)	0858
00.06.1961	Tonygroes West GF - Aberavon Town	W(PTR)	G(All)	0859
05.06.1961	Canning Street North - Birkenhead Cathcart Jn	LM(Birk)	G(All)	0860
06.06.1961	Mount Vernon North - Bothwell	Sc(NBR)	G(All)	0861
05.06.1961	Gellyrhaidd Jn - Britannia Colliery	W(GWR)	G(All)	0862
11.06.1961 [3]	Tottenham North Jn - Tottenham West Jn	E(GER)	G(All)	0863
12.06.1961	Prospect Hill - WHITBY (West Cliff)	NE(NER)	P(All)	0864
12.06.1961	Botolph Bridge British Sugar Siding - Longville Jn	E(GNR)	G(All)	0865 *
12.06.1961	Robertsbridge (Hodson's Siding) - Tenterden Town	S(KESLR)	G(All)	0866 *
12.06.1961	PADDOCK WOOD - HAWKHURST	S(SEC)	P(All)	0867
00.07.1961	Swansea Valley Jn - Six Pit Jn	W(Mid)	G(All)	0868
03.07.1961	GRIMSBY (Cleveland Bridge) - IMMINGHAM DOCK	E(GI)	P(All)	0869
03.07.1961	IMMINGHAM TOWN - IMMINGHAM DOCK	E(GI)	P(All)	0870
17.07.1961	Keighley GN Jn - Keighley South Goods	NE(GNR)	G(All)	0871
31.07.1961	WOOFFERTON - TENBURY WELLS	W(SHJt)	P(All)	0872
31.07.1961	Nostell North Jn - Wharncliffe Woodmoor	NE(GCR)	G(All)	0873
31.07.1961	Nostell South Jn - Wintersett Jn	NE(GCR)	G(All)	0874
31.07.1961	Chilton Bank Foot - Chilton Colliery	NE(NER)	G(All)	0875
31.07.1961	Maryhill East Jn - Balmore	Sc(NBR)	G(All)	0876
01.08.1961	Turriff - Macduff	Sc(GNoSR)	G(All)	0877
14.08.1961	ASHCHURCH - UPTON ON SEVERN	W(Mid)	P	0878
14.08.1961	Tewkesbury - Tewkesbury Engine Shed	W(Mid)	G(All)	0879
26.08.1961 [1]	CHESTERFIELD (Central) [Killamarsh North Jn] - SKEGNESS [Waleswood Jn]	E(GCR)	P*	0880
31.08.1961	Churchbridge Sidings - Hawkins Colliery Sidings	LM(LNW)	G(All)	0881
00.09.1961	Abertillery Old Yard - Cwmtillery Colliery	W(GWR)	G(All)	0882
04.09.1961	Halliwell Goods - Astley Bridge	LM(L&Y)	G(All)	0883
11.09.1961 [1]	AMBERGATE [Crich Jn] - MANSFIELD (Town) [Pye Bridge Jn]	LM(Mid)	P*	0884
11.09.1961	Wolfhall Jn - Ludgershall	W(MSWJ)	G(All)	0885
11.09.1961	Marlborough L.L. - Swindon Town	W(MSWJ)	G(All)	0886
11.09.1961	Stoke Gifford West - Filton Jn	W(GWR)	P	0887
11.09.1961	Crigglestone Jn - Horbury Station	NE(L&Y)	P	0888
11.09.1961	ANDOVERSFORD [Junction] - ANDOVER (Red Post Jn)	W(MSWJ)	P	0889
11.09.1961	Andoversford Junction - Cirencester Watermoor	W/S(MSWJ)	G(All)	0890
11.09.1961	Wolfhall Jn - Ludgershall	S(MSWJ)	G(All)	0891
11.09.1961	SWINDON [Rushey Platt Jn] - SWINDON (Town) [Rushey Platt Station]	W(GWR/MSWJ))		0892
11.09.1961	WINCHESTER (Chesil) - Shawford Jn	S(GWR/LSW)	P*	0893
16.09.1961	Bushey Lane Jn - White Moss Level Crossing	LM(L&Y)	G(All)	0894
02.10.1961	PLYMSTOCK Jn - Turnchapel (Admiralty Wharves)	W(LSW)	G(All)	0895
02.10.1961	Oreston Bayley's Siding points - Plymouth & Creston Timber Co's Sidings	W(LSW)	G(All)	0896
29.10.1961 [3]	Grange Jn - Burslem Grange Wharf	LM(NSR)	G(All)	0897 *

Date	Line	Region (Company)	Type of Traffic	Reference Number
Date	*Line*	*Region (Company)*	*Type of Traffic*	*Reference Number*
30.10.1961	DUNTON GREEN - WESTERHAM	S(SEC)	P(All)	*0898*
31.10.1961	Port Siding - Port Dinorwic	LM(LNW)	G(All)	*0899*
02.11.1961	Plymstock - Turnchapel	W(LSW)	G(All)	*0900*
05.11.1961	Fisherrow Jn - Fisherrow	Sc(NBR)	G(All)	*0901*
05.11.1961	Branches Fork Jn - Graigddu Brickworks Siding	W(GWR)	G(All)	*0902*
06.11.1961	Sutton Colliery - Stoneyford Lane Siding	LM(Mid)	G(All)	*0903*
06.11.1961	BILLINGHAM ON TEES - HAVERTON HILL	NE(NER)	W(Un)	*0904*
13.11.1961	MERTHYR (Rydycar Jn) - PONTSTICILL JN	W(B&M)	P	*0905*
04.12.1961	GRAVESEND Central [Hoo Jn] - GRAIN	S(SEC)	P	*0906*
04.12.1961	STOKE JUNCTION Halt - ALLHALLOWS ON SEA	S(SR)	P(All)	*0907*
31.12.1961	Brackenhill Jn - Hemsworth Colliery	NE(Brack)	G(All)	*0908*
01.01.1962	LEICESTER London Road [Wigston South] - RUGBY Midland	LM(Mid)	P	*0909*
01.01.1962	Wigston South - Rugby Newbold Wharf	LM(Mid)	G(All)	*0910*
01.01.1962	Upwey Jn - Upwey	S(GWR)	G(All)	*0911*
01.01.1962	HAVERHILL [Colne Valley Jn] - CHAPPEL & WAKES COLNE	E(CVH)	P	*0912*
01.01.1962	Haverhill [Colne Valley Jn] - Yeldham	E(CVH)	G(All)	*0913*
01.01.1962	Ackworth Moor Top - Hemsworth Colliery	NE(Brack)	G(All)	*0914*
01.01.1962	KEIGHLEY - OXENHOPE	NER(Mid)	P	*0915*
22.01.1962	BARNARD CASTLE [Tees Valley] - PENRITH [Clifton Moor]	NE(NER)	P	*0916*
22.01.1962	Tees Valley - Merrygill Quarry	NE(NER)	G(All)	*0917*
22.01.1962	Appleby Jn - Clifton Moor	NE(NER)	G(All)	*0918*
22.01.1962	Kirkby Stephen Jn - Tebay	NE(NER)	G(All)	*0919*
05.02.1962	BURNMOUTH - EYEMOUTH	Sc(NBR)	P(All)	*0920*
05.02.1962	ROSEHILL & HAWTHORNDEN [Jn] - GALASHIELS [Kilnknowe Jn]	Sc(NBR)	P(All)	*0921*
18.02.1962	Bottesford North Jn - Bottesford South Jn	E(GN&LNWJt)	G(All)	*0922*
23.02.1962	Kiltonthorpe Jn - Lingdale Mine	NE(NER)	G(All)	*0923*
25.02.1962	Lilliehill Jn - Muircockhall Opencast Site	Sc(NBR)	G(All)	*0924*
00.03.1962 [8]	Hall Farm Jn - Copper Mill Jn	E(GER)	G(All)	*0925*
04.03.1962	Hull (Albert Dock) - Hessle Road Crossing - Jn with new spur	NE(HBR)	G(All)	*0926*
05.03.1962	ORMSKIRK [Burscough Jn] - SOUTHPORT [Burscough Bridge]	LM(L&Y)	P	*0927*
12.03.1962 [3]	BASFORD (North) - NOTTINGHAM (Victoria) [Netherfield & Colwick]	E(GNR)	P	*0928*
02.04.1962	NEILSTON HIGH - UPLAWMOOR	Sc(Cal)	P	*0929*
03.04.1962	Foxfield - Coniston	LM(Furn)	G(All)	*0930*
30.04.1962	CHESTER (General) [Mold Jn] - DENBIGH	LM(LNW)	P	*0931*
30.04.1962	NEWPORT (High Street) [Llantarnam] - BLAENAVON L.L.	W(GWR)	P	*0932* *
30.04.1962	Snatchwood Sidings - Blaenavon L.L. Goods	W(GWR)	G(All)	*0933* *
30.04.1962	PANTEG & GRIFFITHSTOWN [Coed-y-Gric Jn] - PONTYPOOL ROAD	W(GWR)	P	*0934*
30.04.1962	NEWPORT (High Street) [Bassaleg Jn] - BRYNMAWR via Crumlin	W(GWR/LNW)	P	*0935*
30.04.1962	NEWPORT (High Street) [Aberbeeg Jn] - EBBW VALE L.L.	W(GWR)	P	*0936*
30.04.1962	Botley - Bishops Waltham	S(LSW)	G(All)	*0937*
30.04.1962	Knowle Jn - Droxford	S(LSW)	G(All)	*0938*
30.04.1962	EDINBURGH (Princes Street) [Dalry Middle Jn] - LEITH (North)	Sc(Cal)	P	*0939*
00.05.1962 [8]	Caelliau Jn - Brynhenllys Colliery	W(Mid)	G(All)	*0940*
03.05.1962	Hoddlesden Jn - Shaw's Siding	LM(L&Y)	G(All)	*0941*
07.05.1962	Hooton - West Kirby	LM(Birk)	G(All)	*0942*
27.05.1962	Corbridge tunnel old alignment	NE(NER)	P(All)	*0943*
03.06.1962	Pelham Street Jn - Washingborough Jn	E(GNR)	P(All)	*0944*
04.06.1962 [3]	Northop Hall Siding - Connah's Quay Dock	LM(GCR)	G(All)	*0945*
04.06.1962	Huntingdon North No.1 - Godmanchester	E(GN&GEJt)	G(All)	*0946*
04.06.1962	Dykes Jn - Cronberry Jn	Sc(GSW)	G(All)	*0947*
18.06.1962	OXFORD [Witney Jn] - FAIRFORD	W(GWR)	P	*0948*
18.06.1962	Witney - Fairford Goods	W(GWR)	G(All)	*0949*
18.06.1962	CAMBRIDGE [Coldham Jn] - MILDENHALL via Burwell	E(GER)	P	*0950*

Date	Line	Region (Company)	Type of Traffic	Reference Number
03.12.1962	Briton Ferry West - Aberavon Seaside (Cambrian Wagon Works)	W(RSB)	G(All)	1006
03.12.1962	Bridport - West Bay	W(GWR)	G(All)	1007
03.12.1962	Chipping Norton - Great Rollright Siding	W(GWR)	G(All)	1008
03.12.1962	KINGHAM - CHIPPING NORTON	W(GWR)	P	1009
03.12.1962	Llanharan West - Wern Tarw East GF	W(GWR)	G(All)	1010
31.12.1962	Builth Road H.L. No.2 - Builth Road L.L.	W(LNW)	G(All)	1011
31.12.1962	Fleur–de–Lis - Bedwas Colliery North	W(B&M)	G(All)	1012
31.12.1962	Henley in Arden - Henley in Arden Goods	W(GWR)	G(All)	1013
31.12.1962	HIRWAUN [Gelli Tarw Jn] - MERTHYR [Rhydycar Jn]	W(GWR)	P	1014
31.12.1962	MOAT LANE JN - TALYLLYN JN	W(Cam)	P	1015
31.12.1962	Llanidloes - Talyllyn Jn	W(Cam)	G(All)	1016
31.12.1962	Talyllyn East Jn - Talyllyn North Jn	W(Cam)	P(All)	1017
31.12.1962	Brecon (Mount Street Sidings) - Brecon (Watton Goods GF)	W(B&M)	G(All)	1018
31.12.1962	HEREFORD (Brecon Curve Jn) - BRECON (via Three Cocks Jn)	W(Mid/Cam)	P	1019
31.12.1962	Eardisley - Three Cocks Jn	W(Mid)	G(All)	1020
31.12.1962	Ludlow - Bitterley	W(S&HJt)	G(All)	1021
31.12.1962	PLYMOUTH (North Road) [Tavistock Jn] - LAUNCESTON (South)	W(GWR/LSW)	P	1022
31.12.1962	Marsh Mill (Coypool WD Siding) - Tavistock South (SWGB Siding)	W(GWR)	G(All)	1023 *
31.12.1962	Lifton Launceston - Jn with 1943 spur	W(GWR)	G(All)	1024
31.12.1962	NEWPORT (High Street) [Gaer Jn] - BRECON (via Dowlais Top)	W(B&M)	P	1025
31.12.1962	NEWPORT (High Street) [Gaer Jn] - NEW TREDEGAR	W(B&M)	P	1026
31.12.1962	Aberbargoed Jn - New Tredegar	W(B&M)	G(All)	1027
07.01.1963	Alsager East Jn - Silverdale	LM(NSR)	G(All)	1028
07.01.1963	Chadderton Jn - Oldham Werneth	LM(L&Y)	G(All)	1029
07.01.1963	Diglake Jn - Bignall Hill Opencast Disposal Centre	LM(NSR)	G(All)	1030
07.01.1963	NOTTINGHAM (Victoria) [Awsworth Jn] - PINXTON SOUTH	LM(GCR/GNR)	P	1031
07.01.1963	Eastwood & Langley North - Pinxton South	LM(GNR)	G(All)	1032
07.01.1963	Whitchurch - Tattenhall Jn	LM(LNW)	G(All)	1033
07.01.1963	PRINCES RISBORO - BANBURY	LM(GW&GCJt)	P(Locals)	1034
07.01.1963	Gunhouse Jn - Gunness & Burringham Goods	E(GCR)	G(All)	1035
07.01.1963	STRATFORD (Low Level) - PALACE GATES	E(GER)	P	1036
07.01.1963	COATBRIDGE CENTRAL - HAMILTON CENTRAL	Sc(Cal)	P(Locals)	1037
27.01.1963	Berkeley Road South Jn - Berkeley Loop Jn	W(GWR)	G(All)	1038
04.02.1963	CHACEWATER - NEWQUAY [Tolcarn Jn]	W(GWR)	P	1039
04.02.1963	Chacewater - Trevemper Siding	W(GWR)	G(All)	1040
04.02.1963	Kiltonthorpe Jn - Kilton Mine	NE(NER)	G(All)	1041
11.02.1963	Burnbank Jn - Peacock Cross (Allenshaw Foundry)	Sc(NBR)	G(All)	1042
11.02.1963	Burnbank Jn - Jn with new spur	Sc(NBR)	G(All)	1043 *
11.02.1963	Bidston Yard - Bidston Locomotive Depot	LM(GCR)	G(All)	1044
01.03.1963	Drope Jn - Peterston West	W(Barry)	G(All)	1045
04.03.1963 [2]	Bethseda Jn - Port Penrhyn Quay Sidings	LM(LNW)	G(All)	1046
04.03.1963	Llanelly Docks [St Davids Jn] - Dafen Goods	W(GWR)	G(All)	1047
04.03.1963	Amesbury - Ratfyn Siding	S(LSWR)	G(All)	1048
04.03.1963	Grateley - Bulford Camp (Sling Army Coal Yard)	S(LSW)	G(All)	1049
04.03.1963	Stamford Jn - Stamford East	E(GNR)	G(All)	1050
06.03.1963	Tirydail - Gulston Siding	W(GWR)	G(All)	1051
27.03.1963	Duffryn Jn No.1 - Cwmavon (Margam Forge)	W(PTR)	G(All)	1052
31.03.1963	Burton on Trent (Anderstaff Lane) - Salt's Engine Shed	LM(Mid)	G(All)	1053
31.03.1963	Cadoxton South - Tonteg Jn	W(Barry)	G(All)	1054 *
31.03.1963	Walnut Tree West - Tynycaeau North	W(Barry)	G(All)	1055 *
01.04.1963	Marehay Crossing - Ripley	LM(Mid)	G(All)	1056
01.04.1963	Abertillery Jn - Abertillery Old Yard	W(GWR)	G(All)	1057
01.04.1963	Pant Jn - Deri Jn	W(B&M)	G(All)	1058

Date	Line	Region (Company)	Type of Traffic	Reference Number
18.06.1962	Birstall Jn - Birstall Lower	NE(LNW)	G(All)	0951
18.06.1962	BISHOP AUCKLAND [East] - BARNARD CASTLE [East]	NE(NER)	P(All)	0952
18.06.1962	Keighley GN Jn - Oxenhope	NE(Mid)	G(All)	0953 *
02.07.1962	DUNSTABLE NORTH - LEIGHTON BUZZARD	LM(LNW)	P	0954
02.07.1962	Haydon Square Jn - Aldgate Haydon Square	E(LNW)	G(All)	0955
22.07.1962	Wharncliffe Branch Siding - Rockingham Colliery	E(Mid)	G(All)	0956
23.07.1962	WELLINGTON [Ketley Jn] - MUCH WENLOCK	W(GWR)	P	0957
23.07.1962	Ketley Jn - Ketley	W(GWR)	G(All)	0958
30.07.1962	BEWDLEY - TENBURY WELLS	W(GWR)	P	0959
30.07.1962	STOURBRIDGE Jn [North Jn] - WOLVERHAMPTON L.L. [Priestfield Jn]	W(GWR)	P	0960
06.08.1962	SWINDON [Highworth Jn] - HIGHWORTH	W(GWR)	W(Un)	0961
06.08.1962	Foulford Jn - Auchtertool	Sc(NBR)	G(All)	0962
18.08.1962 [1]	SHIREBROOK (North) - NOTTINGHAM (Victoria) [Kirkby South Jn]	E(GNR)	P*	0963
18.08.1962 [1]	BLACKPOOL (North) [Foxlow Jn] - RADFORD [Elmton & Creswell Jn] .	E(Mid)	P*	0964
03.09.1962	Aldridge - Brownhills	LM(Mid)	G(All)	0965
08.09.1962 [1]	LEICESTER (London Road) [Woodville Jn] - BLACKPOOL (North) [Swadlincote Jn]	LM(Mid)	P*	0966
08.09.1962 [1]	EDWINSTOWE [Clipstone East Jn] - NOTTINGHAM (Victoria) [Kirkby South Jn]	E(GCR)	P*	0967
08.09.1962 [1]	HUCKNALL (Central [Bulwell South Jn] - BASFORD (North) [Basford West Jn]	E(GC&GNJt)	P*	0968
10.09.1962	DITTON JN - Timperley Jn (via WARRINGTON Bank Quay L.L.)	LM(LNW)	P	0969
10.09.1962	Timperley Jn - Broadheath (No.1)	LM(LNW)	P(All)	0970
10.09.1962	ELLESMERE - WREXHAM (Central)	LM(Cam)	P	0971
10.09.1962	Ellesmere - Pickhill (Cadbury's Siding)	LM(Cam)	G(All)	0972
10.09.1962	BLACKBURN (Daisyfield Jn) - HELLIFIELD	LM(L&Y)	P	0973
10.09.1962	CADOXTON [Cadoxton Jn] - PONTYPRIDD [Treforest Jn]	W(Barry)	P	0974
10.09.1962	CARDIFF (General) [St Fagan's East Jn] - CREIGIAU	W(Barry)	P	0975
10.09.1962	St Fagan's East - Tynycaeau North Jn	W(Barry)	G(All)	0976
10.09.1962	CASTLE CARY - TAUNTON	W(GWR)	P(Locals)	0977
10.09.1962	COALEY JN - DURSLEY	W(Mid)	P	0978
10.09.1962	DIDCOT (East Jn) - NEWBURY	W(GWR)	P	0979
10.09.1962	Highworth Jn - Highworth	W(GWR)	G(All)	0980
10.09.1962	TAUNTON [Creech Jn] - CHARD JN	W(GWR/LSW)	P	0981
10.09.1962	Totnes Ashburton Jn - Ashburton	W(GWR)	G(All)	0982 *
10.09.1962	WEST DRAYTON - UXBRIDGE (Vine Street)	W(GWR)	P	0983
10.09.1962	WHITLAND [Cardigan Jn] - CARDIGAN	W(GWR)	P	0984
10.09.1962	Bottesford East Jn - Bottesford South Jn	E(GN&LNWJt)	P	0985
10.09.1962	Saxondale Jn - Barnstone APCM Siding	E(GN&LNWJt)	G(All)	0986
10.09.1962	Pilmoor South - Husthwaite Gate	NE(NER)	G(All)	0987
10.09.1962	Watergate Colliery Siding - Tanfield Lea Margaret Pit	NE(NER)	G(All)	0988
23.09.1962 [5]	Hayle Penpol Sidings - Hayle Gasworks	W(GWR)	G(All)	0989
01.10.1962 [1]	Redditch - Evesham	LM(Mid)	P(All)	0990
01.10.1962	Finchley Central - High Barnet	E(GNR)	G(All)	0991 *
01.10.1962	Kelvedon - Tudwick Road Siding	E(GER)	G(All)	0992
04.10.1962	Burry Port - Pwll Brickworks	W(BPGV)	G(All)	0993
14.10.1962	Blochairn Jn - Blochairn Ironworks	Sc(NBR)	G(All)	0994
15.10.1962	Andoversford Jn - Andoversford & Dowdeswell	W(MSWJ)	G(All)	0995
15.10.1962	Craig-y-Nos - Brecon Mount Street Sidings	W(N&B)	G(All)	0996
15.10.1962	KINGHAM - CHELTENHAM SPA (Malvern Road) [Lansdown Jn]	W(GWR)	P	0997
15.10.1962	Bourton on the Water - Lansdown Jn	W(GWR)	G(All)	0998
15.10.1962	Ludlow - Bitterley	W(S&HJt)	G(All)	0999
15.10.1962	NEATH (Riverside) - BRECON	W(N&B)	P	1000 *
05.11.1962	Napton & Stockton - Southam & Long Itchington (Rugby Portland Cement Works)	LM(LNW)	G(All)	1001
05.11.1962	Salmons Lane Jn - Millwall Jn	E(GER)	G(All)	1002
12.11.1962	Little Somerford - Malmesbury	W(GWR)	G(All)	1003
19.11.1962	Blackhill Jn - Germiston Jn	Sc(Cal)	G(All)	1004
03.12.1962	BRITON FERRY [West] - TREHERBERT [Cymmer]	W(RSB)	P	1005

Date	Line	Region (Company)	Type of Traffic	Reference Number
01.04.1963	Lytham Goods - Lytham Old Yard	LM(P&W)	G(All)	1059
08.04.1963	Niddrie North - Wanton Wells	Sc(NBR)	G(All)	1060
06.05.1963	Hengord H.L. - Ystrad Mynach North	W(GWR)	G(All)	1061
06.05.1963	Sheerness Triangle North - Sheerness Dockyard Goods	S(SEC)	G(All)	1062
13.05.1963	CHURSTON - BRIXHAM	W(GWR)	P(All)	1063
20.05.1963	Highbridge A - Burnham on Sea	W(S&DJt)	G(All)	1064
27.05.1963	Cardigan Jn - Cardigan	W(GWR)	G(All	1065
00.06.1963 [2]	Cransley - Loddington	LM(Mid)	G(All)	1066 *
01.06.1963	Gresley - Netherseal Colliery	LM(Mid)	G(All)	1067
01.06.1963	Sheffield No 4 - Park Goods	E(GCR)	G(All)	1068
01.06.1963	Swadlincote Jn - Bretby Colliery	LM(Mid)	G(All)	1069
03.06.1963	Middleton Bottom - Middleton Top	LM(LNW)	G(All)	1070
03.06.1963	Hopton Wood Branch Jn - Hopton Wood Quarry	LM(LNW)	G(All)	1071
10.06.1963	Congresbury - Wrington	W(GWR)	G(All)	1072
14.06.1963 [1]	CHILWELL ROF [Lenton South Jn] - ELMTON & CRESWELL [Lenton North Jn]	LM(Mid)	W(Un)	1073
17.06.1963	Atherton Jn (Bag Lane) - Pennington South Jn	LM(LNW)	G(All)	1074
17.06.1963 [3]	REDDITCH - ASHCHURCH	LM(Mid)	P	1075
17.06.1963	Alcester - Evesham	LM(Mid)	G(All)	1076
17.06.1963	Seacombe Jn - Seacombe & Egremont Goods	LM(Wirral)	G(All)	1077
17.06.1963	BOSTON [Grand Sluice] - LINCOLN (Central)	E(GNR)	P	1078
17.06.1963	Grand Sluice - Coningsby Jn	E(GNR)	G(All)	1079
17.06.1963	CHEADLE - CRESSWELL	LM(NSR)	P	1080
17.06.1963	CHESTERFIELD (Central) - NOTTINGHAM (Victoria) [Springwood Jn]	E(GCR)	P(All)	1081
17.06.1963	Chesterfield Hydes Sidings - Heath Jn	E(GCR)	G(All)	1082
17.06.1963	IMMINGHAM DOCK [Goxhill] - NEW HOLLAND (Pier)	E(GCR)	P	1083
17.06.1963	Killingholme Yorkshire Tar Distillers - Goxhill	E(GCR)	G(All)	1084
17.06.1963	Westcraigs Jn - Shotts East	Sc(NBR)	G(All)	1085
21.06.1963	Dubton North Jn - Broomfield Jn	Sc(Cal)	G(All)	1086
22.06.1963	Simpasture - Stillington North	NE(NER)	G(All)	1087
01.07.1963	Claydale Sidings - Hemel Hempstead Midland Road	LM(Mid)	G(All)	1088
01.07.1963	Cleator Moor Jn - Distington Joint Jn	LM(C&WJt)	G(All)	1089
01.07.1963	Moor Row No.1 - Distington Joint Jn	LM(C&WJt)	G(All)	1090
01.07.1963	Tewkesbury - Upton on Severn	W(Mid)	G(All)	1091
01.07.1963	Uffington - Faringdon	W(GWR)	G(All)	1092
20.07.1963	Ruchill Hospital Branch GF - Ruchill Hospital	Sc(Cal)	G(All)	1093
20.07.1963	Robroyston East Jn - Robroyston Hospital	Sc(Cal)	G(All)	1094
22.07.1963	Tryddyn Jn - Coed Talon (Star Quarry Siding)	LM(LNW)	G(All)	1095
27.07.1963	Holwell (Welby Sidings West GF) - Wycombe Jn	LM(Mid)	G(All)	1096
29.07.1963	Cwmavon - Aberavon Town	W(RSB)	G(All)	1097
31.07.1963	Garstang Town - Pilling	LM(GKER)	G(All)	1098
31.07.1963	Perham - Tidworth	WD(MSWJ)	G(All)	1099
05.08.1963	Deri Jn - Pant Jn	W(B&M)	G(All)	1100
12.08.1963	Whitworth - Facit	LM(L&Y)	G(All)	1101
12.08.1963	Bullo Pill West - Bullo Pill Docks	W(GWR)	G(All)	1102
12.08.1963	Coleford Jn - Speech House Road	W(SWJt)	G(All)	1103 *
12.08.1963	Staveley South Jn - Sheepbridge Sidings	E(GCR)	G(All)	1104
12.08.1963	Boosbeck - Guisborough Jn	NE(NER)	G(All)	1105
12.08.1963	Crag Hall - Loftus	NE(NER)	G(All)	1106
19.08.1963	Coalburn - Bankend Colliery	Sc(Cal)	G(All)	1107
19.08.1963	Tottington Jn - Tottington	LM(L&Y)	G(All)	1108
25.08.1963	Lydney West - Lydney Docks Pine End Plywood Factory	W(SWJt)	G(All)	1109
00.09.1963 [7]	North Parade Crossing - North Roskear Holman Boiler Works	W(GWR)	G(All)	1110
02.09.1963	CHESTER (General) [Mold Jn] - BROUGHTON & BRETTON	LM(LNW)	W(Un)	1111
02.09.1963	Whitemyre Jn - Lilliehill Jn	Sc(NBR)	G(All)	1112
09.09.1963	Hincaster Jn - Sandside	LM(Furn)	G(All)	1113

Date	Line	Region (Company)	Type of Traffic	Reference Number
09.09.1963	Woodville Goods Jn - Swadlincote (Wraggs Sidings)	LM(Mid)	G(All)	1114
09.09.1963	BEWDLEY - SHREWSBURY [Abbey Jn]	W(GWR)	P	1115
09.09.1963	Evesham - Ashchurch	W(Mid)	G(All)	1116
09.09.1963	LLANDILO [Carmarthen Valley Jn] - CARMARTHEN [Abergwili Jn]	W(LNW)	P(All)	1117
09.09.1963	PYLE - PORTHCAWL	W(GWR)	P	1118
09.09.1963	Pyle West - Heol–y–Sheet Crossing	W(GWR)	P*	1119
09.09.1963	RADLEY - ABINGDON	W(GWR)	P	1120
09.09.1963	TIVERTON JN - HEMYOCK	W(GWR)	P	1121
09.09.1963	WELLINGTON [Market Drayton Jn] - NANTWICH [Market Drayton Jn]	W/LM(GWR)	P	1122
09.09.1963	WITHAM - YATTON	W(GWR)	P	1123
09.09.1963	Hertford North - Hertford East	E(GNR)	G(All)	1124
09.09.1963	NEWCASTLE (Central) [Pelaw Jn] - WASHINGTON	NE(NER)	P	1125
09.09.1963	Balerno Goods GF - Ravelrig Jn	Sc(Cal)	G(All)	1126
16.09.1963	BRENT - KINGSBRIDGE	W(GWR)	P(All)	1127
29.09.1963	Moffatt Mills Branch Jn - Springbank Quarry	Sc(NBR)	G(All)	1128
30.09.1963	Epworth - Hatfield Moor Depot	E(IAJR)	G(All)	1129
30.09.1963	Exchange Jn - Liverpool (Great Howard St. Goods)	LM(L&Y)	G(All)	1130
30.09.1963	Randolph Colliery GF - Butterknowle	NE(NER)	G(All)	1131
30.09.1963	Wrangbrook Jn - Moorhouse & South Elmsall	NE(HBR)	G(All)	1132
00.10.1963 [5]	Monmouth Troy - Monmouth May Hill	W(GWR)	G(All)	1133
00.10.1963	Garden Lane - Laygate Lane Sidings	NE(NER)	G(All)	1134
01.10.1963	Brymbo East - Ffrith (Bwlchgwyn Siding)	LM(LNW&GW)	G(All)	1135
05.10.1963 [7]	Newhaven Town - Newhaven West Quay	S(LBSC)	G(All)	1136
06.10.1963	Bristol T.M. High Level Goods - Wapping Wharf	W(GWR)	G(All)	1137
07.10.1963	Bethesda Jn - Bethesda	LM(LNW)	G(All)	1138
07.10.1963	Clay Cross Ironworks - Clay Cross Town Goods	LM(Mid)	G(All)	1139
07.10.1963	Shepshed (Charnwood Granite Co. Sid) - Loughborough East	LM(LNW)	G(All)	1140
07.10.1963	Hartington - Ashbourne	LM(LNW)	G(All)	1141
07.10.1963	Humber Road Jn - Gosford Green Goods	LM(LNW)	G(All)	1142
07.10.1963	Colbren Jn - Craig–y–nos	W(N&B)	G(All)	1143 *
07.10.1963	EXETER (St Davids) [Stoke Canon] - DULVERTON [Morebath Jn]	W(GWR)	P	1144
07.10.1963	Thorverton - Tiverton	W(GWR)	G(All)	1145
07.10.1963	Tiverton - Morebath Jn	W(GWR)	G(All)	1146
07.10.1963	Nutbrook Jn - Heanor South	LM(GNR)	G(All)	1147
14.10.1963	Rhos Jn GF - Pant (Brickworks Siding)	W(GWR)	G(All)	1148
14.10.1963	Legacy - Manweb Siding	W(GWR)	G(All)	1149
14.10.1963	Old Kent Road Jn - Deptford Lift Bridge	S(LBSC)	G(All)	1150
15.10.1963 [5]	New Cross Gate East London Down Jn - Deptford Wharf	S(LBSC)	G(All)	1151
15.10.1963 [5]	New Cross Gate East London Up Jn - Deptford Lift Bridge	S(LBSC)	G(All)	1152
27.10.1963	Cwmbran Oakfield Sidings - Newport Mill St	W(GWR)	G(All)	1153
28.10.1963	HAYWARDS HEATH - HORSTED KEYNES	S(LBSC)	P	1154 *
28.10.1963	Ardingly - Horsted Keynes	S(LBSC)	G(All)	1155
28.10.1963	Cranford (East Sidings) - Kimbolton	LM(Mid)	G(All)	1156
28.10.1963	Tolcarn Jn - Trevemper Lane Siding	W(GWR)	G(All)	1157
28.10.1963	Paisley St.James's - Barrhead South	Sc(GSW)	G(All)	1158
01.11.1963	Arbroath North - Arbroath Harbour	Sc(NBR)	G(All)	1159
04.11.1963	Adderbury - Hook Norton	W(GWR)	G(All)	1160
04.11.1963	Delph Jn - Delph	LM(LNW)	G(All)	1161
04.11.1963	Harborne Jn - Harborne	LM(LNW)	G(All)	1162
04.11.1963	Skelmersdale - White Moss Level Crossing	LM(L&Y)	G(All)	1163
04.11.1963	Whitchurch - Tattenhall Jn	LM(LNW)	G(All)	1164
04.11.1963	Coalbrookvale - Brynmawr No.1	W(GW&LNW)	G(All)	1165
04.11.1963	Looe - Looe Goods	W(GWR)	G(All)	1166
04.11.1963	Tredegar - Sirhowy	W(LNW)	G(All)	1167
04.11.1963	HAVANT - HAYLING ISLAND	S(LBSC)	P(All)	1168

Date	Line	Region (Company)	Type of Traffic	Reference Number
04.11.1963	Marefield Jn - North Welham Jn	E/LM(GN&LNW)	G(All)	*1169*
04.11.1963	Castle Eden West - Wingate	NE(NER)	G(All)	*1170*
04.11.1963	Trimdon Grange - Kelloe Bank Foot GF	NE(NER)	G(All)	*1171*
04.11.1963	Wingate Colliery - Grange Level Crossing	NE(NER)	G(All)	*1172*
10.11.1963 [4]	Frome South Jn - Frome West Jn GF	W(GWR)	G(All)	*1173*
11.11.1963	Blaydon Mineral Yard - Blaydon South	NE(NER)	G(All)	*1174*
11.11.1963	Blaydon South Loop West - Rowlands Gill	NE(NER)	G(All)	*1175*
11.11.1963	Hetton North - Murton	NE(NER)	G(All)	*1176*
11.11.1963	Melmerby North - Masham	NE(NER)	G(All)	*1177*
11.11.1963	Swalwell North - Blaydon Main	NE(NER)	G(All)	*1178*
11.11.1963	Reedsmouth - Bellingham (North Tyne)	NE(NBR)	G(All)	*1179*
11.11.1963	Rowlands Gill - Blackhill	NE(NER)	G(All)	*1180* *
11.11.1963	Thornton - Cullingworth	NE(GNR)	G(All)	*1181*
11.11.1963	Scotsgap - Rothbury	NE(NBR)	G(All)	*1182*
11.11.1963	Woodburn - Reedsmouth	NE(NBR)	G(All)	*1183*
18.11.1963	Ormskirk Branch Sidings - Skelmersdale	LM(L&Y)	G(All)	*1184*
24.11.1963	Darlaston Jn - Fallings Heath (Lloyds Works Sidings)	LM(LNW)	G(All)	*1185*
25.11.1963	High St Kensington - High St Kensington Coal Yard	LM(Mid)	G(All)	*1186*
00.12.1963 [2]	Farnsfield Jn - Bilsthorpe	LM(MNJt)	G(All)	*1187*
01.12.1963	Netley - Netley Hospital	S(LSW)	G(All)	*1188*
01.12.1963	Congleton Upper Jn - Congleton Lower Jn GF	LM(NSR)	G(All)	*1189*
02.12.1963	Buckingham - Banbury Merton St	LM(LNW)	G(All)	*1190* *
02.12.1963	Cheddington - Aylesbury High St	LM(LNW)	G(All)	*1191*
02.12.1963	Penygroes - Nantlle	LM(LNW)	G(All)	*1192*
02.12.1963	Stanton Jn - Nutbrook Sidings	LM(GNR)	G(All)	*1193*
02.12.1963	Weedon - Napton & Stockton	LM(LNW)	G(All)	*1194*
02.12.1963	Buildwas East Jn - Alveley Sidings	W(GWR)	G(All)	*1195* *
02.12.1963	Buildwas - Longville	W(GWR)	G(All)	*1196*
02.12.1963	Buildwas - Shrewsbury S&M Jn GF	W(GWR)	G(All)	*1197*
02.12.1963	Lassodie - Lindsay Colliery	Sc(NBR)	G(All)	*1198*
02.12.1963 [3]	Thornton West Jn - West Wemyss (Wimpey's Siding)	Sc(NBR)	G(All)	*1199*
09.12.1963	Robin Hood - Newmarket Colliery	NE(EWYU)	G(All)	*1200*
11.12.1963	Whitwick Colliery - Shepshed (Charnwood Granite Co's Siding)	LM(LNW)	G(All)	*1201*
23.12.1963	Normacot Jn - Park Hall Colliery	LM(NSR)	G(All)	*1202*
23.12.1963	Niddrie North - Niddrie West (Lothian Lines)	Sc(NBR)	G(All)	*1203*
30.12.1963	Shefford - Hitchin Midland Goods Yard	E(Mid)	G(All)	*1204*
06.01.1964	Bewdley - Tenbury Wells	LM(GWR)	G(All)	*1205*
06.01.1964 [3]	Blodwell Jn - Llanrhaiadr Mochnant	LM(Cam)	G(All)	*1206* *
06.01.1964	Halesowen - Rubery	LM(HJt)	G(All)	*1207*
06.01.1964	Norton Crossing Jn - East Cannock Jn	LM(LNW)	G(All)	*1208*
06.01.1964	Oakley Jn - Piddington (Yardley Chase OESD Siding)	LM(Mid)	G(All)	*1209* *
06.01.1964	Tintern Quarry - Monmouth Troy	W(GWR)	G(All)	*1210*
06.01.1964	Cambridge Jn - Hitchin Midland Goods Yard	E(Mid)	G(All)	*1211* *
06.01.1964	CHURCH FENTON - WETHERBY	NE(NER)	P	*1212*
06.01.1964	LEEDS [Cross Gates] - HARROGATE [Crimple Jn]	NE(NER)	P	*1213*
06.01.1964	Wetherby South Jn - Crimple	NE(NER)	G(All)	*1214*
06.01.1964	Kelty - Blairenbathie	Sc(NBR)	G(All)	*1215*
08.01.1964	Ashby–de–la–Zouch - Burton Road Crossing (Standard Soap Co.)	LM(Mid)	G(All)	*1216*
13.01.1964	Plymouth (North Road) - Plymouth Millbay	W(GWR)	G(All)	*1217*
13.01.1964	Cornwall Jn - Devonport Jn	W(GWR)	G(All)	*1218*
13.01.1964	Chesterfield Central - Hydes Sidings	E(GCR)	G(All)	*1219*
19.01.1964	Kentish Town Jn - Highgate Road Jn	LM(Mid)	G	*1220*
20.01.1964 [2]	North Skelton Jn - Priestcroft Jn	NE(NER)	G(All)	*1221*

Date	Line	Region (Company)	Type of Traffic	Reference Number
24.01.1964	Cobnarwood Jn - Monkwood	E(Mid)	G(All)	1222
31.01.1964 [3]	PYLE - PORTHCAWL	W(GWR)	P*	1223
00.02.1964	Pontypool Road South Jn - Pontypool Road West Jn	W(GWR)	G(All)	1224
03.02.1964	Axminster - Lyme Regis	W(LSW)	G(All)	1225
03.02.1964	Blisworth (RTB Siding) - Woodford West Jn	LM(SMJ)	G(All)	1226
03.02.1964	Seaton Jn - Seaton	W(LSW)	G(All)	1227
03.02.1964	Blackfriars - Blackfriars Goods	S(SEC)	G(All)	1228
17.02.1964	Bestwood Jn - Bulwell Forest	LM(GNR)	G(All)	1229
17.02.1964	Tunstall Jn - Longport Jn	LM(NSR)	G(All)	1230
24.02.1964	Embankment GF - Uxbridge High St	W(GWR)	G(All)	1231
24.02.1964	West Drayton & Yiewsley - Uxbridge Vine St	W(GWR)	G(All)	1232 *
24.02.1964	Crombie RNAD Branch Jn - GF Charlestown	Sc(NBR)	G(All)	1233
24.02.1964	Menstrie & Glenochil - Alva	Sc(NBR)	G(All)	1234
26.02.1964	Lochore Mary Pit - Westfield Lurgi Plant Siding	Sc(NBR)	G(All)	1235
02.03.1964	Burton–on–Trent Uxbridge St.Jn - Bond End Wharf	LM(Mid)	G(All)	1236
02.03.1964	Cadley Hill Colliery - Wraggs Sidings	LM(Mid)	G(All)	1237
02.03.1964	ETRURIA - KIDSGROVE (Liverpool Road) via Hanley	LM(NSR)	P	1238
02.03.1964	Kidsgrove Liverpool Road - Newchapel & Goldenhill	LM(NSR)	G(All)	1239
02.03.1964	Old Dinting Goods GF - Waterside	LM(GCR)	G(All)	1240
02.03.1964	STOKE ON TRENT - SILVERDALE	LM(NSR)	P	1241
02.03.1964	Swains Park Crossing - Woodville Goods	LM(Mid)	G(All)	1242
02.03.1964	Duckmanton South Jn - Duckmanton East Jn	E(GCR)	G(All)	1243
02.03.1964	MIDDLESBROUGH [Nunthorpe] - GUISBOROUGH	NE(NER)	P	1244
02.03.1964	Dalry Middle Jn - Haymarket West Jn	Sc(Cal)	P(All)	1245
02.03.1964	Kipps (Sun Foundry) - Rigghead Coup	Sc(NBR)	G(All)	1246
02.03.1964	Lanridge Jn - Mannieshall Siding	Sc(Cal)	G(All)	1247
08.03.1964	Pleasley Jn - Hollins Siding	LM(Mid)	G(All)	1248
08.03.1964	Lydney Jn - Otters Pool Jn	W(SWJt)	G(All)	1249
09.03.1964	North Acton Jn - Wood Lane (United Dairies Siding)	W(GWR)	G(All)	1250
09.03.1964	Dalry Jn - Coltbridge Jn	Sc(Cal)	G(All)	1251
16.03.1964	ABERCYNON - ABERDARE L.L.	W(Taff)	P	1252 *
16.03.1964	CARDIFF (General) - CARDIFF (Clarence Road)	W(GWR)	P	1253
16.03.1964	Riverside Branch North Curran's Siding - Cardiff Clarence Road	W(GWR)	G(All)	1254
23.03.1964	Tattenhall Jn - Whitchurch Chester Jn	LM(LNW)	G(All)	1255
31.03.1964	Moredon Siding - Cirencester Watermoor	W(MSWJ)	G(All)	1256
00.04.1964	Crumlin Jn - Llanhilleth Middle	W(GWR)	G(All)	1257
01.04.1964	Swinton Town - Cirencester Watermoor	W(MSWJ)	G(All	1258
06.04.1964	Buckminster Siding - South Witham Pains Siding	LM(Mid)	G(All)	1259 *
06.04.1964	Carr Mill Jn - Fleet Lane LC (Marsh's Siding)	LM(LNW)	G(All)	1260
06.04.1964	Cradley Road Bridge GF - Old Hill Goods	LM(GWR)	G(All)	1261
06.04.1964	Haydock Jn - Old Ford Colliery	LM(LNW)	G(All)	1262
06.04.1964	Shackerstone Jn - Hugglescote	LM(A&NJt)	G(All)	1263
06.04.1964	Bovey - Moretonhampstead	W(GWR)	G(All)	1264
06.04.1964	KEMBLE - TETBURY	W(GWR)	P(All)	1265
06.04.1964	KEMBLE - CIRENCESTER (Town)	W(GWR)	P	1266
06.04.1964	AYR [Dalrymple Jn] - DALMELLINGTON	Sc(GSW)	P	1267
06.04.1964	Beattock - Moffat	Sc(Cal)	G(All)	1268
06.04.1964	ELGIN [Lossie Jn] - LOSSIEMOUTH	Sc(GNosR)	P	1269
06.04.1964	KILMARNOCK [Crosshouse Jn] - IRVINE	Sc(GSW)	P	1270
06.04.1964	KILMARNOCK [Hurlford Jn] - DARVEL	Sc(GSW)	P	1271
13.04.1964	Oldham Waterloo Sidings - Greenfield	LM(LNW)	G(All)	1272
13.04.1964	Quakers Yard East - Quakers Yard LL Jn	W(GWR)	G(All)	1273
15.04.1964	TAUNTON [Curry Rivell Jn] - YEOVIL (Town)	W(GWR)	P	1274
15.04.1964	TAUNTON [Durston] - ATHELNEY [Athelney Jn]	W(GWR)	P	1275
20.04.1964	Ferniegair Jn - Swinehill	Sc(Cal)	G(All)	1276

▲A C2X class 32546 is at Grange Road with a Three Bridges to Tunbridge Wells West local on 12th January 1950. The line between Ashurst and Three Bridges survived until 2nd January 1967. (R.C.Riley)

▲ Class O1 31370 built in 1903, stands at Headcorn with a single coach passenger train for the Kent & East Sussex line on 27th July 1953. Passenger services ceased to ran after 4th January 1954. (R.C.Riley)

►LMS design Class 2 2-6-2T 41293 with an ancient three coach set rests at Horsted Keynes on 4th September 1953. The branch from Haywards Heath was operated by third rail. (R.C.Riley)

Date	Line	Region (Company)	Type of Traffic	Reference Number
24.04.1964	Newton - Dechmont Briquette Works	Sc(Cal)	G(All)	1277
27.04.1964	Croft Jn GF - Croft Depot	NE(NER)	G(All)	1278
27.04.1964	Cross Gates - Wetherby Goods	NE(NER)	G(All)	1279
27.04.1964	Redmile - Hawes	NE(NER)	G(All)	1280
04.05.1964	Caernarvon - Llanberis	LM(LNW)	G(All)	1281
04.05.1964	Caernarvon - Afonwen	LM(LNW)	G	1282
04.05.1964	Gotham Co's Siding - Gotham Goods	LM(GCR)	G(All)	1283
04.05.1964	Harbourne Jn - Harbourne	LM(LNW)	G(All)	1284
04.05.1964	Oundle - Thrapston Bridge Street	LM(LNW)	G(All)	1285
04.05.1964	Tibshelf Town - Tibshelf Colliery	LM(GCR)	G(All)	1286
04.05.1964	Tibshelf & Newton - Tibshelf Colliery	LM(Mid)	G(All)	1287
04.05.1964	Aberdovey - Aberdovey Harbour	W(Cam)	G(All)	1288
04.05.1964	Pontiscill Jn - Dowlais Central	W(B&M)	G(All)	1289
04.05.1964	Vaynor Siding - Brecon Watton Goods	W(B&M)	G(All)	1290
04.05.1964	BROCKENHURST [Lymington Jn] - POOLE [Hokes Bay Jn] (Via Ringwood)	S(LSW)	P	1291
04.05.1964	Lymington Jn - Ringwood	S(LSW)	G(All)	1292
04.05.1964	BROADSTONE - HAMWORTHY JN	S(LSW)	P	1293
04.05.1964	Broadstone (Doulton Siding) - Hamworthy Jn	S(LSW)	G(All)	1294
04.05.1964	SALISBURY [Aldenbury Jn] - WEST MOORS	S(LSWR)	P(All)	1295
04.05.1964	Scalford - Waltham on the Wolds	E(GNR)	G(All)	1296
04.05.1964	Waltham Jn - Eaton Siding	E(GNR)	G(All)	1297
04.05.1964 [1]	Finsbury Park No.7 - Edgware	E(GNR)	G(All)	1298 *
04.05.1964	BISHOP AUCKLAND - DURHAM [Reilly Mill Jn]	NE(NER)	P	1299
04.05.1964	DURHAM [Newton Hall Jn] - SUNDERLAND	NE(NER)	P	1300
04.05.1964	EDINBURGH (Waverley) - BERWICK ON TWEED	Sc(NBR)	P(Local)	1301
04.05.1964	Kilsyth Jn GF - Banknock Siding	Sc(K&B)	G(All)	1302
04.05.1964	Wilsontown Jn - Kingshill No.2 Colliery	Sc(Cal)	G(All)	1303
04.05.1964	Twechar - Kilsyth Old	Sc(NBR)	G(All)	1304
06.05.1964	NORTHAMPTON (Castle) - PETERBOROUGH (East) [Yarwell Jn]	LM(LNW)	P	1305
11.05.1964	Plodder Lane (Highfield Siding) - Little Hulton Colliery	LM(LNW)	G(All)	1306
11.05.1964	Southampton Yard - SOUTHAMPTON (C&I Boat Shed)	S(LSW)	P*(All)	1307
18.05.1964	Stanton Fork Jn No.1 GF Stanton Old Works (GNR)	LM(GNR)	G(All)	1308
18.05.1964	Esk Valley Jn - Polton	SC(NBR)	G(All)	1309
19.05.1964	Marlborough L.L - Marlborough H.L.	W(GWR)	G(All)	1310
21.05.1964	Gartverrie Branch GF - Gartverrie Fireclay Works	Sc(NBR)	G(All)	1311
01.06.1964	Cockermouth Jn - Cockermouth Old Goods	LM(LNW)	G(All)	1312
01.06.1964	Leen Valley Jn - Daybrook	LM(GNR)	G(All)	1313
01.06.1964	Rocester - Ashbourne	LM(LNW)	G(All)	1314
01.06.1964	Seaton - Uppingham	LM(LNW)	G(All)	1315
01.06.1964	Salisbury East - Salisbury Market House Sidings	S(LSW)	G(All)	1316
01.06.1964	Humberstone - Melton Mowbray North	E(GNR/LNWJt)	G(All)	1317
01.06.1964 [3]	Park Jn - Edgware	E(GNR)	G(All)	1318 *
15.06.1964	North Rode Jn - Leek	LM(NSR)	G(All)	1319
15.06.1964	Harrington Jn - Distington Ironworks	LM(WCEJt)	G(All)	1320
15.06.1964	Harrington Jn - Wilkinson's Wagon Works	LM(C&WJt)	G(All)	1321
15.06.1964	Windsor Bridge No.2 - New Barns Jn	LM(L&Y)	G(All)	1322
15.06.1964	Cowbridge Road Jn - Coity Goods	W(Barry)	G(All)	1323
15.06.1964	BARRY (Town) - BRIDGEND	W(Barry)	P	1324
15.06.1964	Hengoed H.L. - Penalltau Jn	W(GWR)	G(All)	1325
15.06.1964	Maesycwmmer Jn - Hengoed H.L.	W(GWR)	G(All)	1326
15.06.1964	Ocean & Taff Merthyr Collieries - Cresselley Crossing	W(GWR)	G(All)	1327
15.06.1964	Hafodrynys West - Sirhowy Jn	W(GWR)	G(All)	1328
15.06.1964	Pontypool Road Station South - Trosnant Jn	W(GWR)	G(All)	1329 *
15.06.1964	Swansea Eastern Depot - Wind Street Jn	W(GWR)	G(All)	1330
15.06.1964	Windsor Colliery North GF - Senghenydd	W(Taff)	G(All)	1331

Date	Line	Region (Company)	Type of Traffic	Reference Number
15.06.1964	Chesterfield Tube Works Sidings - Brampton Goods	E(Mid)	G(All)	1332
06.07.1964	Curry Rivell Jn - Hendford (Yeovil)	W(GWR)	G(All)	1333
06.07.1964	Bramley - Cutlers Jn (Laisterdyke)	NE(GNR)	G(All)	1334
06.07.1964	Spring Bank North - Springhead Locomotive	NE(H&B)	G(All)	1335
06.07.1964	Springfield Jn - Little Weighton	NE(H&B)	G(All)	1336
06.07.1964	Brackenhill Jn - Catrine	S(LSW)	G(All)	1337
06.07.1964	Calder - Airdrie East	Sc(Cal)	G(All)	1338
06.07.1964	CRAIGENDORAN - ARROCHAR & TARBERT	Sc(NBR)	P(Locals)	1339
06.07.1964	EDINBURGH (Princes Street) - KINGSKNOWE	Sc(Cal)	P	1340
06.07.1964	GLENEAGLES - CRIEFF	Sc(Cal)	P	1341 *
06.07.1964	Gleneagles - Muthill	Sc(Cal)	G(All)	1342
06.07.1964	Crieff - Comrie	Sc(Cal)	G(All)	1343
06.07.1964	Imperial Tube Works Siding - Airdrie East	Sc(Cal)	G(All)	1344
06.07.1964	Kipps Incline Foot - Airdrie North	Sc(NBR)	G(All)	1345
06.07.1964	Manuel Brickworks - Bowhouse	Sc(NBR)	G(All)	1346
06.07.1964	Maryhill Central Jn - Kelvin Bridge	Sc(Cal)	G(All)	1347
06.07.1964	Mayfield Jn GF - Darvel	Sc(GSW)	G(All)	1348
06.07.1964 2	South Renfrew No.2 - Kings Inch	Sc(G&PJt)	G(All)	1349
06.07.1964	TILLYNAUGHT - BANFF	Sc(GNoSR)	P	1350
06.07.1964	Waterside - Dalmellington	Sc(GSW)	G(All)	1351
13.07.1964	Denham - Uxbridge High Street	W(GWR)	G(All)	1352
13.07.1964	West Drayton - Uxbridge Vine Street	W(GWR)	G(All)	1353
13.07.1964	Hengoed H.L. - Hengoed L.L.	W(Rhy)	G(All)	1354
13.07.1964	Wells East Somerset - Wells Priory Road GF	W(S&DJt)	G(All)	1355
13.07.1964	Barnwell - Burwell	E(GER)	G(All)	1356
13.07.1964	Fordham - Mildenhall	E(GER)	G(All)	1357
13.07.1964	Ely Dock Jn - Sutton	E(GER)	G(All)	1358
13.07.1964	Mellis - Eye	E(GER)	G(All)	1359
13.07.1964	Somersham - Warboys	E(GN&GEJt)	G(All)	1360
13.07.1964	Three Horseshoes - Benwick	E(GER)	G(All)	1361
19.07.1964 3	Babbington Jn - Cinderhill Colliery	LM(GNR)	G(All)	1362
20.07.1964	Caerphilly East - Machen (via Waterloo Halt up line)	W(B&M)	G(All)	1363
22.07.1964	Dereham South - Dereham West	E(GER)	G(All)	1364
27.07.1964	Boskell Siding - Lansalson	W(GWR)	G(All)	1365
27.07.1964	Virginia Water B - Virginia Water C	S(LSW)	G(All)	1366
29.07.1964	Milngavie - Ellangowie Paper Works	Sc(NBR)	G(All)	1367
03.08.1964	Burrows Jn - Aberavon Seaside Cambrian Wagon Works	W(RSB)	G(All)	1368
03.08.1964	Ditchingham - Bungay	E(GER)	G(All)	1369
10.08.1964	Endborne Jn - Winnal Sidings	W(GWR)	G(All)	1370
10.08.1964	Didcot East Jn - Newbury East Jn	W(GWR)	G(All)	1371
10.08.1964	Lye Goods Yard - Lye Hayes Lane	W(GWR)	G(All)	1372
10.08.1964	Amotherby - Husthwaite Gate	NE(NER)	G(All)	1373
10.08.1964	Gilling - Kirby Moorside	NE(NER)	G(All)	1374
10.08.1964	Pickering Mill Lane - Thornton Dale	NE(NER)	G(All)	1375
10.08.1964	Rawdon Jn - Yeadon Goods	NE(Mid)	G(All)	1376
10.08.1964	East Fife Central Jn - Lochty	Sc(NBR)	G(All)	1377 *
10.08.1964	Bathgate - Fauldhouse	Sc(NBR)	G(All)	1378
10.08.1964	Glenesk Jn - Dalkeith	Sc(NBR)	G(All)	1379
10.08.1964	ROXBURGH - JEDBURGH	Sc(NBR)	P(All)	1380
17.08.1964	Charnwood Forest Jn - Hugglescote	LM(A&NJt)	G(All)	1381
17.08.1964	Gleneagles - Crieff	Sc(Cal)	G(All)	1382
22.08.1964	Ilkeston Jn - Ilkeston Town	LM(Mid)	G(All)	1383
24.08.1964	Heckmondwike Jn - Gildersome	NE(LNW)	G(All)	1384
31.08.1964	Ruabon North - Ruabon (Brick & Terracotta Siding)	W(GWR)	G(All)	1385
31.08.1964	Duffryn Yard - Maesteg (Neath Road)	W(PTR)	G(All)	1386

Date	Line	Region (Company)	Type of Traffic	Reference Number
31.08.1964	Maesteg (Neath Road) - Cwmdu	W(PTR)	G(All)	1387 *
31.08.1964	Mill Hill East - Edgware	E(GNR)	G(All)	1388
31.08.1964	Nunthorpe East - Guisborough	NE(NER)	G(All)	1389
00.09.1964	Northeys Siding GF (Sutton Harbour) - Northey s Siding	W(GWR)	G(All)	1390
01.09.1964	Croftengea Siding - Jamestown	Sc(NBR)	G(All)	1391
06.09.1964 [5]	WESTON SUPER MARE Excursion Platform - Locking Road GF	W(GWR)	P*	1392
07.09.1964	WOLVERTON NEWPORT - PAGNALL	LM(LNW)	P	1393
07.09.1964	DERBY (Friargate) - NOTTINGHAM (Victoria) [Bagthorpe Jn]	LM(GNR)	P	1394
07.09.1964	MIDDLETON JN - MIDDLETON	LM(L&Y)	P	1395
07.09.1964	LEICESTER (London Road) [Knighton North Jn] - BURTON ON TRENT [Leicester Jn]	LM(Mid)	P	1396 *
07.09.1964	STALYBRIDGE - DIGGLE via Micklehurst	LM(LNW)	P	1397
07.09.1964	SOUTHPORT [St Lukes] - PRESTON [Whitehouse Jn]	LM(L&Y)	P	1398
07.09.1964	Hesketh Bank - Penwortham Jn	LM(L&Y)	G(All)	1399
07.09.1964	STAFFORD - WELLINGTON	LM(LNW)	P	1400
07.09.1964	VERNEY JN - BUCKINGHAM	LM(LNW)	P	1401
07.09.1964	WELLINGTON - SHREWSBURY	LM(SH&WJt)	P(Locals)	1402
07.09.1964	Olive Mount Jn - Edge Hill No.4	LM(LNW)	G(All)	1403
07.09.1964	CARLISLE [Port Carlisle Jn] - SILLOTH	LM(NBR)	P(All)	1404
07.09.1964	Roe Lane Jn - Hawkeshead Street Jn	LM(L&Y)	G(All)	1405
07.09.1964	Cahnc & Hunt's Siding - Oldbury Goods Yard	LM(GWR)	G(All))	1406
07.09.1964	Caernarvon - Llanberis	LM(LNW)	G(All)	1407
07.09.1964	BRISTOL (Temple Meads) [Parson Street Jn] - PORTISHEAD	W(GWR)	P	1408
07.09.1964	Bude - Bude Basin Siding	W(LSW)	G(All)	1409
07.09.1964	Kingham - Chipping Norton	W(GWR)	G(All)	1410
07.09.1964	Barnstaple Jn - Rolles Quay Siding	W(LSW)	G(All)	1411
07.09.1964	Devonport Kings Road - St Budeaux Victoria Road	W(LSW)	P(All)	1412 *
07.09.1964	Kingham - Bourton on the Water	W(GWR)	G(All)	1413
07.09.1964	Saversnake L.L. - Marlborough L.L.	W(GWR)	G(All)	1414 *
07.09.1964	Tavistock South SWGB Siding - Lydford	W(LSW&GW)	G(All)	1415
07.09.1964	WORCESTER (Shrub Hill) [Leominster Jn] - BROMYARD	W(GWR)	P(All)	1416
07.09.1964	ANDOVER JN - ROMSEY [Kimbridge Jn]	S(LSW)	P	1417
07.09.1964	Andover Town - Kimbridge Jn	S(LSW)	G(All)	1418
07.09.1964	Frimley Jn - Sturt Lane Jn East	S(LSW)	P(All)	1419
07.09.1964	Frimley Jn - Sturt Lane Jn West	S(LSW)	P(All)	1420
07.09.1964	Melton Mowbray North - Stathern Ironside Sidings	E(GN&LNWJt)	G(All	1421
07.09.1964	WITHAM - MALDON EAST & HEYBRIDGE	E(GER)	P	1422
07.09.1964	AUDLEY END - BARTLOW	E(GER)	P	1423
07.09.1964	MANCHESTER (Piccadilly) [Beighton Jn] - SKEGNESS [Pyewipe Jn]	E(GCR)	P*	1424
07.09.1964	NORTH WALSHAM (Main) - MUNDESLEY ON SEA	E(N&SJt)	P	1425
07.09.1964	SCARBOROUGH [Tuxford North] - NOTTINGHAM (Midland) [Tuxford West]	E(GCR)	P*	1426
07.09.1964	SCARBOROUGH [Warsop Jn] - NOTTINGHAM (Midland) [Shirebrook West]	E(GCR)	P*	1427
07.09.1964	WAKEFIELD (Westgate) [Wrenthorpe Jn] - BRADFORD (Exchange) [Dudley Hill]	NE(NER)	P	1428
07.09.1964	Cudworth Station - Monk Spring Jn	NE(Mid)	G(All)	1429 *
07.09.1964	Alyth Jn - Alyth	Sc(Cal)	G(All)	1430
07.09.1964	Alyth Jn - Newtyle Goods	Sc(Cal)	G(All)	1431
07.09.1964	Brechin - Edzell	Sc(Cal)	G(All)	1432
07.09.1964	Caraston - Justinhaugh	Sc(Cal)	G(All)	1433
07.09.1964	EDINBURGH (Waverley) - MUSSELBURGH (via Abbeyhill)	Sc(NBR)	P	1434
07.09.1964	GLASGOW (Queens Street) [Campsie Branch Jn] - KIRKINTILLOCH	Sc(NBR)	P(Locals)	1435
07.09.1964	Justinhaugh - Careston	Sc(Cal)	G(All)	1436
07.09.1964	Rutherglen London Road - Balornock Jn	Sc(Cal)	G(All)	1437
07.09.1964	Strathord - Bankfoot	Sc(Cal)	G(All)	1438
14.09.1964	Brotton - Boosbeck	NE(NER)	G(All)	1439
21.09.1964	Ardwick Jn - Ashburys Midland Jn	LM(Mid)	G(All)	1440
21.09.1964	Chinley East Jn - Chinley South Jn	LM(Mid)	G(All)	1441

Date	Line	Region (Company)	Type of Traffic	Reference Number
21.09.1964	Ross Jn - Fernigair Jn	Sc(Cal)	G(All)	*1442*
27.09.1964	Castle Caereinon - Sylfaen	LM(WLLR)	G(All)	*1443 **
28.09.1964	Short Heath - Birchills PS	LM(Mid)	G(All)	*1444*
28.09.1964	Blaencaegurwen Colliery - Brynamman West	W(Mid/GWR)	G(All)	*1445*
28.09.1964	Brecon Curve Jn - Eardisley	W(Mid)	G(All)	*1446*
28.09.1964	Kington Jn - Kington	W(GWR)	G(All)	*1447*
28.09.1964	Titley Jn - Presteigne	W(GWR)	G(All)	*1448*
28.09.1964 [5]	Treforest Jn - Llantwit Fardre Cwm Colliery GF	W(Taff)	G(All)	*1449*
28.09.1964 [5]	Waterhall Jn - Creigiau Quarry Siding	W(Taff)	G(All)	*1450*
28.09.1964	Blane Valley Jn - Lennox Castle Hospital Siding	Sc(NBR)	G(All)	*1451*
01.10.1964	Yatton - Cheddar	W(GWR)	G(All)	*1452*
05.10.1964	HARROW & WEALDSTONE - BELMONT	LM(LNW)	P(All)	*1453*
05.10.1964	LIVERPOOL (Central) [Hough Green East] - WARRINGTON (Central) [Widnes Jn]	LM(GC&MidJt)	P	*1454 **
05.10.1964	Hough Green Jn - Widnes East	LM(GC&MidJt)	P(All)	*1455*
05.10.1964	Lancaster Freeman's Wood Siding - Glasson Dock	LM(LNW)	G(All)	*1456*
05.10.1964	Lowton St Marys - Hindley South	LM(GCR)	G(All)	*1457*
05.10.1964	Gwinear Road - Helston	W(GWR)	G(All)	*1458*
05.10.1964	PLYMOUTH (North Road) - PENZANCE	W(GWR)	P(Locals)	*1459*
05.10.1964	TAUNTON - EXETER (St Davids)	W(GWR)	P(Locals)	*1460*
05.10.1964	TAUNTON - WESTON SUPER MARE	W(GWR)	P(Locals)	*1461*
05.10.1964	TIVERTON JN - TIVERTON	W(GWR)	P	*1462*
05.10.1964	DEREHAM - WELLS NEXT THE SEA	E(GER)	P	*1463*
05.10.1964	Fakenham East - Wells next the Sea	E(GER)	G(All)	*1464*
05.10.1964	Needingworth Jn - Bluntisham	E(GER)	G(All)	*1465*
05.10.1964	Knaresborough Jn - Brafferton	NE(NER)	G(All)	*1466*
05.10.1964	Barrmill Jn GF - Beith Town	Sc(GB&KJt)	G(All)	*1467*
05.10.1964	COATBRIDGE (Central) - BRIDGETON CROSS	Sc(Cal)	P	*1468 **
05.10.1964	RUTHERGLEN - DUMBARTON (East) (via Glasgow Central L.L.)	Sc(Cal)	P	*1469 **
05.10.1964	Old Kilpatrick - Dunglass Jn	Sc(Cal)	G(All)	*1470*
05.10.1964	STOBCROSS - POSSIL	Sc(Cal)	P	*1471*
05.10.1964	Partick North Jn - Partick East Jn	Sc(Cal)	G(All)	*1472*
05.10.1964	Tollcross - Partick Central Goods	Sc(Cal)	G(All)	*1473*
05.10.1964	Bridgeton Cross Jn - Strathcylde Jn	Sc(Cal)	G(All)	*1474*
05.10.1964	LANARK - MUIRKIRK	Sc(GSW)	P	*1475*
05.10.1964	Ponfeigh - Muirkirk	Sc(Cal)	G(All)	*1476*
05.10.1964	Mawcarse - Auchtermuchty	Sc(NBR)	G(All)	*1477*
05.10.1964	Millisle - Garlieston Harbour	Sc(PWJt)	G(All)	*1478*
05.10.1964	Newton Stewart - Whithorn	Sc(PWJt)	G(All)	*1479*
05.10.1964	St Fort - Lindores	Sc(NBR)	G(All)	*1480*
07.10.1964	Plean Jn - Plean Quarry	Sc(Cal)	G(All)	*1481*
12.10.1964	NOTTINGHAM (Midland) [Radford Jn] - WORKSOP [Shireoaks East Jn]	LM/E(Mid)	P	*1482 **
12.10.1964	Midhurst Goods - Petworth	S(LBSC)	G(All)	*1483*
18.10.1964	Chatterley Jn - Chesterton Jn	LM(NSR)	G(All)	*1484 **
19.10.1964	HULL (Paragon) [West Parade Jn] - WITHERNSEA	NE(NER)	P	*1485*
19.10.1964	HULL (Paragon) [West Parade Jn] - HORNSEA	NE(NER)	P	*1486*
19.10.1964	Hornsea Bridge - Hornsea Town	NE(NER)	G(All)	*1487*
19.10.1964	Malton East - Malton (Scarborough Road)	NE(NER)	G(All)	*1488*
19.10.1964	Malton (Scarborough Road) - Amotherby	NE(NER)	G(All)	*1489*
22.10.1964	Newton Hall - Leamside	NE(NER)	G(All)	*1490*
22.10.1964	Frankland - Finchale Siding	NE(NER)	G(All)	*1491*
01.11.1964	New Cross Gate (East London Up Jn) - Surrey Docks (Deptford Rd Jn)	S(ELR)	G(All)	*1492*
02.11.1964	MANCHESTER (Exchange) [Tydesley] - WIGAN (North Western) [Springs Branch No.1]	LM(LNW)	P(Locals)	*1493*
02.11.1964	BLACKPOOL (North) - FLEETWOOD	LM(PWYJt)	P(Locals)	*1494*
02.11.1964	Poulton No.4 - Poulton No.5	LM(PWYJt)	P(All)	*1495*
02.11.1964	Great Harewood Jn - Padiham	LM(L&Y)	G(All)	*1496*

▶0-4-2T 1447 stands at Wallingford on 14th May 1951 having propelled its autocoach from Cholsey & Moulsford. This service was withdrawn on 15th June 1959. The ABM maltings was served until 28th May 1981. (R.C.Riley)

▼0-6-0T 5715 is seen running round its train at Watlington on 21st June 1952. The passenger service from Princes Risborough ceased on 1st July 1957, and the goods survived until 2nd January 1961. (R.C.Riley)

▼A 799XX series single railcar departs from Banbury Merton Street station with a local to Buckingham, on 26th November 1961. From 2nd January 1961 passenger services were withdrawn from this line. Goods continued until 6th June 1966. (R.C.Riley)

Date	Line	Region (Company)	Type of Traffic	Reference Number
02.11.1964	Spen Dyke - BLACKPOOL (South)	LM(PWYJt)	P*	1497
02.11.1964	Middleton Branch Jn - Middle Peak Wharf	LM(LNW)	G(All)	1498 *
02.11.1964	Woodville Jn - Church Gresley Colliery	LM(Mid)	G(All)	1499
02.11.1964	Venables GF - Stafford (Doxey Road Goods)	LM(GNR)	G(All)	1500
02.11.1964	Radcliffe North Jn - Bradley Fold Jn	LM(L&Y)	G(All)	1501
02.11.1964	Radcliffe West - Radcliffe Central	LM(L&Y)	G(All)	1502
02.11.1964	GLAZEBROOK [West Jn] - WIGAN (Central)	LM(GCR)	P	1503
02.11.1964	Wigan Central Goods - Wigan Central	LM(GCR)	G(All)	1504
02.11.1964	Ashchurch - Tewkesbury Goods	W(Mid)	G(All)	1505
02.11.1964	CHELTENHAM (St James) - SWANSEA (High Street)	W(GWR)	P(Locals)	1506
02.11.1964	Duffryn Rhondda West - Cwmavon	W(RSB)	G(All)	1507
02.11.1964	GLOUCESTER (Central) [Grange Court] - HEREFORD [Rotherwas Jn]	W(GWR)	P	1508
02.11.1964	Oakwood GF - Garth Tonmawr Colliery	W(RSB)	G(All)	1509
02.11.1964	Ross on Wye - Rotherwas Jn (ROF Sidings)	W(GWR)	G(All)	1510
02.11.1964	SWINDON - GLOUCESTER (Central)	W(GWR)	P(Locals)	1511
02.11.1964	BERKELEY ROAD - SHARPNESS	W(SWJt)	P	1512
02.11.1964	Old Kent Road Jn - New Cross Gate (East London Up Jn)	S(ELR)	G(All)	1513
02.11.1964	County School - Foulsham	E(GER)	G(All)	1514
02.11.1964	Fakenham East - Wells next the Sea	E(GER)	G(All)	1515
02.11.1964	Forcett Valley Jn - Forcett Goods	NE(NER)	G(All)	1516
02.11.1964	Laisterdyke (English Electric Siding) - Idle	NE(GNR)	G(All)	1517
02.11.1964	LEEDS (Central) [Lofthouse Jn] - CASTLEFORD (Central) [Methley Jn]	NE(GN/MJt)	P	1518
02.11.1964	CASTLEFORD (Central) - PONTEFRACT (Baghill)	NE(NER/L&Y)	P	1519
02.11.1964	Pontefract East - PONTEFRACT (Baghill)	NE(S&KJt)	P(All)	1520
02.11.1964	NEWCASTLE CENTRAL [Benton Jn] - BLYTH	NE(NER)	P	1521
02.11.1964	Blyth SB - Blyth	NE(NER)	G(All)	1522
02.11.1964	MONKSEATON - NEWBIGGIN	NE(NER)	P	1523
02.11.1964	Monkseaton - Hartley	NE(NER)	G(All)	1524
02.11.1964	Woodhorn - New Biggin	NE(NER)	G(All)	1525
02.11.1964	Ripley - Pateley Bridge	NE(NER)	G(All)	1526
02.11.1964	Galashiels (Galafoot SGB Siding) - Selkirk	Sc(NBR)	G(All)	1527
02.11.1964	Muthill - Crieff	Sc(Cal)	G(All)	1528
09.11.1964	Cart Jn - Johnstone No.1	Sc(GSW)	G(All)	1529
16.11.1964	ST MARGARETS - BUNTINGFORD	E(GER)	P	1530
17.11.1964	Stockingford Colliery Sidings - Stockingford Colliery	LM(Mid)	G(All)	1531
23.11.1964	SEVERN BEACH - PILNING LL	W(GWR)	P	1532
23.11.1964	BRISTOL T.M. [Filton Jn] - ST ANDREWS ROAD	W(GWR)	P	1533
29.11.1964	Bugle - Wheal Rose Great Beam Siding	W(GWR)	G(All)	1534
30.11.1964	GLAZEBROOK [East Jn] - STOCKPORT (Tiviot Dale)	LM(CLC)	P	1535
30.11.1964	Berkeley Road - Lydney Town	W(SWJt)	G(All)	1536
30.11.1964	DARLINGTON (North Road) [Hopetown Jn] - MIDDLETON IN TEESDALE	NE(NER)	P	1537
03.12.1964	Rigleys Wagon Works - Bestwood Jn	LM(GNR)	G(All)	1538
07.12.1964	CAERNARVON - AFON WEN	LM(LNW)	P(All)	1539
07.12.1964	GAERWEN - AMLWCH	LM(LNW)	P	1540
07.12.1964	Associated Octel Sidings - Amlwch	LM(LNW)	G(All)	1541
07.12.1964	DIDCOT - SWINDON	W(GWR)	P(Locals)	1542
07.12.1964	Caernarvon - Llanberis	LM(LNW)	G(All)	1543
07.12.1964	Low Gill - Ingleton LNW Goods	LM(LNW)	G(All)	1544 *
07.12.1964	Willenhall (Stafford Street) - Short Heath	LM(Mid)	G(All)	1545
07.12.1964	Angel Road Jn - Edmonton Jn GF	E(GER)	G(All)	1546
14.12.1964	Strata Florida - Aberystwyth	W(GWR)	G(All)	1547
14.12.1964	Llangollen Goods - Bala Jn	LM(GWR)	G(All)	1548
14.12.1964	Greenhill Lower Jn - Bonnybridge Canal PS	Sc(Cal)	G(All)	1549
14.12.1964	Lugton Jn - Neilston High	Sc(Cal)	G(All)	1550
21.12.1964 [5]	Stonefield Jn - Cardiff (Adam Street Goods)	W(Rym)	G(All)	1551

Date	Line	Region (Company)	Type of Traffic	Reference Number
28.12.1964	Cardington (Air Ministry Siding) - Shefford	LM(Mid)	G(All)	1552
28.12.1964	Audley End - Bartlow	E(GER)	G(All)	1553
28.12.1964	Halstead - Yeldham	E(CVH)	G(All)	1554
28.12.1964	Heacham - Burnham Market	E(GER)	G(All)	1555
28.12.1964	Murrow West - Wisbech North	E(BR/MGN)	G(All)	1556
28.12.1964	NORTH WALSHAM (Main) - MUNDESLEY ON SEA	E(NSJt)	P(All)	1557
28.12.1964	Seven Sisters - Palace Gates	E(GER)	G(All)	1558
28.12.1964	SHERINGHAM - MELTON CONSTABLE	E(MGN)	P(All)	1559 *
28.12.1964	Dearness Valley - Waterhouses	NE(NER)	G(All)	1560
28.12.1964	Westfield Paper Mill - Avonbridge	Sc(NBR)	G(All)	1561
31.12.1964	Basford North - Leen Valley Jn	LM(GC&GNJt)	G(All)	1562
31.12.1964	Leen Valley Jn - Bulwell Forest	LM(GNR)	G(All)	1563
31.12.1964	Brentford Town Goods - Brentford Dock	W(GWR)	G(All)	1564
31.12.1964	Wheldrake - Cliff Common	DVLR	G(All)	1565 *
31.12.1964	Dover Wellington Dock Swing Bridge - Dover East Pier	S(SEC)	G(All)	1566 *
01.01.1965	Bestwood Jn - Bulwell Forest	LM(GNR)	G(All)	1567
04.01.1965	Ashton in Makerfield - St Helens Central	LM(GCR)	G(All)	1568
04.01.1965	Bootle Oriel Road - Bankfield Goods	LM(L&Y)	G(All)	1569 *
04.01.1965	Pleasley East GF - Hollins Siding	LM(Mid)	G(All)	1570
04.01.1965	LEEK - UTTOXETER	LM(LNW)	P	1571
04.01.1965	Oakamoor BIS Co's Siding - Uttoxeter North Shell Mex BP Siding	LM(NSR)	G(All)	1572
04.01.1965	Lowton St Marys - Hindley South	LM(GCR)	G(All)	1573
04.01.1965	BRISTOL (Temple Meads) - WORCESTER (Shrub Hill)	W(Mid)	P(Locals)	1574
04.01.1965	LOSTWITHIEL - FOWEY	W(GWR)	P	1575
04.01.1965	SWINDON - BRISTOL (Temple Meads)	W(GWR)	P(Locals)	1576
04.01.1965	Horseshoe Crossing - Wisbech Harbour North	E(MGN)	G(All)	1577
04.01.1965	Murrow East - Wisbech North Horseshoe Lane Crossing	E(MGN)	G(All)	1578
04.01.1965	GLASGOW (Central) - CARLISLE	Sc(Cal)	P(Locals)	1579 *
18.01.1965	BIRMINGHAM (New Street) [Castle Bromwich Jn] - WALSALL [Ryecroft Jn]	LM(Mid)	P	1580
18.01.1965	NUNEATON - LEAMINGTON SPA (Avenue)	LM(LNW)	P	1581 *
18.01.1965	Berkswell Jn - Kenilworth Jn	LM(LNW)	P	1582
18.01.1965	WOLVERHAMPTON HL - BURTON ON TRENT [Wichnor Jn]	LM(LNW)	P	1583 *
18.01.1965	WALSALL - RUGELEY (Trent Valley)	LM(LNW)	P	1584 *
18.01.1965	Atherton Jn - Howe Bridge West	LM(LNW)	G(All)	1585
18.01.1965	WHITCHURCH [Cambrian Jn] - BUTTINGTON [Jn]	LM(Cam)	P	1586
18.01.1965	Ellesmere - Oswestry	LM(Cam)	G(All)	1587
18.01.1965	Llynclys Jn - Buttington Jn	LM(Cam)	G(All)	1588
18.01.1965 [3]	RUABON [Llangollen Line Jn] - MORFA MAWDDACH	LM(GWR)	P	1589 *
18.01.1965	Llangollen Goods Jn - Morfa Mawddach	LM(GWR)	G(All)	1590
18.01.1965	LLANYMYNCH - LLANFYLLIN	LM(Cam)	P(All)	1591
18.01.1965	BALA JN - BALA	LM(GWR)	P(All)	1592 *
25.01.1965	Penwortham GF - Preston West Lancs	LM(L&Y)	G(All)	1593
25.01.1965	Whitehouse South - Penwortham GF	LM(L&Y)	G(All)	1594
25.01.1965	Alyth Jn - Alyth	Sc(Cal)	G(All)	1595
25.01.1965	Fairmuir Jn - Maryfield Jn	Sc(Cal)	G(All)	1596
25.01.1965	Guthrie Jn - Colliston	Sc(Cal)	G(All)	1597
25.01.1965	Methven Jn - Methven Town	Sc(Cal)	G(All)	1598
01.02.1965	Whaley Bridge - Shallcross Yard	LM(LNW)	G(All)	1599
01.02.1965	Llanharry Colliery - Cowbridge	W(GWR)	G(All)	1600
01.02.1965	Pyle East Jn - Porthcawl	W(GWR)	G(All)	1601
01.02.1965	Pyle West Jn - Heol–y–Sheet Crossing	W(GWR)	G(All)	1602
01.02.1965	Llanharry - Cowbridge	W(Taff)	G(All)	1603
01.02.1965	Clydach on Tawe North (Mond Nickel GF) - Trebanos Daren Colliery	W(GWR)	G(All)	1604

◄ The branch between Wickham Market and Framlingham lost passenger trains on 3 November 1952. However a J15 65389 shunts in the thriving goods yard at Framlingham on 3rd May 1958. (R.C.Riley)

▼ D16/3 4-4-0 62574 crosses over the East Coast Mainline at Sandy with an Oxford to Cambridge service in May 1952. Bedford St Johns to Cambridge lost its passenger service from 1st January 1968. (P.J.Lynch)

▼ Ex Great Eastern F5 672... hauls a two coach train fro... Ongar to Epping on 26th Aug... 1956. The third and middle ra... are for the future Central line ... tension to Epping. British Ra... ways services ceased on 1... November 1957. (R.C.Riley)

Date	Line	Region (Company)	Type of Traffic	Reference Number
01.02.1965	Haddiscoe Yard - Aldeby	E(GER)	G(All)	1605
10.02.1965	Crockham Siding - Trusham	W(GWR)	G(All)	1606
15.02.1965	Adwalton Jn - Batley West	NE(GNR)	G(All)	1607
15.02.1965	Batley - Roundwood Colliery	NE(GNR)	G(All)	1608 *
15.02.1965	Wrenthorpe West - Wrenthorpe South	NE(GNR)	G(All)	1609
22.02.1965	Hindley South - Amberswood Jn East	LM(LNW)	G(All)	1610
22.02.1965 3	CARMARTHEN - ABERYSTWYTH	W(GWR)	P	1611 *
22.02.1965 3	Pont Llanio - Aberystwyth	W(GWR)	G(All)	1612 *
27.02.1965	Stalybridge Jn - GF Stalybridge North	LM(L&Y)	G(All)	1613
00.03.1965 5	Reading L.L. Yard - Huntley & Palmers Siding	W(GWR)	G(All)	1614
01.03.1965	Baggeridge Jn - Oxley North Jn	LM(GWR)	G(All)	1615
01.03.1965	Blidworth Jn - Rolleston Jn	LM(Mid)	G(All)	1616
01.03.1965	Burton Dassett - Stratford upon Avon Racecourse Jn	LM(SMJ)	G(All)	1617
01.03.1965 2	Clapham - Ingleton LNW Goods	LM(Mid)	G(All)	1618
01.03.1965	Denbigh - Ruthin	LM(LNW)	G(All)	1619
01.03.1965	Oxley Branch Jn - Oxley Middle	LM(GWR)	G(All)	1620
01.03.1965	Rolleston Jn - Fiskerton Jn	LM(LMS)	G(All)	1621
01.03.1965	Stratford upon Avon Old Town - Evesham Road Crossing	LM(SMJ)	G(All)	1622 *
01.03.1965	Letterston Jn - Letterston	W(GWR)	G(All)	1623
01.03.1965	Mountain Ash (Cardiff Road) - Cresselley Crossing	W(GWR)	G(All)	1624
01.03.1965	TORRINGTON - HALWILL	W(SR)	P	1625
01.03.1965	Meeth North Devon Clay Co's Sid. No.1 GF - Halwill	W(SR)	G(All)	1626 *
01.03.1965	Paisley Abercorn Pitts Siding - Cart Harbour	Sc(GSW)	G(All)	1627
08.03.1965	SHEFFIELD (Victoria) [Mexborough South Jn] - YORK [Mexborough West Jn]	E(GCR)	P	1628
08.03.1965	SHEFFIELD (Victoria) [Mexborough West Jn] - YORK [Dearne Junction]	NE(S&KJt)	P	1629
08.03.1965	SWINTON (Town) - MEXBOROUGH [West Jn]	E(GCR)	P(All)	1630 *
08.03.1965	BISHOP AUCKLAND - CROOK	NE(NER)	P	1631
08.03.1965	WHITBY (Town) [Grosmont] - YORK [Rillington Jn]	NE(NER)	P	1632
08.03.1965	Pickering - Grosmont	NE(NER)	G(All)	1633 *
08.03.1965	SCARBOROUGH - WHITBY (Town)	NE(NER)	P(All)	1634
08.03.1965	Scarborough Gallows Close Goods - Whitby Prospect Hill	NE(NER)	P(All)	1635
08.03.1965	Whitby Prospect Hill - Whitby Bog Hall	NE(NER)	P(All)	1636
22.03.1965	Staines B - Staines C	S(LSW)	G(All)	1637
22.03.1965	LEEDS (City) [Arthington Jn] - ILKLEY [Milner Wood Jn]	NE(NER/Mid	P	1638
22.03.1965	LEEDS (City) - BRADFORD (Forster Square)	NE(Mid)	P(Locals)	1639
22.03.1965	ILKLEY - SKIPTON	NE(Mid)	P	1640
22.03.1965	Bellahouston No.1 - Shields Jn No.2	Sc(Cal)	G(All)	1641
22.03.1965	Pollok Jn – Bellahouston No.1	Sc(G&PJt)	G(All)	1642
29.03.1965	Whitchurch Cambrian Jn - Ellesmere	LM(Cam)	G(All)	1643
29.03.1965	WEST DRAYTON - STAINES (West)	W(GWR)	P	1644
29.03.1965	Cobnarwood GF - Nesfield	E(Mid)	G(All)	1645
29.03.1965	Coldstream - Wooler	NE(NER)	G(All)	1646
31.03.1965	Ingliston Jn - Ingliston Anchor Paper Works	Sc(Cal)	G(All)	1647
29.03.1965	Tweedmouth - Kelso	NE/Sc(NER/NBR)	G(All)	1648
01.04.1965	Bawtry - Misson	E(GNR)	G(All)	1649
01.04.1965	Hamilton No.1 - Hamilton Gas Works	Sc(Cal)	G(All)	1650
04.04.1965	Mexborough West Jn - Dearne Jn	NE(S&KJt)	G(All)	1651
05.04.1965 5	Hindley South - Amberswood Jn West	LM(LNW)	G(All)	1652
05.04.1965	Felin Fach (Green Grove Siding) - Aberayron	W(GWR)	P(All)	1653
05.04.1965	Reading General ML East - Reading Jn (SR)	S(LSW)	P(All)	1654 *
05.04.1965	Parkandillack Clay Works Sid. - St.Dennis Jn	W(GWR)	G(All)	1655 *
05.04.1965	Tavistock Jn - Marsh Mills (Jn with new curve)	W(GWR)	G(All)	1656 *
05.04.1965	Weymouth Jn - Easton	S(W&PJt)	G(All)	1657
05.04.1965	Bourne East - Morton Road (Haconby Siding)	E(GNR)	G(All)	1658
05.04.1965	Mexborough West Jn - Dearne Jn	E(S&KJt)	G(All)	1659

Date	Line	Region (Company)	Type of Traffic	Reference Number
05.04.1965	Spalding No.1 - Sutton Bridge	E(MGN)	G(All)	1660
05.04.1965	Spalding No.1 - Bourne	E(MGN)	G(All)	1661
05.04.1965	Barnard Castle East - Barnard Castle Old station	NE(NER)	G(All)	1662
05.04.1965	Deighton ICI - Kirkburton	NE(LNW)	G(All)	1663
05.04.1965	Forcett Jn - Middleton in Teesdale	NE(NER)	G(All)	1664
05.04.1965	Marshland Jn - Epworth	NE(IAJt)	G(All)	1665
05.04.1965	Lockwood No.2 - Meltham	NE(L&Y)	G(All)	1666
05.04.1965	Lofthouse North Jn - Newmarket Silkstone Colliery	NE(MJt)	G(All)	1667
05.04.1965	Lofthouse South Jn - Lofthouse East Jn	NE(MJt)	G(All)	1668
05.04.1965	Reedness Jn - Fockerby	NE(IAJt)	G(All)	1669
05.04.1965	Reilly Mill Jn - Waterhouses	NE(NER)	G(All)	1670
05.04.1965	Maybole Jn - Maybole Goods	Sc(LSW)	G(All)	1671
09.04.1965	Forth & Clyde Jn - Croftengea Siding	Sc(NBR)	G(All)	1672
10.04.1965	Bewdley - Cleobury Mortimer	W(GWR)	G(All)	1673
12.04.1965	Cradley East – Corngreaves Siding	LM(GWR)	G(All)	1674
12.04.1965	Fieldon Bridge - Bishop Auckland East	NE(NER)	G(All)	1675
16.04.1965	Bewdley North Jn - Tenbury Wells	LM(GWR)	G(All)	1676
16.04.1965	Cleobury Mortimer - Ditton Priors	MOD(CMDPLR)	G(All)	1677 *
19.04.1965	Bewdley North - Cleobury Mortimer	LM(GWR)	G(All)	1678
19.04.1965	Abbey & West Dereham BSc Sidings - Stoke Ferry	E(GER)	G(All)	1679
19.04.1965	Beccles - Ditchingham	E(GER)	G(All)	1680
19.04.1965	Bentley - Hadleigh	E(GER)	G(All)	1681
19.04.1965	Bury St Edmunds - Lavenham	E(GER)	G(All)	1682
19.04.1965	Chappel & Wakes Colne - Halstead	E(CV)	G(All)	1683
19.04.1965	Haverhill North - Colne Valley Jn GF	E(GER)	G(All)	1684
19.04.1965	Colne Valley Jn GF - Haverhill South	E(CVR)	G(All)	1685
19.04.1965	Fordham - Burwell	E(GER)	G(All)	1686
19.04.1965	Murrow West Jn - Murrow East	E(BR/MGN)	G(All)	1688
19.04.1965	Watton - Swaffham	E(GER)	G(All)	1687
19.04.1965	Wickham Market Jn - Framlingham	E(GER)	G(All)	1688
25.04.1965 [7]	Newton - Blantyreferme Colliery	Sc(Cal)	G(All)	1689
26.04.1965	WELWYN GARDEN CITY - DUNSTABLE (North)	E(GNR)	P	1690
29.04.1965	New Cauldedown South GF - Gunheath	W(GWR)	G(All)	1691
29.04.1965	Gunheath - Carbean Siding	W(GWR)	G(All)	1692
30.04.1965	Denham East - Harefield Embankment GF	W(GWR)	G(All)	1693
03.05.1965	Conduit Jn - Norton Crossing Jn	LM(LNW)	G(All)	1694
03.05.1965	Harrisons Siding - Coppice Colliery (The Norton Branch)	LM(LNW)	G(All)	1695
03.05.1965	Rugby Midland - Newbold Wharf	LM(Mid)	G(All)	1696
03.05.1965	South Acton - Hammersmith & Chiswick	W(N&SWJn)	G(All)	1697
03.05.1965	Brockholes - Holmfirth	NE(L&Y)	G(All)	1698
03.05.1965	Hedon - Withernsea	NE(NER)	G(All)	1699
03.05.1965	Stoneferry - Hornsea Bridge	NE(NER)	G(All)	1700
03.05.1965	SUNDERLAND [Tile Shed Jn] - SOUTH SHIELDS	NE(NER)	P	1701
03.05.1965	ABERDEEN [Maud Jn] - PETERHEAD	Sc(GNoSR)	P	1702
03.05.1965	BALLINLUIG - ABERFELDY	Sc(High)	P(All)	1703
03.05.1965	CASTLE DOUGLAS - KIRKCUDBRIGHT	Sc(GSW)	P	1704
03.05.1965	Fraserburgh - St.Combs	Sc(GNoSR)	G(All)	1705
03.05.1965	INVERNESS - ELGIN	Sc(High)	P(Locals)	1706
03.05.1965	PERTH [Buckingham Jn] - DUNDEE (West)	Sc(Cal)	P	1707
03.05.1965	PERTH - INVERNESS	Sc(High)	P(Locals)	1708 *
03.05.1965	TAYPORT - NEWPORT ON TAY (East)	Sc(NBR)	P	1709
03.05.1965 [2]	Whiteinch West Jn - Whiteinch Victoria Road	Sc(NBR)	G(All)	1710
06.05.1965	Clydebridge Jn - Farme Siding	Sc(Cal)	G(All)	1711
11.05.1965	Hessle Road - Cottingham South	NE(NER)	P*(All)	1712
11.05.1965	Dam Lane Jn - Glazebrook Moss Jn	LM(CLC)	G(All)	1713

Date	Line	Region (Company)	Type of Traffic	Reference Number
15.05.1965	CRAIGENDORAN - ARROCHAR & TARBET	Sc(NBR)	P(Locals)	*1714*
17.05.1965	Highbridge East - Highbridge Wharf	W(S&DJt)	G(All)	*1715*
17.05.1965	Highbridge West - Highbridge B	W(GWR)	G(All)	*1716*
17.05.1965	Tufts Jn - Princess Royal Colliery EWS	W(SWJt)	G(All)	*1717*
19.05.1965	Butterwick Cold Storage Sidings - St Albans Abbey	LM(GNR)	G(All)	*1718*
24.05.1965	Elliot Jn Metal Box Siding - Carmyllie	Sc(D&AJt)	G(All)	*1719*
24.05.1965	Smeaton Jn - Saltoun	Sc(NBR)	G(All)	*1720*
00.06.1965	Heath - Williamthorpe Colliery	E(GCR)	G(All)	*1721*
00.06.1965	Heath - Holmewood Colliery	E(GCR)	G(All)	*1722*
00.06.1965	Byfield - Ironstone Siding Fenny Compton	W(SMJ)	G(All)	*1723*
07.06.1965	Anniesland - Knightswood Mineral Depot	Sc(NBR)	G(All)	*1724*
07.06.1965	Irthingborough - Thrapston Bridge Street	LM(LNW)	G(All)	*1725*
07.06.1965	Stourton Jn - Lofthouse E&W Sidings GF	NE(EWYU)	G(All)	*1726*
13.06.1965	Retford - Thrumpton LC	E(GCR)	P(All)	*1727*
13.06.1965	Whisker Hill Jn - Retford South (Retford Avoider)	E(GCR)	P(All)	*1728* *
14.06.1965	Pool Hey Jn - Southport St Lukes	LM(L&Y)	P(All)	*1729*
14.06.1965	Ashley Hill Jn - Kingswood Jn	W(Mid)	G(All)	*1730*
14.06.1965	Ashton Bridge Jn - Canon Marsh Goods	W(GWR)	G(All)	*1731*
14.06.1965	ERIDGE [Redgate Mill Jn] - HAILSHAM	S(LBSC)	P	*1732*
14.06.1965	Redgate Mill Jn - Heathfield	S(LBSC)	G(All)	*1733*
14.06.1965	CHRIST HOSPITAL [Stammerham Jn] - GUILDFORD [Peasmarsh Jn]	S(LBSC)	P(All)	*1734*
14.06.1965	Harworth Glass Bulbs Siding - Scrooby Sidings	E(GNR)	G(All)	*1735*
14.06.1965	BRADFORD (Exchange) [Low Moor] - HUDDERSFIELD [Mirfield No.4]	NE(L&Y)	P	*1736*
14.06.1965	Heckmondwike Jn - Mirfield No.4	NE(L&Y)	G(All)	*1737*
14.06.1965	BRADFORD (Exchange) - HUDDERSFIELD (via Halifax)	NE(L&Y)	P(Locals)	*1738* *
14.06.1965	LEEDS [Farnley Jn] - HUDDERSFIELD [Spen Valley Jn] (Via New line)	NE(LNW)	P	*1739*
14.06.1965	MARKET WEIGHTON [East] - DRIFFIELD	NE(NER)	P(All)	*1740*
14.06.1965	SELBY [Barlby North] - MARKET WEIGHTON [West]	NE(NER)	P	*1741*
14.06.1965	Barlby North - Holme Moor Goods	NE(NER)	G(All)	*1742*
14.06.1965	South Gosforth East - South Gosforth West	NE(NER)	G(All)	*1743*
14.06.1965	Tile Shed - Harton	NE(NER)	G(All)	*1744*
14.06.1965	Castle Douglas - Kirkcudbright	Sc(GSW)	G(All)	*1745*
14.06.1965	DUMFRIES - STRANRAER [Challoch Jn]	Sc(GSW)	P	*1746*
14.06.1965	Maxwelltown [ICI Siding] - Challoch Jn	Sc(GSW/PPWJt)	G(All)	*1747*
21.06.1965	Moorgate - Aldersgate (deviation of old route)	LT(Met)	P(All)	*1748*
21.06.1965	Kirriemuir Jn - Kirriemuir	Sc(Cal)	G(All)	*1749*
24.06.1965	Stratton (Green Lane Level Crossing) - South Marston Factory	W(GWR)	G(All)	*1750*
28.06.1965	Lancing Station GF - LANCING WORKS Platform	S(LBSC)	W(All)	*1751*
28.06.1965	Keighley Jn - Ingrow East	NE(Mid/GNR)	G(All)	*1752* *
28.06.1965	Horton Park - Thornton	NE(GNR)	G(All)	*1753*
01.07.1965	Bolton No.2 - Highfield Siding	LM(LNW)	G(All)	*1754*
05.07.1965	Aldridge Brixancole PS - Walsall Wood end of line	LM(Mid)	G(All)	*1755*
05.07.1965	Buckley Jn - Northop Hall Siding	LM(GCR)	G(All)	*1756*
05.07.1965	Stourbridge Jn Middle - Stourbridge Town Goods	LM(GWR)	G(All)	*1757* *
05.07.1965	Windmill End Jn - Netherton Goods	LM(GWR)	G(All)	*1758*
05.07.1965 [3]	Woodford No.4 - Byfield Ironstone Siding	LM(SMJ)	G(All)	*1759*
05.07.1965	CROOK - TOW LAW	NE(NER)	P(All)	*1760*
05.07.1965	Ilkley - Embsay Jn	NE(Mid)	G(All)	*1761* *
05.07.1965	Menston Jn - Milnerwood Jn	NE(OIJt))	G(All)	*1762*
05.07.1965	Arthington Jn South - Burley Jn	NE(OIJt)	G(All)	*1763*
05.07.1965	Arthington Jn North - Arthington Jn West	NE(NER)	G(All)	*1764*
10.07.1965	International & Ocean Collieries - Glyngarw	W(GWR)	G(All)	*1765* *
12.07.1965	Llanelly Sandy Yard - Albert Road Goods	W(LMM)	G(All)	*1766*
12.07.1965	Morriston East - Clydach on Tawe South (Mond Nickel Sid.)	W(Mid)	G(All)	*1767*
12.07.1965	Grimesthorpe No.1 - Sheffield Wicker Goods	E(Mid)	G(All)	*1768*

Date	Line	Region (Company)	Type of Traffic	Reference Number
12.07.1965 [2]	Nunnery Goods - Sheffield Wharf Street Goods	E(LNW)	G(All)	1769
14.07.1965	West Kensington - West Kensington Goods	LM(Mid)	G(All)	1770
19.07.1965	Ravenswood Jn - Greenlaw	Sc(NBR)	G(All)	1771
19.07.1965	Garstang & Catterall - Garstang Town Coal Yard	LM(GKER)	G(All)	1772
19.07.1965	Kinneil Colliery - Bridgeness	Sc(NBR)	G(All)	1773
20.07.1965	Denny West Jn GF - Carmuirs West Jn	Sc(Cal)	G(All)	1774
26.07.1965	Swinton Jn - Mexborough (Dale Brown Siding)	E(GCR)	G(All)	1775
02.08.1965	Carlisle No.3 - Viaduct Goods	LM(Cal)	G(All)	1776
02.08.1965	Upperby Yard - Carlisle Crown Street	LM(LNW)	G(All)	1777
02.08.1965	LEEDS [Farnley Jn] - HUDDERSFIELD [Spen Valley Jn (Leeds New Line)]	NE(LNW)	P	1778
02.08.1965	BOURNEMOUTH (Central) [Boscombe Jn] - BOURNEMOUTH (West)	S(LSW)	P	1779
02.08.1965	Branksome - Bournemouth West Jn	S(LSW)	P(All)	1780
02.08.1965	Battersby - Stokesley	NE(NER)	G(All)	1781
02.08.1965	Market Weighton West - Holme Moor	NE(NER)	G(All)	1782
02.08.1965	Drumshoreland - Broxburn Oil Works	Sc(NBR)	G(All)	1783
02.08.1965	Crew Jn - Pilton West GF	Sc(Cal)	G(All)	1784
09.08.1965	Warrington Allied Brewery Siding - Foundry Street Coal Yard	LM(LNW)	G(All)	1785
14.08.1965	Bolton No.1 - Bolton Great Moor Street	LM(LNW)	G(All)	1786
02.09.1965	Daubhill St Helens Road Coop Coal Yd - Rumworth & Daubhill Coal Yd	LM(LNW)	G(All)	1787
06.09.1965	Reading New Spur Jn - READING (Southern)	S(LSW)	P(All)	1788
06.09.1965	NOTTINGHAM (Midland) [Pye Bridge] - KIRKBY IN ASHFIELD (East)	LM(Mid)	P	1789
06.09.1965	Pendleton Broad Street - Pendlebury (Fast Lines)	LM(L&Y)	P(All)	1790
06.09.1965	Haverthwaite - Lake Side	LM(Furn)	G(All)	1791
06.09.1965	Farnley Jn - Cleckheaton Spen	NE(L&Y)	G(All)	1792 *
06.09.1965	LEVEN - ST ANDREWS	Sc(NBR)	P	1793
06.09.1965	Crail - St Andrews	Sc(NBR)	G(All)	1794
06.09.1965	AYR - STRANRAER	Sc(GSWR)	P(Locals)	1795
06.09.1965	Saracen Goods - Ruchill	Sc(NBR)	G(All)	1796
06.09.1965	SLATEFORD [Jn] - EDINBURGH (Princes Street)	Sc(Cal)	P	1797
06.09.1965	Morrison Street Goods - Edinburgh (Princes Street)	Sc(Cal)	G(All)	1798
13.09.1965	Pennington South Jn - Bickershaw Colliery	LM(LNW)	G(All)	1799
13.09.1965	Glascoed ROF - Usk	W(GWR)	G(All)	1800
13.09.1965	Acton Lane Jn - Bollo Lane Jn	S(LSW)	G(All)	1801
13.09.1965	NEWMARKET [Warrenhill Jn] - FORDHAM [Snailwell Jn]	E(GER)	P(All)	1802
16.09.1965	Wear Valley Jn - Crook	NE(NER)	G(All)	1803
20.09.1965	St Margarets - Buntingford	E(GER)	G(All)	1804
20.09.1965	CHIPPENHAM [East] - CALNE	W(GWR)	P(All)	1805
20.09.1965	Hurlford Mineral Sidings - Hurlford Fireclay Sidings	Sc(GSW)	G(All)	1806
20.09.1965	Hawkins Lane Jn - Wetmore Sidings	LM(NSR)	G(All)	1807 *
27.09.1965 [5]	EARBY - BARNOLDSWICK	LM(Mid)	P	1808
28.09.1965 [5]	CALLENDAR - BALQUHIDDER	Sc(Cal)	P(All)	1809
28.09.1965 [5]	KILLIN JN - KILLIN	Sc(Cal)	P(All)	1810
28.09.1965 [5]	Killin Jn - Lower Loch Tay	Sc(Cal)	G(All)	1811
29.09.1965	Yoker Caledonian Yard - new spur to Rothesey Dock Green Road	Sc(Cal)	G(All)	1812
03.10.1965 [4]	Fawcett Street - Sunderland	NE(NER)	G(All)	1813
04.10.1965	BARNSTAPLE JN - TORRINGTON	W(LSW)	P	1814
04.10.1965	ABERDEEN [Dyce Jn] - FRASERBURGH	Sc(GNoSR)	P	1815
04.10.1965	Argosy PSiding - Mount Vernon North	Sc(NBR)	G(All)	1816
04.10.1965	HAMILTON - COALBURN	Sc(Cal)	P	1817
04.10.1965	Auchlochan Colliery - Coalburn	Sc(Cal)	G(All)	1818
04.10.1965	HAMILTON - STRATHAVEN	Sc(Cal)	P	1819
04.10.1965	Stonehouse - Strathaven	Sc(Cal)	G(All)	1820
04.10.1965	Kemble - Cirencester Town	W(GWR)	G(All)	1821
04.10.1965	Cart Jn - Johnstone Cartside	Sc(GSW)	G(All)	1822
04.10.1965	Felin Fran West - Hafod Jn	W(GWR)	G(All)	1823

▲A LSW Adams Class 0415 No. 30584 (72A) hauling a single coach is seen leaving Combpyne on 8th July 1959 with a Lyme Regis service. This passenger service was withdrawn on 29th November 1965. (R.C.Riley)

▲British Railways Standard Class 3MT 2–6–2T 82009 (83A) simmers at Moretonhampstead with the 10.15 a.m. local to Newton Abbot on 22nd May 1956. This service was withdrawn from 2nd March 1959. The goods service lasted a little longer until 6th April 1964. (R.J.Buckley)

▶An M7 0-4-4T 30129 stands at Yeovil Junction on a 2 coach evening train to Yeovil Town on 22nd July 1958. This shuttle service was withdrawn from 6th May 1968. (R.C.Riley)

Date	Line	Region (Company)	Type of Traffic	Reference Number
04.10.1965	Swansea Victoria No.1 - Swansea Victoria	W(LNW)	G(All)	1824
04.10.1965	Swansea No.1 - Swansea South Dock	W(LNW)	G(All)	1825
04.10.1965	Lonlas Jn - Skewen East	W(GWR)	G(All)	1826
04.10.1965	Chingford Goods Yard - Chingford Goods	E(GER)	G(All)	1827
11.10.1965	Middleton Jn - Middleton	LM(LNW)	G(All)	1828
11.10.1965	Crosshouse - Irvine Goods	Sc(GSW)	G(All)	1829
13.10.1965	Honeybourne South Loop - Honeybourne East Loop	W(GWR)	G(All)	1830
13.10.1965	Bolton No.1 - Magees Brewery (Bolton High Street)	LM(LNW)	G(All)	1831
18.10.1965	AVIEMORE - CRAIGELLACHIE	Sc(HR/GNoS)	P	1832
18.10.1965	AVIEMORE - FORRES	Sc(High)	P	1833
18.10.1965	Boat of Garten - Forres Dallasdhu Distillery	Sc(High)	G(All)	1834
18.10.1965	KEITH JN - ELGIN via Dufftown	Sc(GNoSR)	P	1835
18.10.1965	Possil - Balornock Jn	Sc(Cal)	G(All)	1836
18.10.1965 [3]	Smyllum West Jn - Lanark Racecourse	Sc(Cal)	G(All)	1837
25.10.1965	Oxted Crowhurst Jn North - Oxted Crowhurst Jn South	S(C&OJt)	G(All)	1838 *
25.10.1965	Kidwelly - Coedbach Washery	W(BPGV)	G(All)	1839
30.10.1965	Shirland Sidings - Shirland Colliery	LM(Mid)	G(All)	1840
01.11.1965	ROSE GROVE [Stansfield Hall] - TODMORDEN [Todmorden East]	LM(L&Y)	P	1841
01.11.1965	Wapping Bank Head - Liverpool Park Lane Goods	LM(LNW)	G(All)	1842
01.11.1965	Wednesfield - Willenhall (Stafford Street)	LM(Mid)	G(All)	1843
01.11.1965	Gas Works Jn - Bournemouth West Jn	S(LSW)	G(All)	1844
01.11.1965	Grange Court - Ross on Wye	W(GWR)	G(All)	1845
01.11.1965	Pillbank Jn - Pillgwenlly	W(GWR)	G(All)	1846
01.11.1965	Ross on Wye - Lydbrook Jn AEI Siding	W(GWR)	G(All)	1847
01.11.1965	Swansea High Street - Swansea Victoria No.2	W(GWR)	G(All)	1848
01.11.1965	Swansea Victoria - No.2 Wind Street	W(GWR)	G(All)	1849
01.11.1965	GRANTHAM [Honington Jn] - LINCOLN (Central) [Pelham St. Jn]	E(GNR)	P	1850
01.11.1965	Honington Jn - Bracebridge Gas Sidings	E(GNR)	G(All)	1851
01.11.1965	LINCOLN (Central) - BARNETBY	E(GCR)	P(Locals)	1852
01.11.1965	Stanhope - Stanhope Goods	NE(NER)	G(All)	1853
01.11.1965	Westgate in Weardale - St Johns Chapel	NE(NER)	G(All)	1854
01.11.1965	Wrenthorpe North - Roundwood Colliery	NE(GNR)	G(All)	1855
01.11.1965	DUNBLANE - CALLANDER	Sc(Cal)	P	1856
01.11.1965	Springbank Mill Siding - Callander	Sc(Cal)	G(All)	1857
01.11.1965	DUNBLANE - CRIANLARICH LOWER [Jn]	Sc(Cal)	P(All)	1858
03.11.1965	Houghton Colliery Sidings - Houghton Main Colliery	NE(Mid)	G(All)	1860
18.11.1965	Cockett - Cockett Goods	W(GWR)	G(All)	1861
22.11.1965	Coldblow LC - Deptford Lift Bridge	S(LBSC)	G(All)	1862
22.11.1965	Cemetery South - Cemetery West	NE(NER)	G(All)	1863
29.11.1965	HULL (Paragon) - YORK (via Beverley)	NE(NER)	P	1864
29.11.1965	Beverley North SB - Bootham SB	NE(NER)	G(All)	1865
29.11.1965	Spen Valley Jn - Heckmondwike Spen Goods (Jn new spur)	NE(LNW)	G(All)	1866 *
30.11.1965	PERTH [Buckingham Jn] - DUNDEE (West)	Sc(Cal)	P(All)	1867
06.12.1965	Coupar Angus - Blairgowrie	Sc(Cal)	G(All)	1868
06.12.1965	GLASGOW (St Enoch) - CARLISLE (via Kilmarnock)	Sc(GSW)	P(Locals)	1869
06.12.1965	Moorgate - Aldersgate (deviation of old line)	LT(Met)	P(All)	1870
16.12.1965	Lochhead Colliery - West Wemyss (Wimpey Siding)	Sc(NBR)	G(All)	1871
20.12.1965	Neasden North Jn - Brent North	LM(GCR)	G(All)	1872
28.12.1965	Bilson Jn - Northern United Colliery	W(GWR)	G(All)	1873
00.00.1966	Gatewen Colliery ODE - Brymbo North	LM(GCR)	G(All)	1874
01.01.1966	North Walsham Main - Jn with MGN	E(BRB)	G(All)	1875
01.01.1966	Jn with 1958 spur - North Walsham Town	E(MGN)	G(All)	1876
03.01.1966	Brinnington Jn - Reddish Jn	LM(Mid)	G(All)	1877
03.01.1966	Chorley No.4 - Feniscowles	LM(LUJt)	G(All)	1878

Date	Line	Region (Company)	Type of Traffic	Reference Number
03.01.1966	LANCASTER (Castle) - MORECAMBE	LM(Mid)	P	1879
03.01.1966	MORECAMBE - HEYSHAM (Harbour)	LM(Mid)	P	1880
03.01.1966	WENNINGTON [Jn] - LANCASTER (Green Ayre)	LM(Mid)	P	1881
03.01.1966	Waterloo Road York Street Wharf - Newchapel & Goldenhill	LM(NSR)	G(All)	1882
03.01.1966	CHELTENHAM SPA (Malvern Road) - CHELTENHAM SPA (St.James)	W(GWR)	P	1883
03.01.1966	Blackbridge Siding - Luton Vauxhall South GF	E(GNR)	G(All)	1884
03.01.1966	Hunslet East GN Goods - Parkside Jn	NE(GNR)	G(All)	1885
03.01.1966	Inverurie - Old Meldrum	Sc(GNoSR)	G(All)	1886
03.01.1966	Inveramsay - Turriff	Sc(GNoSR)	G(All)	1887
03.01.1966	Paradise Siding - Alford	Sc(GNoSR)	G(All)	1888
04.01.1966	Seafield Jn - Seafield	Sc(Cal)	G(All)	1889
10.01.1966	LEIGHTON BUZZARD - DUNSTABLE (North)	LM(LNW)	P(All)	1890
11.01.1966	Farnley Jn - Heckmondwyke Spen Goods	NE(LNW)	G(All)	1891
23.01.1966	Ryde Esplanade - Ryde Pierhead (Tramway)	S(IWR)	P(All)	1892 *
24.01.1966	Morfa Jn - Llandeilo Jn East	W(GWR)	G(All)	1893
24.01.1966	Hurlford Jn - Hurlford Mineral Sidings	Sc(GSW)	G(All)	1894
24.01.1966	East Kilbride - East Kilbride Mavor & Coulson	Sc(Cal)	G(All)	1895
31.01.1966	Uttoxeter North - Uttoxeter	LM(NSR)	G(All)	1896
31.01.1966	Court House Jn - Barnsley Court House Goods	E(Mid)	G(All)	1897
31.01.1966	Norwich Victoria Coal Yard - Norwich Victoria Goods	E(GER)	G(All)	1898
31.01.1966	Bellshaugh Jn - Dawsholm Kelvindale Siding	Sc(Cal)	G(All)	1899
31.01.1966	Crow Park - Partick Hill Mineral Yard	Sc(Cal)	G(All)	1900
31.01.1966	Partick West Jn - Possil	Sc(Cal)	G(All)	1901
31.01.1966	Possil - Lambhill Ironworks	Sc(Cal)	G(All)	1902
05.02.1966	Hawkins Lane Jn - Anderstaff Lane	LM(Mid)	G(All)	1903
07.02.1966	Camp Hill - Camp Hill Goods	LM(Mid)	G(All)	1904
07.02.1966	Irk Valley - Smedley Viaduct	LM(L&Y)	P(All)	1905
07.02.1966	Dalmeny - Kirkliston	Sc(NBR)	G(All)	1906
07.02.1966	Dalmeny - South Queensferry	Sc(NBR)	G(All)	1907
09.02.1966 [3]	Harpur Hill - Old Harpur SMRE Siding	LM(LNW)	G(All)	1908
14.02.1966	Newcastle Jn - Brampton Sidings	LM(NSR)	G(All)	1909
14.02.1966 [2]	Silverdale Jn - Madeley Chord	LM(NSR)	G(All)	1910
14.02.1966	TOTTON - FAWLEY	S(SR)	P	1911
21.02.1966	Greenock Upper - Weymess Bay	Sc(Cal)	G	1912
21.02.1966	RYDE Pier [Smallbrook Jn] - COWES	S(IWC)	P(All)	1913
22.02.1966	Woodhill - Hillhead	Sc(GSW)	G(All)	1914
27.02.1966 [5]	Chinley East Jn - Chinley South Jn	LM(Mid)	G(All)	1915
28.02.1966	Blaydon Mineral GF - Blaydon South	NE(NER)	(All)	1916
28.02.1966	Scotswood Bridge - Blydon Main	NE(NER)	G(All)	1917
28.02.1966	Lydford - Launceston North	W(GWR)	G(All)	1918 *
28.02.1966	Launceston North 1943 Spur - Launceston South	W(GWR/LSW)	G(All)	1919
28.02.1966	Garngaber Jn - Bedlay	Sc(NBR)	G(All)	1920
28.02.1966	ABERDEEN [Ferryhill Jn] - BALLATER	Sc(GNoSR)	P	1921
00.03.1966	Saxby - Pain's Siding	LM(Mid)	G(All)	1922
07.03.1966	BATH (Green Park) - TEMPLECOMBE	W(S&DJt)	P(All)	1923
07.03.1966	MANGOTSFIELD - BATH (Green Park)	W(Mid)	P	1924
07.03.1966	Mangotsfield Station Jn - Mangotsfield South Jn	W(Mid)	P(All)	1925
07.03.1966	Bath Midland Road Bridge - BATH Green Park	W(Mid)	G(All)	1926
07.03.1966	Bath Coop Coal Siding - Writhington Colliery	W(S&DJt)	G(All)	1927
07.03.1966	Radstock North New spur Jn - Blandford Forum	S/W(S&DJt)	G(All)	1928
07.03.1966	Bason Bridge Wilts Utd Dairies Sidings - Evercreech Jn North	W(S&DJt)	G(All)	1929
07.03.1966	EVERCREECH JN - HIGHBRIDGE & BURNHAM	W(S&DJt)	P	1930
07.03.1966	Evercreech Jn - Bason Bridge (United Dairies Siding)	W(S&DJt)	G(All)	1931
07.03.1966	TEMPLECOMBE - POOLE [Broadstone Jn]	S(S&DJt)	P	1932
07.03.1966	Templecombe No.3 - Templecombe Lower Yard	S(S&DJt)	G(All)	1933

◀ 3582 2-4-0T awaits its departure with the 12 noon auto from Fowey to Lostwithel on 7th June 1949. Passenger trains continued to serve this line until 4th January 1965. The line was cut back to Carne Point on 4th August 1968. *(R.J.Buckley.)*

▼The curved platform at Yelverton sees 4402 awaiting departure with a train over the moors to Princetown on 21st August 1947. The line totally closed on 5th March 1956. *(R.J.Buckley.)*

▼ A 4500 Class tank 5502 sits at Padstow (the furthest western part of the Southern Region). Soon to depart with the 9.8 a.m. to Bodmin Road on 7th June 1949. This line ended its days under Western Region control. The passenger service was withdrawn from 30th January 1967 and totally closed after Wadebridge. *(R.J.Buckley.)*

Date	Line	Region (Company)	Type of Traffic	Reference Number
07.03.1966	Templecombe Jn - Templecombe	W(S&DJt)	G(All)	*1934*
07.03.1966	SEATON JN - SEATON (Devon)	W(LSW)	P(All)	*1935*
07.03.1966	CHRISTS HOSPITAL [Itchingfield Jn] - SHOREHAM	S(LBSC)	P	*1936*
07.03.1966	Itchingfield Jn - Beeding Cement Works Siding	S(LBSC)	G(All)	*1937*
07.03.1966	SALISBURY - EXETER (Central)	S/W(LSW)	P(Locals)	*1938*
07.03.1966	Rockingham South - Smithywood Colliery	E(GCR)	G(All)	*1939*
07.03.1966	Greenock (Mearns Street) - Lynedoch Goods	Sc(GSW)	G(All)	*1940*
27.03.1966 [4]	Copley Hill No.3 - Leeds Central B	E(LNW)	G(All)	*1941*
27.03.1966 [4]?	Copley Hill No.3 - Whitehall Road GF	E(LNW)	G(All)	*1942* *
28.03.1966	CONNEL FERRY - BALLACHULISH	Sc(Cal)	P(All)	*1943*
28.03.1966	Orbliston Jn - Fochabers Town	Sc(High)	G(All)	*1944*
28.03.1966	Lossie Jn - Lossiemouth	Sc(GNoSR)	G(All)	*1945*
04.04.1966	Marton Jn - Leamington Spa Avenue	LM(LNW)	G(All)	*1946*
04.04.1966 [5]	North Stafford Jn - Horninglow Jn	LM(NSR)	G(All)	*1947*
04.04.1966	Bentley - Bordon	S(LSW)	G(All)	*1948* *
04.04.1966	Bordon - Martinque	LMilR	G(All)	*1949*
04.04.1966	Shawford Jn - Winchester Chesil	S(LSW)	G(All)	*1950*
04.04.1966	Tadcaster - Wetherby	NE(NER)	G(All)	*1951*
04.04.1966	Bellside Jn - Chapelhall	Sc(Cal)	G(All)	*1952*
04.04.1966	Kelvin Valley GF - Twechar No.1 Colliery	Sc(NBR)	G(All)	*1953*
04.04.1966	Lenzie - Lennoxtown Old Goods	Sc(NBR)	G(All)	*1954*
04.04.1966	Middlemuir Jn - Woodleys Jn	Sc(NBR)	G(All)	*1955*
04.04.1966	Symington - Broughton	Sc(Cal)	G(All)	*1956*
04.04.1966	Tollcross East - Tollcross	Sc(Cal)	G(All)	*1957*
04.04.1966	Woodleys Jn - Kirkintilloch Basin	Sc(NBR)	G(All)	*1958*
18.04.1966	CREWE - CHESTER (General)	LM(LNW)	P(Locals)	*1959*
18.04.1966	KESWICK - WORKINGTON [Derwent Jn]	LM(CK&P/LNW)	P(All)	*1960*
18.04.1966	ROYTON JN - ROYTON	LM(L&Y)	P	*1961*
18.04.1966	Higginshaw Gas Siding - Royton	LM(L&Y)	G(All)	*1962*
18.04.1966	WYRE DOCK - FLEETWOOD	LM(PWYJt)	P(All)	*1963*
18.04.1966	CHIPPENHAM [Thingley Jn] - TROWBRIDGE [Bradford South Jn]	W(GWR)	P	*1964* *
18.04.1966	NEWBURY - WESTBURY	W(GWR)	P(Locals)	*1965*
18.04.1966	PATNEY & CHIRTON - HOLT JN via Devizes	W(GWR)	P	*1966*
18.04.1966	Canal Jn - New Cross (Up Side)	S(ELR)	G(All)	*1967*
18.04.1966	SHANKLIN - VENTNOR	S(IofWR)	P(All)	*1968*
18.04.1966	Tivetshall - Harleston	E(GER)	G(All)	*1969*
18.04.1966	Eye Green - Murrow West	E(MGN)	G(All)	*1970*
18.04.1966	Southside GF - Silvertown	E(GER)	G(All)	*1971*
18.04.1966	East London Jn - Shoreditch	E(ELR)	G(All)	*1972*
18.04.1966	Custon House Jn - Albert Dock Jn H.L.	E(GER)	G(All)	*1973*
18.04.1966	Felsted - Dunmow	E(GER)	G(All)	*1974*
18.04.1966	Witham Goods - Maldon East & Heybridge	E(GER)	G(All)	*1975*
18.04.1966	EDINBURGH (Waverley) [Silvermuir Jn East] - LANARK [Silvermuir Jn South]	Sc (Cal)	P(Locals)	*1976*
18.04.1966	Dumfries Goods Jn - Lockerbie	Sc(Cal)	G(All)	*1977*
18.04.1966	GLASGOW (St Enoch) [Gorbals Jn] - KILMARNOCK [Strathbungo Jn]	Sc(GSW)	P	*1978*
20.04.1966 [5]	Hayle Wharf - Penpol Sidings	W(GWR)	G(All)	*1979*
02.05.1966 [5]	Cheadle Village Jn - Davenport Jn	LM(LNW)	G(All)	*1980*
02.05.1966	Desford - Leicester West Bridge	LM(Mid)	G(All)	*1981*
02.05.1966	Rolleston Jn - Southwell	LM(Mid)	G(All)	*1982*
02.05.1966	Crwys Sidings - Cardiff Adam Street Goods	W(Rhy)	G(All)	*1983*
02.05.1966	Coxhoe Jn - Bishop Auckland East	NE(NER)	G(All)	*1984*
02.05.1966 [3]	Spitalfields - Bishopsgate Goods	E(GER)	G(All)	*1985*
02.05.1966	Nickstream Chemical & Insulating Co's Sd - Forcett East [Layton Quarry]	NE(NER)	G(All)	*1986*
02.05.1966	Fauldhouse & Crofthead - Levenseat Sand Quarry	Sc(NBR)	G(All)	*1987*
02.05.1966	South Queensferry - Port Edgar	Sc(NBR)	G(All)	*1988*

Date	Line	Region (Company)	Type of Traffic	Reference Number
02.05.1966	Whitburn - Fauldhouse & Crofthead	Sc(NBR)	G(All)	*1989*
12.05.1966	Mapperley Jn - Mapperley Colliery	LM(Mid)	G(All)	*1990*
16.05.1966	Medina Wharf - Cowes	S(IWCR)	G(All)	*1991*
16.05.1966	Awsworth Jn - Eastwood & Langley Mill North	LM(GNR)	G(All)	*1992*
22.05.1966	NEWPORT ON TAY (East) - TAYPORT	Sc(NBR)	P	*1993*
23.05.1966	Hardham Jn - Petworth	S(LBSC)	G(All)	*1994*
23.05.1966	Wisbech East - Upwell	E(GER)	G(All)	*1995*
23.05.1966	Attimore Hall Siding - Hertford North	E(GNR)	G(All)	*1996*
23.05.1966	Broomfield Siding - Inverbervie	Sc(NBR)	G(All)	*1997*
23.05.1966	Newport on Tay East - Tayport Morton's Siding	Sc(NBR)	G(All)	*1998*
27.05.1966	Leamington Spa General Station North - Leamington Spa Avenue Coal Yard	W(GWR)	G(All)	*1999*
01.06.1966	Dudbridge Jn - Stroud Wallbridge	W(Mid)	G(All)	*2000*
01.06.1966	Stonehouse Bristol Road - Nailsworth	W(Mid)	G(All)	*2001*
03.06.1966	CHELTENHAM (Malvern Road) East - CHELTENHAM SPA (St James)	W(GWR)	P	*2002*
03.06.1966	Lando GF - Lando ROF Exchange Sidings	W(GWR)	G(All)	*2003*
05.06.1966	ST DENYS [Northam Jn] - SOUTHAMPTON (Terminus)	S(LSW)	P	*2004*
06.06.1966	BUSHEY & OXHEY [Colne Jn] - CROXLEY GREEN [Croxley Green Jn]	LM(LNW)	P	*2005*
06.06.1966	MELTON MOWBRAY - NOTTINGHAM (Midland) [London Road Jn]	LM(Mid)	P	*2006*
06.06.1966	KETTERING [Glendon South] - LEICESTER (London Road) via Melton Mowbray	LM(Mid)	P	*2007* *
06.06.1966	RUGBY (Midland) - PETERBOROUGH (East)	LM/E(LNW)	P	*2008*
06.06.1966	Rugby Midland - Kingscliffe	LM(LNW)	G(All)	*2009*
06.06.1966	SEATON JN - STAMFORD [Luffenham Jn]	LM(LNW/Mid)	P(All)	*2010*
06.06.1966	Trent Lane Jn - Nottingham Manvers Street Goods	LM(LNW)	G(All)	*2011*
06.06.1966	Wellingborough Midland Jn - Irthingborough	LM(LNW)	G(All)	*2012*
06.06.1966	Kings Cliffe - Market Harborough No.3	LM(LNW)	G(All)	*2013*
06.06.1966	Market Harborough No.1 - Clifton Mill	LM(LNW)	G(All)	*2014*
06.06.1966	Banbury General - Banbury Merton Street	W(GWR)	G(All)	*2015*
06.06.1966	Panteg Jn - Panteg Steelworks	W(GWR)	G(All)	*2016*
06.06.1966	Lumphinnans Central Jn - Foulford NCB Workshops	Sc(NBR)	G(All)	*2017*
13.06.1966	Ynyscedwyn Colliery - Easton Bros. Siding	W(Mid)	G(All)	*2018*
19.06.1966 [3]	Clapham - Low Gill	LM(Mid/LNW	G(All)	*2019*
20.06.1966	Ashton Moss South Jn - Ashtom Oldham Road Goods	LM(LNW)	G(All)	*2020*
20.06.1966	Baxter Wood No.1 - Consett South	NE(NER)	G(All)	*2021*
27.06.1966	Bradwell Sidings - Kidsgrove Central (Old Harecastle line)	LM(LNW)	P(All)	*2022*
27.06.1966	GLASGOW (St.Enoch) - Shield Jn	Sc(GSW)	P	*2023*
27.06.1966	PAISLEY (Gilmour St.) [Cart Jn] - DALRY [Brownhill Jn]	Sc(GSW)	P	*2024*
27.06.1966	Port Eglinton Jn - Bellahouston No.2	Sc(GSW)	P(All)	*2025*
27.06.1966 [4]	Troon Jn - Troon Harbour (Templehill Sidings)	Sc(GSW)	G(All)	*2026*
04.07.1966 [3]	Dalston Jn - Eastern Jn	LM(NLR)	G(All)	*2027*
04.07.1966	Rillington Jn - Pickering	NE(NER)	G(All)	*2028*
07.07.1966	Redmarshall East - Redmarshall North	NE(NER)	G(All)	*2029*
07.07.1966	Redmarshall South - Wingate South	NE(NER)	G(All)	*2030*
09.07.1966	Llandebie Limestone Branch GF - Cilrychen Lime Works	LM(GWR)	G(All)	*2031*
11.07.1966	Hickleton Colliery Sidings - Hickleton Main Colliery	NE(DVR)	G(All)	*2032*
11.07.1966	Crofton South Jn - Crofton East Jn	NE(DVR)	G(All)	*2033*
11.07.1966	Shafton Jn - Brierley	NE(DVR)	G(All)	*2034*
11.07.1966	Thurnscoe Jn - Hickleton Main Colliery Sidings	NE(DVR)	G(All)	*2035*
11.07.1966	Houghton Colliery Sidings - Hickleton BR Spur Jn	NE(DVR)	G(All)	*2036*
11.07.1966	Goldthorpe Colliery - Yorkshire Main Sidings	NE(DVR)	G(All)	*2037*
11.07.1966	Shafton NCB Workshops - Crofton West Jn	NE(L&Y)	G(All)	*2038*
18.07.1966	Leven - Crail	Sc(NBR)	G(All)	*2039*
18.07.1966	Culter - Ballater	Sc(GNoSR)	G(All)	*2040*
20.07.1966 [3]	Birkenhead Blackpool Street - Monks Ferry Depot	LM(BJt)	G(All)	*2041*
20.07.1966	Murrow West - Dogsthorpe Siding	E(MGN)	G(All)	*2042*
01.08.1966	Earby Barnoldswick Jn - Barnoldswick Goods	LM(Mid)	G(All)	*2043*

Date	Line	Region (Company)	Type of Traffic	Reference Number
01.08.1966	Hardingstone Jn - Wellingborough (London Road)	LM(LNW)	G(All)	2044
01.08.1966	Hanley Jn - Hanley Goods	LM(NSR)	G(All)	2045
01.08.1966	Stafford [Universal Grinding Wheel Co. Sd] - Newport (Salop)	LM(LNW)	(All)	2046
01.08.1966	Barrs Court Jn - Show Yard Siding	W(GWR)	G(All)	2047
01.08.1966	Barton Curve Jn - Moorfields Jn	W(Mid)	G(All)	2048
01.08.1966	Merthyr - Yaynor Quarry	W(B&M/LNWJt)	G(All)	2049
01.08.1966	Red Hill Jn - Hereford Barton	W(GWR)	G(All)	2050
01.08.1966	Ollerton Colliery EWS GF - Eakring Road Siding	E(MNJt)	G(All)	2051
01.08.1966	Kirkhill Jn - Westburn Jn	Sc(Cal)	G(All)	2052
02.08.1966	Pontypool Road Down Yard - Panteg Jn	W(GWR)	G(All)	2053
02.08.1966	Don Bridge East Jn - Roundwood Colliery	E(GC&MidJt)	G(All)	2054
15.08.1966	Slateford Jn - Edinburgh (Morrison Street Goods)	Sc(Cal)	G(All)	2055
15.08.1966 [4]	Forres South - Forres West	Sc(High)	G(All)	2056
15.08.1966	Neath General West - Neath Jn	W(GWR)	G(All)	2057
26.08.1966	West Hallam LWS GF - Shipley Colliery	LM(Mid)	G(All)	2058
00.09.1966	Pain's Siding - Buckminster Siding	LM(Mid)	G(All)	2059 *
05.09.1966	AYLESBURY (Town) - RUGBY (Central)	LM(GCR)	P	2060
05.09.1966	Calvert Jn - Rugby Central	LM(GCR)	G(All)	2061
05.09.1966	BANBURY [Banbury Jn] - WOODFORD HALSE [Culworth Jn]	LM(GCR)	P(All)	2062
05.09.1966 [1]	Ashendon Jn - Grendon Underwood Jn	LM(GCR)	P(All)	2063
05.09.1966 [1]	Ashendon Jn - Akeman Street (MOA Siding)	LM(GCR)	G(All)	2064
05.09.1966	NOTTINGHAM (Victoria) - SHEFFIELD (Victoria) [Woodhouse East Jn]	LM/E(GCR)	P	2065
05.09.1966	Bulwell North Jn - Annesley North Jn	LM(GCR)	G(All)	2066
05.09.1966	New Hucknall Sidings - Duckmanton North Jn	LM/E(GCR)	G(All)	2067 *
05.09.1966	Pilsley - Pilsley Colliery	LM(GCR)	G(All)	2068
05.09.1966	Kirkby South Jn - Sutton in Ashfield Central	LM(GCR)	G(All)	2069
05.09.1966 [5]	Tondu North - Tondu Ogmore Jn	W(GWR)	G(All)	2070
05.09.1966	SOUTHAMPTON (Central) [Tunnel Jn] - SOUTHAMPTON (Terminus)	S(LSW)	P	2071
12.09.1966	SHEFFIELD (Victoria) [Woodburn Jn] - YORK/DONCASTER [Aldwarke North Jns]	E(GCR)	P	2072 *
12.09.1966	SAXMUNHAM - ALDEBURGH	E(GER)	P	2073
12.09.1966	Sizewell Siding - Aldeburgh	E(GER)	G(All)	2074
19.09.1966	Croxley Green Jn - Colne Jn	LM(LNW)	G(All)	2075
26.09.1966	Kilmacolm - Greenock (Albert Harbour)	Sc(GSW)	G(All)	2076 *
30.09.1966	Treherbert RSB Jn - Fernhill Upper GF	W(Taff)	G(All)	2077
31.10.1966	Silverwood Sidings - Thurcroft Sidings	E(GC&MidJt)	G(All)	2078
03.10.1966	Blidworth Jn - Blidworth Colliery GF	LM(LMS)	G(All)	2079
03.10.1966	Codnor Park Jn - Ironville Jn	LM(Mid)	G(All)	2080
03.10.1966	Diggle Jn - Staley & Millbrook	LM(LNW)	G(All)	2081
03.10.1966	Rufford Jn - Blidworth Jn	LM(Mid)	G(All)	2082
03.10.1966	BATHAMPTON - DORCHESTER (West)	W(GWR)	P(Locals)	2083
03.10.1966	HALWILL [Jn] - BUDE	W(LSW)	P(All)	2084
03.10.1966	HALWILL [Meldon Jn] - WADEBRIDGE [East]	W(LSW)	P	2085
03.10.1966	TAUNTON [Norton Fitzwarren] - BARNSTAPLE JN [South Loop GF]	W(GWR)	P(All)	2086
03.10.1966	YATTON - CLEVEDON	W(GWR)	P(All)	2087
03.10.1966	YEOVIL JN [South Jn] - YEOVIL (Town)	W(LSW)	P(All)	2088
03.10.1966	Lewes East Yard - Friars Walk Goods	S(LBSC)	G(All)	2089
03.10.1966	Bridge House - Baxter Wood No.1	NE(NER)	G(All)	2090
03.10.1966	Dearness Valley - Baxter Wood No.2	NE(NER)	G(All)	2091
03.10.1966	Flatts Lane LC - Normanby Brickworks	NE(NER)	G(All)	2092
03.10.1966	Morpeth - Woodburn	NE(NBR)	G(All)	2093
03.10.1966	Reilly Mill - Baxter Wood No.1	NE(NER)	G(All)	2094
03.10.1966	South Bank Gasworks Siding - Eston	NE(NER)	G(All)	2095
03.10.1966	Stourton Jn - Lofthouse North Jn	NE(EWYU)	G(All)	2096
03.10.1966	Thirsk - Thirsk Town Jn	NE(NER)	G(All)	2097
03.10.1966	Thirsk Town Jn - Thirsk Town Goods	NE(NER)	G(All)	2098

Date	Line	Region (Company)	Type of Traffic	Reference Number
03.10.1966	Keith Jn - Altmore	Sc(High)	G(All)	*2099*
03.10.1966	Misk Siding GF - Ardeer Platform	Sc(GSW)	G(All)	*2100*
12.10.1966 [5]	Dalton - Stainton	LM(Furn)	G(All)	*2101*
15.10.1966 [3]	Methil West - Lochhead Colliery	Sc(NBR)	G(All)	*2102*
17.10.1966	Great Mountain Colliery - Cross Hands	W(LMM)	G(All)	*2103*
17.10.1966	Dumfries No.1 - Dumfries Goods Jn	Sc(Cal)	G(All)	*2104*
17.10.1966	Dumfries Goods Jn - St Marys Goods	Sc(Cal)	G(All)	*2105*
24.10.1966	Smallbrook Jn - Medina Wharf	S(IWCR)	G(All)	*2106*
29.10.1966	Port Glasgow Jn - Port Glasgow Harbour	Sc(Cal)	G(All)	*2107*
30.10.1966 [5]	Dove Jn - Marston Jn	LM(NSR)	G(All)	*2108*
31.10.1966 [3]	Bickershaw Jn - Moss Hall Colliery	LM(LNW)	G(All)	*2109*
31.10.1966	Sudbury - Sudbury Old Goods	E(GER)	G(All)	*2110*
31.10 1966	Culters Jn - Laisterdyke Coal Yard	NE(GNR)	G(All)	*2111*
31.10.1966	Galashiels - Selkirk Jn Galafoot SGB Siding	Sc(NBR)	G(All)	*2112*
07.11.1966	GUNNISLAKE - CALLINGTON	W(PD&SWJn)	P(All)	*2113*
07.11.1966	GOBOWEN - OSWESTRY	LM(GWR)	P	*2114*
07.11.1966	CAMBRIDGE - BURY ST EDMUNDS	E(GER)	P(Locals)	*2115*
07.11.1966	Belmont - Durham (Gilesgate)	NE(NER)	G(All)	*2116*
07.11.1966	BARRHEAD - KILMARNOCK	Sc(GBKJt)	P(Locals)	*2117*
07.11.1966	Burghead - Burghead Harbour	Sc(High)	G(All)	*2118*
07.11.1966	GLASGOW (Buchanan Street) - CUMBERNAULD [Sighthill West]	Sc(Cal)	P(All)	*2119*
07.11.1966	Reston - Duns	Sc(NBR)	G(All)	*2120*
07.11.1966	Kintore - Paradise Sidings	Sc(GNoSR)	G(All)	*2121*
14.11.1966 [5]	Brynmenyn Jn - Tynycoed Jn	W(GWR)	G(All)	*2122*
21.11.1966	West Boldon Goods - Washington Chemical Works	NE(NER)	G(All)	*2123*
27.11.1966	Milton Jn - Provan Gasworks Siding	Sc(Cal)	G(All)	*2124*
28.11.1966	Newport (Dock Street) - Newport (Mill Street)	W(GWR)	G(All)	*2125*
28.11.1966	Germiston Jn - Robroyston West Jn	Sc(Cal)	G(All)	*2126*
30.11.1966 [2]	Stoke Canon - Thorverton	W(GWR)	G(All)	*2127*
30.11.1966	Church Fenton - Tadcaster	NE(NER)	G(All)	*2128*
05.12.1966	BLETCHLEY [Verney Jn] - BUCKINGHAM	LM(LNW)	P	*2129*
05.12.1966	Verney Jn - Buckingham	LM(LNW)	G(All)	*2130*
05.12.1966	MANCHESTER (Victoria) [Clifton Jn] - ACCRINGTON [Radcliffe North Jn]	LM(L&Y)	P(All)	*2131*
05.12.1966	RAMSBOTTOM [Stubbins Jn] - ACCRINGTON [North Jn]	LM(L&Y)	P	*2132*
05.12.1966	Stubbins Jn - Accrington South Jn	LM(L&Y)	G(All)	*2133*
05.12.1966	Accrington West Jn - Accrington South Jn	LM(L&Y)	G(All)	*2134*
05.12.1966	Rawtenstall - Bacup	LM(L&Y)	G(All)	*2135*
05.12.1966	South Hetton Colliery - Pesspool	NE(NER)	G(All)	*2136*
11.12.1966 [4]	Mansfield North Jn - Mansfield East Jn	LM(Mid)	G(All)	*2137*
12.12.1966	Charity - Stooperdale	NE(NER)	G(All)	*2138*
19.12.1966	MORLEY [Farnley Jsw - LEEDS (City) [West]	NE(LNW)	P(All)	*2139* *
30.12.1966	Metal Box Co's Siding - Neath Canalside	W(RSB)	G(All)	*2140*
02.01.1967	DERBY (Midland) [Ambergate] - SHEFFIELD (Midland) [Crich Jn]	LM/E(Mid)	P(Locals)	*2141*
02.01.1967 [3]	Earlestown No.1 - Earlestown No.3	LM(LNW)	G(All)	*2142*
02.01.1967	Goodyear Tyre Siding - Rickmansworth (Church Street)	LM(LNW)	G(All)	*2143*
02.01.1967	Heaton Mersey Station Jn - Heaton Mersey East Jn	LM(Mid)	P(All)	*2144*
02.01.1967	Heaton Mersey East Jn - Bredbury Jn	LM(CLC)	P	*2145*
02.01.1967	Bredbury Jn - Romiley Jn	LM(GC&MidJt)	P	*2146*
02.01.1967	NOTTINGHAM (Midland) [Long Eaton Jn] - SHEFFIELD (Midland) [Trowell Jn]	LM/E(Mid)	P(Locals)	*2147*
02.01.1967	Bridgwater Bath Crossing - Bridgwater Docks	W(GWR)	G(All)	*2148*
02.01.1967	Bridgwater Church Street 1954 spur - Bridgwater North Goods	W(S&DJt/BR)	G(All)	*2149*
02.01.1967	Penrhos Jn - Glyntaff Interchange Sidings GF	W(ADR)	G(All)	*2150*
02.01.1967	GROOMBRIDGE [Ashurst West] - THREE BRIDGES	S(LBSC)	P	*2151*

▲ A 5700 Class Pannier tank 9667 (86A) having just arrived at Blaenavon Low Level with 6.15 a.m. from Newport High Street on 24th June 1956. Although the service was later dieselised, the savings did not reprieve it and passenger trains ceased after 30th April 1962. *(R.J.Buckley)*

▲ On 13th September 1952, 4406 2-6-2T pauses with its three coach train at Pyle, with the 12.40 p.m. Porthcawl to Tondu service. The Pyle to Porthcawl service was withdrawn from 9th September 1963. *(R.J.Buckley)*

► The 0-4-2T 5819 stands at Newcastle Emlyn with the 8.10 a.m. departure for Pencader on 3rd September 1952, the last day of service. Pannier tank 7425 sits at the buffers having brought the 7.30 a.m. from Pencader. Milk traffic enabled the branch to survive until 1st October 1973. *(R.J.Buckley)*

Date	Line	Region (Company)	Type of Traffic	Notes
02.01.1967	Ashurst West Jn - East Grinstead H.L. Goods	S(LBSC)	G(All)	2152
02.01.1967	East Grinstead B - Three Bridges	S(LBSC)	G(All)	2153
02.01.1967	East Grinstead A (H.L.) - St Margarets Jn	S(LBSC)	P(All)	2154
02.01.1967	IPSWICH - NORWICH (Thorpe)	E(GER)	P(Locals)	2155
02.01.1967	SHERINGHAM (New) - SHERINGHAM (Old)	E(MGN)	P(All)	2156 *
02.01.1967	WAKEFIELD (Kirkgate) - PONTEFRACT (Monkhill)	E(L&Y)	P	2157
02.01.1967	BARASSIE - KILMARNOCK [No.2]	Sc(GSW)	P	2158
02.01.1967	Ferryhill Jn - Culter	Sc(GNoSR)	G(All)	2159
02.01.1967	Tay Bridge South - Newport on Tay (East)	Sc(NBR)	G	2160
05.01.1967	Copper Works Jn - Port Talbot Station	W(PTR)	G(All)	2161
07.01.1967	Sunderland Deptford - Lambton Staithes	NE(NER)	G(All)	2162
08.01.1967	Killamarsh Jn - Waleswood Jn	E(GCR)	G(All)	2163
09.01.1967	Cadzow Jn GF - Hamilton Allanshaw Siding	Sc(Cal)	G(All)	2164
09.01.1967	Niddrie South Jn - Leith South Jn	Sc(NBR)	G(All)	2165
09.01.1967	Langwith Colliery Jn Jn with new spur) - Spinkhill	E(GCR)	G(All)	2166
23.01.1967	Haigh Jn - Whelley Jn	LM(LNW)	R(All)	2167
30.01.1967	Horwich Fork Jn - Loco Jn	LM(L&Y)	G(All)	2168
30.01.1967	St Helens Pilkington's Siding - Old Mill Lane	LM(LNW)	G(All)	2169
30.01.1967	Stretton Jn - Horninglow	LM(NSR)	G(All)	2170
30.01.1967	BODMIN ROAD - PADSTOW	W(GWR/LSW)	P	2171
30.01.1967	Wadebridge Goods - Padstow	W(LSW)	G(All)	2172
30.01.1967	Dunmere Jn GF - Bodmin North	W(LSW)	G(All)	2173
03.02.1967	Mary Pit - Lochore Coup	Sc(NBR)	G(All)	2174
06.02.1967	Port Talbot General - East Abbey Works West (Via Copper Works Jn)	W(GWR)	G(All)	2175
06.02.1967	Copper Works Jn - Duffryn Yard	W(PTR)	G(All)	2176
13.02.1967	KIRKHAM & WESHAM [Kirkham North Jn] - BLACKPOOL (South) (via Marton)	LM(P&WJt)	P(All)	2177
13.02.1967 [2]	Wenford Bridge EEC Sidings - Wenford Bridge Goods	W(LSW)	G(All)	2178
20.02.1967	Ynys–y–Geinon Jn - Abercrave International Colliery	W(Mid)	G(All)	2178
26.02.1967 [5]	Ambergate North Jn - Ambergate West Jn	LM(Mid)	G(All)	2180
26.02.1967 [5]	Ambergate Station Jn - Ambergate North Jn	LM(Mid)	G(All)	2181
28.02.1967	Brownieside Jn GF - Airdrie (Boots Siding)	Sc(NBR)	G(All)	2182
00.03.1967	Dairycoates East - St Andrews Fish Dock	NE(NER)	G(All)	2183
06.03.1967	DERBY (Midland) - MANCHESTER (Central)	LM(Mid/CLC)	P(Locals)	2184
06.03.1967	MANCHESTER (Central) - SHEFFIELD (Midland)	LM/E(CLC/Mid)	P(Locals)	2185
06.03.1967	MILLERS DALE - BUXTON (Midland)	LM(Mid)	P	2186
06.03.1967	CHINLEY [Peak Forest Jn] - BUXTON (Midland) [Blackwell Jn]	LM(Mid)	P	2187
06.03.1967	Buxton East Jn - Buxton Midland	LM(Mid)	G(All)	2188
06.03.1967	Bredbury Jn - Romiley Jn	LM(GC&MidJt)	G(All)	2189
06.03.1967	Millers Dale Jn - Buxton Jn	LM(Mid)	G(All)	2190
06.03.1967	Church Road Jn - Birmingham Central Goods	LM(Mid)	G(All)	2191
06.03.1967	SIDMOUTH JN - SIDMOUTH	W(LSW)	P	2192
06.03.1967	TIPTON ST JOHN - EXMOUTH	W(LSW)	P(All)	2193
06.03.1967	APPLEDORE - NEW ROMNEY	S(SEC)	P	2194
06.03.1967	Lydd Town CEGB Siding - New Romney	S(SER)	G(All)	2195
06.03.1967	CAMBRIDGE [Shelford Jn] - SUDBURY	E(GER)	P(All)	2196
06.03.1967	MARCH [South Jn] - ST IVES	E(GN&GEJt)	P	2197
06.03.1967	March South Jn - St Ives (Cambs)	E(GER)	G(All)	2198
06.03.1967	HARROGATE [Dragon Jn] - NORTHALLERTON [Cordio Jn]	NE(NER)	P	2199 *
06.03.1967	Melmerby South - Northallerton Cordio Jn	NE(NER)	G(All)	2200
06.03.1967	Cordio Jn - Boroughbridge Road	NE(NER)	G(All)	2201
06.03.1967	Dragon Jn - Bilton Jn	NE(NER)	G(All)	2202
07.03.1967	Cwmbran Jn - Oakfield Sidings	W(GWR)	G(All)	2203
24.03.1967	Bury Loop Jn - Bury Loco Jn	LM(L&Y)	G(All)	2204
27.03.1967	Methley South - Whitwood Jn	NE(NER)	G(All)	2205
27.03.1967	Hardengreen Jn - Penicuik	Sc(NBR)	G(All)	2206

Date	Line	Region (Company)	Type of Traffic	Reference Number
01.04.1967	Lawrence Hill Jn - Bristol Midland Road (St Philips)	W(Mid)	G(All)	2207
01.04.1967 [2]	Hawarden Bridge Jn - Connah's Quay	LM(GCR)	G(All)	2208
03.04.1967 [3]	Billington Road Crossing - Dunstable North	LM(LNW)	G(All)	2209
03.04.1967	High Peak Jn - Middleton Branch Sidings	LM(LNW)	G(All)	2210
03.04.1967	Coed Ely - Clydach Vale Cambrian Colliery	W(GWR)	G(All)	2211
10.04.1967	East Grinstead H.L. - East Grinstead L.L. (through siding)	S(LBSC)	G(All)	2212
17.04.1967	Charnwood Forest Jn-Whitwick Colliery	LM(LNW)	G(All)	2213
17.04.1967	Coalville Jn-Charnwood Forest Jn	LM(A&NJt)	G(All)	2214 *
17.04.1967	Hessle Road - Dairycoates East	E(NER)	G(All)	2215
24.04.1967	Plumpton Jn - Backbarrow Charcoal Iron Co s Sid	LM(Furn)	G(All)	2216 *
24.04.1967	Eastbourne - Eastbourne Gas Works	S(LBSC)	G(All)	2217
27.04.1967	Friden - Middleton Branch Sidings	LM(LNW)	G(All)	2218
30.04.1967 [5]	TRENT [Station North] - SAWLEY JN (Via North Curve)	LM(Mid)	P(All)	2219
00.05.1967	Stairfoot Jn - Wharncliffe Woodmoor Colliery	E(GCR)	G(All)	2220
01.05.1967	Cruckmeole Jn GF - Minsterley	LM(Sh&WJt)	G(All)	2221
01.05.1967	Friden - Middleton Top	LM(LNW)	G(All)	2222
01.05.1967	Wellington No.4 - Nantwich Market Drayton Jn	LM(GWR)	G(All)	2223
01.05.1967	North Walsall Jn - Lichfield Road Jn	LM(Mid)	G(All)	2224
01.05.1967	1964 Spur Jn - Humberstone Coal Yard	LM(BR/GNR)	G(All)	2225
01.05.1967 [1]	Bilson Jn - Berry Wiggins Siding	W(GWR)	G(All)	2226
01.05.1967	Caerphilly West - Penrhos Jn	W(Rhy)	G(All)	2227
01.05.1967	Cwmmawr Colliery - Cwmmawr	W(BPGV)	G(All)	2228
01.05.1967	Redruth Jn - Redruth West Yard	W(GWR)	G(All)	2229
01.05.1967	Thame Shell Mex BP Siding - Morris Cowley	W(GWR)	G(All)	2230
01.05.1967	Watford Crossing - Beddau Loop	W(Rhy)	G(All)	2231
01.05.1967	Holbeck East - LEEDS (Central)	E(GN/LCJt)	P(All)	2232
01.05.1967	Wortley Jn - LEEDS (Central)	E(NER/LCJt)	P	2233
01.05.1967	Summer Lane - Dodworth (old alignment)	E(GCR)	P(All)	2234
01.05.1967	Bathgate Lower - Westfield Paper Mill	Sc(NBR)	G(All)	2235
06.05.1967	Annesley Jn (GNR) - Annesley Colliery	LM(GNR)	G(All)	2236
08.05.1967	Sidmouth Jn - Sidmouth	W(LSW)	G(All)	2237
08.05.1967	Singer Jn - SINGER WORKS Platform	Sc(NBR)	W(All)	2238
21.05.1967	Albert Hill - Lingfield Lane (Paton & Baldwins Siding)	E(NER)	G(All)	2239
21.05.1967 [4]	Forres East - Dallasdhu Siding	Sc(High)	G(All)	2240
22.05.1967	Sheepwashers Lane - OAGBJn	LM(OAGBJt)	G(All)	2241
22.05.1967	Triangle GF - Newport Pagnall	LM(LNW)	G(All)	2242
01.06.1967	Gwaunton Opencast Site (OCS) - Abercrave International Colliery	W(Mid)	G(All)	2243
05.06.1967	Wennington Jn - Torrisholme Jn No.1	LM(Mid)	G(All)	2244
05.06.1967	Tiverton Jn - Tiverton Goods	W(GWR)	G(All)	2245
05.06.1967	Glasgow St.Enoch - Clyde Jn	Sc(GSW)	R(All)	2246
05.06.1967	HILLINGTON (West) [Arkleston Jn] - RENFREW WHARF	Sc(GSW)	P	2247
05.06.1967	Wennington Lancaster Ladies Walk - CEGB Siding	LM(Mid)	G(All)	2248
05.06.1967	White Lund NWGB Siding - Lancaster Green Ayre	LM(Mid)	G(All)	2249
05.06.1967 [3]	Winsford Jn - Falks Jn ICI Sidings	LM(CLC)	G(All)	2250
19.06.1967	Montrose North - Broomfield Jn	Sc(NBR)	G(All)	2251
19.06.1967	Broomfield Jn - Broomfield Siding	Sc(NBR)	G(All)	2252
19.06.1967	Broomfield Jn - Montrose East	Sc(Cal)	G(All)	2253
19.06.1967	Montrose South - Montrose Harbour	Sc(NBR)	G(All)	2254
30.06.1967	Daubhill Jn - Daubhill (St Helens Road Coop Coal Yard)	LM(LNW)	G(All)	2255
01.07.1967	Lumphinnans Central Jn - Lumphinnans North Jn	Sc(NBR)	G(All)	2256
01.07.1967	Lumphinnians East Jn - Kelty South	Sc(NBR)	G(All)	2257
03.07.1967	Barrow Shipyard - Ramsden Dock	LM(Furn)	G(All)	2258
03.07.1967	Loco Jn - BARROW SHIPYARD (Island Road)	LM(Furn)	W	2259
03.07.1967	Wigston North Jn - Wigston South	LM(Mid)	G(All)	2260
03.07.1967	Beeston Jn - Parkside Jn	E(GNR)	G(All)	2261

►Black 5 45059 with a 16F shedplate rests at Gloucester Eastgate on a northbound express. The station clock gives the time as 9.45 a.m. The Midland line south from Eastgate station crossed many roads on the level and after 1st December 1975, passenger services were concentrated on a modernised Gloucester Central station. (G.Hurst Collection)

▼Ex Great Western Railcar W19W pulls away from Cleobury Mortimer on 21st May 1955. In the background tank engine 2144 stands with a SLS railtour from Birmingham Snow Hill to Cleobury North Sidings. Passenger services were withdrawn from the Bewdley to Tenbury Wells line on 1st August 1962. Goods traffic continued until 19th April 1965. (R.J.Buckley)

▲Pannier Tank engine 9774 an up freight through Handsworth & Smethwick station on 21st February 1966. Passenger services ceased on 6th March 1972. Cement traffic continues to use Handsworth Goods just beyond the bridge in the background. The former Great Western route is to reopened to BR and later to Metro services. (R.J.Buckley)

Date	Line	Region (Company)	Type of Traffic	Reference Number
03.07.1967	Parkside Jn - Middleton Broom Colliery Exchange Sid.	E(GNR)	G(All)	2262
03.07.1967	Christian Street Jn - Commerical Road Goods	E(LTS)	G(All)	2263
03.07.1967	Cudworth Yard South - Jn with new spur MP55½	E(HBR)	G(All)	2264
03.07.1967 [3]	Bowesfield - Redmarshall North	E(NER)	G(All)	2265
03.07.1967 [3]	Redmarshall South - Redmarshall West	E(NER)	G(All)	2266
10.07.1967	Avonmouth Dock Jn - St Andrews Jn	W(GWR)	G(All)	2267
10.07.1967	MARLOW (New) - MARLOW (Old)	W(GWR)	P(All)	2268
17.07.1967	Mansfield Colliery Jn - Mansfield Colliery EWS	LM(Mid)	G(All)	2269
17.07.1967	Mansfield Colliery Jn - Mansfield Colliery EWS	LM(Mid)	G(All)	2270
17.07.1967	Jn with EWS - Mansfield Colliery LWS	LM(Mid)	G(All)	2271
24.07.1967	Stalybridge No.1 - Bayley Street Coal Depot	LM(GC&LNWJt)	G(All)	2272
31.07.1967	Moira East Jn - Moira South Jn	LM(Mid)	G(All)	2273
31.07.1967	Pontypridd PC&N Jn - Glyntaff Interchange Sidings GF	W(ADR)	G(All)	2274
31.07.1967	Alton Cripples Home Siding GF - Treloar's Siding	S(LSW)	G(All)	2275
01.08.1967 [2]	Gloucester Tramway Jn - Gloucester Hempstead Goods	W(Mid)	G(All)	2276
01.08.1967	Parkend - Whitecroft	W(SWJt)	G(All)	2277
01.08.1967	Whitecroft - Coleford	W(SWJt)	G(All)	2278
01.08.1967 [3]	Bullo Pit West - Cinderford Town	W(GWR)	G(All)	2279
02.08.1967	Oldfield Road - Salford Goods	LM(L&Y)	G(All)	2280
02.08.1967	Knighton North Jn - Saffron Lane Jn	LM(Mid)	G(All)	2281
02.08.1967	Llanelly - Sandy Gate	W(BPGV)	G(All)	2282
07.08.1967	West Moors MOD Siding - Ringwood	S(LSW)	G(All)	2283
07.08.1967	Boldon Colliery Sidings - West Boldon Goods	E(NER)	G(All)	2284
07.08.1967	Hemsworth East - Hemsworth South	E(HBR)	G(All)	2285
07.08.1967	Monkton Empty Sidings - Wrangbrook Jn	E(H&B)	G(All)	2286
07.08.1967	Wrangbrook Jn - Sprotborough Middleton Siding	E(GC&HBJt)	G(All)	2287
07.08.1967	Pickburn & Brodsworth - Brodsworth Main Colliery	E(GC&HBJt)	G(All)	2288
14.08.1967 [3]	Lancaster No.1 - Lancaster Old	LM(LNW)	G(All)	2289
14.08.1967	Prestwick ICI Sidings - Ponteland	E(NER)	G(All)	2290
21.08.1967	Rochdale East Jn - Whitworth	LM(L&Y)	G(All)	2291
21.08.1967	Milford Jn - Salisbury (Milford)	S(LSW)	G(All)	2292
21.08.1967	Penshaw North - Hylton Quarry Sidings	E(NER)	G(All)	2293
04.09.1967	Bournville - Lifford Canal Yard	LM(Mid)	G(All)	2294
04.09.1967	GRANTHAM [Netherfield] - NOTTINGHAM (Victoria) [Weekday Cross Jn]	LM(GNR)	P	2295
04.09.1967	NOTTINGHAM (Victoria) - NOTTINGHAM (Arkwright Street)	LM(GCR)	P	2296
04.09.1967	PERTH [Stanley Jn] - ABERDEEN [Kinnaber Jn]	Sc(Cal)	P	2297
04.09.1967	Forfar North Jn - Bridge of Dun	Sc(Cal)	G(All)	2298
04.09.1967	Forfar South Jn - Justinhaugh	Sc(Cal)	G(All)	2299
04.09.1967	Tredegar Jn Lower - Britannia Colliery	W(GW/B&M)	G(All)	2300
04.09.1967	Granton Jn GF - Associated Deliveries Siding	Sc(Cal)	G(All)	2301
11.09.1967	Ketley's Sidings - Pool Dam (Canal Wharf Sidings)	LM(NSR)	G(All)	2302
11.09.1967	Sheepbridge Glass Works Siding - Chesterfield Central	E(GCR)	G(All)	2303
11.09.1967	Inveralmond (Dewar's Siding) - Crieff	Sc(Cal)	G(All)	2304
18.09.1967	Andover Jn - Andover Town	S(LSW)	G(All)	2305
18.09.1967	Riddings Jn - Langholm	Sc(NBR)	G(All)	2306
30.09.1967	Blisworth - Blisworth (RTB Siding)	LM(SMJ)	G(All)	2307
30.09.1967 [3]	Yate Main Line Jn - Thornbury	W(Mid)	G(All)	2308
02.10.1967	Briggs Sidings - Friden	LM(LNW)	G(All)	2309
02.10.1967	Knutton Gate Jn - Whitebarn Jn reversing loop	LM(NSR)	G(All)	2310
02.10.1967	Mansfield Colliery Sidings - Sutton in Ashfield Central	LM(GCR)	G(All)	2311 *
02.10.1967	Moat Lane Jn - Llanidloes	LM(Cam)	G(All)	2312
02.10.1967	Parsley Hay - Hartington	LM(LNW)	G(All)	2313 *
02.10.1967	Coleford Jn - Coleford	W(SWJt)	G(All)	2314
02.10.1967	Glyn Neath - Hirwaun Pond	W(GWR)	G(All)	2315 *
02.10.1967	Parkend - Coleford Jn	W(SWJt)	G(All)	2316

Date	Line	Region (Company)	Type of Traffic	Reference Number
02.10.1967	Harby & Stathern - Stathern Ironstone Sidings	E(GN&LNWJt)	G(All)	2317
07.10.1967	Knutton Gate Jn - Whitebarn Jn run round loop	LM(NSR)	G(All)	2318
09.10.1967	Broughty Jn - Kingsmuir	Sc(Cal)	G(All)	2319
09.10.1967	Panteg & Coedygric Jn - Pontypool Road South Jn	W(GWR)	G(All)	2320
09.10.1967	Yeovil Town - Yeovil Hendford Goods	W(GWR)	G(All)	2321
09.10.1967	Auchmuty Jn GF - Leslie	Sc(NBR)	G(All)	2322
09.10.1967	Leslie - Fettykil Paper Mill	Sc(NBR)	G(All)	2323
11.10.1967	Marsh's Crossing - Triplex Glass Works	LM(LNW)	G(All)	2324
11.10.1967	Armadale Jn - Bathville	Sc(NBR)	G(All)	2325
12.10.1967	Colbren Jn - Abercrave	W(N&B)	G(All)	2326
16.10.1967 [4]	Courtaulds No.2 GF - Longridge	LM(P&LJt)	G(All)	2327
16.10.1967	Hulton's Sidings - Bolton (Crook Street Goods)	LM(LNW)	G(All)	2328
23.10.1967	Torrisholme No.1 - Morecambe Promenade	LM(Mid)	G(All)	2329
30.10.1967	Kings Cross Goods - Caledonian Road reversing sidings	E(GNR)	G(All)	2330
30.10.1967	Caledonian Road reversing sidings - Caledonian Road Goods	E(GNR)	G(All)	2331
05.11.1967	ROCK FERRY - BIRKENHEAD (Woodside)	LM(BirkJt)	P(All)	2332
06.11.1967	Bickershaw Jn - Wigan Central Goods	LM(GCR)	G(All)	2333
06.11.1967	Court House Jn - Barnsley (Central Goods)	E(GCR)	G(All)	2334
06.11.1967	Kirkley Jn - Lowestoft Goods	E(GER)	G(All)	2335
06.11.1967	Lea Bridge Jn - Hall Farm Jn	E(GER)	G(All)	2336
06.11.1967	SEVEN SISTERS - SOUTH TOTTENHAM [Jn]	E(GER)	P	2337
06.11.1967	SOUTH TOTTENHAM [West Jn] - South Tottenham South Jn	E(GER)	P	2338
06.11.1967	Dalmeny Jn - South Queensferry	Sc(NBR)	G(All)	2339
06.11.1967	Ninewells Jn - Maryfield	Sc(Cal)	G(All)	2340
06.11.1967	Trinity Jn - Edinburgh (Scotland Street Goods)	Sc(NBR)	G(All)	2341
06.11.1967	Blackstone Jn - Linwood Goods	Sc(Cal)	G(All)	2342
10.11.1967	Bethnal Green - Spitalfields Goods	E(GER)	G(All)	2343
12.11.1967 [5]	Subway Jn - Royal Oak	W(GWR)	P(All)	2344
20.11.1967	Halls Road Jn - Penar Jn	W(GWR)	G(All)	2345 *
20.11.1967	Machen - Caerphilly East Jn	W(B&M)	G(All)	2346
26.11.1967	Wigston North Jn - Wigston Central Jn	LM(Mid)	G(All)	2347
27.11.1967	Stamford Jn (Mid) - Stamford Priory Siding	E(GNR)	G(All)	2348
27.11.1967	Brandy Bridge Jn - Vaynor Limestone Quarry	W(B&M/LNW)	G(All)	2349
27.11.1967	Meols Cop - Hesketh Park	LM(L&Y)	G(All)	2350
27.11.1967	Brandy Bridge Jn - Merthyr Plymouth Street	W(Taff)	G(All)	2351
30.11.1967	Bath Jn - Bath Coop Coal Siding	W(S&DJt)	G(All)	2352
04.12.1967	Exmouth - Exmouth Dock	W(LSW)	G(All)	2353
04.12.1967	Heathfield - Crockham Siding	W(GWR)	G(All)	2354
04.12.1967	Totnes - Totnes Quay	W(GWR)	G(All)	2355
04.12.1967	Gorgie Mills Siding - Gorgie Cattle Market Siding	Sc(NBR)	G(All)	2356
04.12.1967	Balerno Jn - Balerno	Sc(Cal)	G(All)	2357
11.12.1967	Jersey Marine Jn South - Danygraig Reception Sidings	W(RSB)	G(All	2358
18.12.1967	Penrhos Jn - Taff Wells Dolomite Works	W(Barry)	G(All)	2359
29.12.1967	Bow Jn (NLR) - Gas Factory Jn	LM(NLR)	G(All)	2360
31.12.1967 [5]	Pontsmill (New Consolidated Siding) - Trevanney Siding	W(GWR)	G(All)	2361
01.01.1968	BEDFORD (St Johns) - CAMBRIDGE	LM/E(LNW)	P	2362
01.01.1968	Goldington GF - Cambridge Goods Yard	LM/E(LNW)	G(All)	2363
01.01.1968	CHINLEY [New Mills South Jn] - MANCHESTER (Central)	LM(Mid/CLC)	P(All)	2364 *
01.01.1968	Denton Jn - Stalybridge No.1 (via Hooley Hill)	LM(LNW)	G(All)	2365
01.01.1968 [3]	Fazakerley North Jn - Langton Dock	LM(Mid)	G(All)	2366 *
01.01.1968	Foryd Jn - Denbigh	LM(LNW)	G(All)	2367
01.01.1968 [3]	Great Bridge South Thomas Pigott's Sid. - Swan Village West WMGB Siding	LM(GWR)	G(All)	2368
01.01.1968	Hawkins Lane Sidings - Burton on Trent Horninglow Street Goods	LM(LNW)	G(All)	2369

Date	Line	Region (Company)	Type of Traffic	Reference Number
01.01.1968 [3]	Horsley Field Jn - Great Bridge South (Thomas Pigott's Sid)	LM(GWR)	G(All)	2370
01.01.1968 [3]	Linacre Branch GF - Lancashire Tar Distillers Sidings	LM(Mid)	G(All)	2371
01.01.1968	Mold (Synthite Siding) - Dolfechlas	LM(LNW)	G(All)	2372 *
01.01.1968	Old Hill Jn - Blowers Green Jn	LM(GWR)	G(All)	2373
01.01.1968	Priestfield Jn - Dudley North	LM(GWR)	G(All)	2374
01.01.1968 [3]	Trevor - Pontcysyllte (Monsanato Sidings)	LM(GWR)	G(All)	2375
01.01.1968	Tydesley - Springs Branch No.2	LM(LNW)	G(All)	2376
01.01.1968	Wednesbury (Patent Shaft Sidings) - Fallings Heath Crossing	LM(LNW)	G(All)	2377
01.01.1968	OXFORD [Wolvercot Jn] - BLETCHLEY [Oxford Jn]	W/LM(GW/LNW)	P	2378 *
01.01.1968	Redmile - Harby & Stathern	E(GN&LNWJt	P(All)	2379
01.01.1968	SHEFFIELD (Midland) [Wath Road Jn] - LEEDS (City) [Goose Hill Jn] via Royston	E(Mid)	P(Locals)	2380 *
01.01.1968	Stathern Jn - Barnstone Cement Works	E(GN&LNWJt	G(All)	2381
01.01.1968	St Rollox West - Fleming Bros. Siding	Sc(Cal)	G(All)	2382
01.01.1968	FALKIRK (Grahamston) - GRANGEMOUTH	Sc(Cal)	P	2383
01.01.1968	EDINBURGH (Waverley) [Haymarket] - CORSTORPHINE	Sc(NBR)	P	2384
01.01.1968	LARBERT - ALLOA	Sc(Cal)	P	2385 *
01.01.1968	Drem Jn - North Berwick	Sc(NBR)	G	2386
15.01.1968	Smyllum Jn - Douglas Colliery	Sc(Cal)	G(All)	2387
19.01.1968	Petrockstow - Meeth (North Devon Clay Co s Siding)	W(SR)	G(All)	2388
20.01.1968	Burton on Trent James Street Jn - Duke Street	LM(Mid)	G(All)	2389
29.01.1968	ALNMOUTH - ALNWICK	E(NER)	P(All)	2390
29.01.1968	Isabella - Blyth Engine Shed	E(NER)	G(All)	2391
05.02.1968	Junction Mill Siding - Leith Central	Sc(NBR)	G(All)	2392
05.02.1968	Haymarket West Jn - Corstorphine	Sc(NBR)	G(All)	2393
12.02.1968	Panteg Steelworks - Pontypool Road Station South	W(GWR)	G(All)	2394
16.02.1968	Wellfield - Wingate South	E(NER)	G(All)	2395
16.02.1968	Wingate South - Trimdon Grange Colliery	E(NER)	G(All)	2396
18.02.1968	Parkhead North Jn - Haghill Jn	Sc(NBR)	G(All)	2397
22.02.1968	Broxburn Jn - Broxburn Oil Works	Sc(NBR)	G(All)	2398
28.02.1968	Alloa East Goods - Alloa Harbour	Sc(NBR)	G(All)	2399 *
28.02.1968	Bonnington Goods Yard GF - Junction Mill Siding	Sc(NBR)	G(All)	2400
28.02.1968	Associated Delivery Siding - Leith North (George Street Depot)	Sc(Cal)	G(All)	2401
00.03.1968 [5]	Accrington South - Accrington West	LM(L&Y)	G(All)	2402
01.03.1968	Hardingstone Jn (CEGB Siding) - Yardley Chase	LM(Mid)	G(All)	2403
04.03.1968	Birmingham Moor Street Jn - BIRMINGHAM (Snow Hill)	LM(GWR)	P(All)	2404 *
04.03.1968	BIRMINGHAM (New Street) - DERBY (Midland)	LM(Mid)	P(Locals)	2405
04.03.1968	BIRMINGHAM (New Street) - LEICESTER (London Road) via Nuneaton Abbey St.	LM(Mid/LNW)	P(Locals)	2406
04.03.1968	WOLVERHAMPTON L.L. - Stafford Road Jn	LM(GWR)	P(All)	2407
04.03.1968	Cannock Road Jn - Bushbury No.1	LM(GWR)	P(All)	2408
04.03.1968	Cannock Road Jn - Wolverhampton L.L.	LM(GWR)	G(All)	2409
04.03.1968	LEICESTER (London Road) - NOTTINGHAM (Midland)	LM(Mid)	P(Locals)	2410
11.03.1968	NEWCASTLE upon TYNE (Central) [Scotswood Jn] - PRUDHOE [West Wylam Coll.Jn]	E(NER)	P	2411 *
11.03.1968	Stella North - West Wylam Colliery Jn	E(NER)	G(All)	2412
15.03.1968 [5]	Northwich (Parks Siding) - New Cheshire Salt Works Siding	LM(CLC)	G(All)	2413
16.03.1968	New Hucknall Sidings - Bentinck Colliery	LM(GCR)	G(All)	2414
16.03.1968	New Hucknall Sidings - South Normanton Colliery	LM(GCR)	G(All)	2415
16.03.1968	Dudley Hill - Birkenshaw & Tong	E(GNR)	G(All)	2416
16.03.1968	Morley Top - Gildersome West	E(GNR)	G(All)	2417
25.03.1968	STRATFORD upon AVON - GLOUCESTER (Central) [Lansdown Jn]	LM(GWR)	P	2418
25.03.1968	Southfleet - Gravesend West	S(SEC)	G(All)	2419
00.04.1968	Finsbury Park No.3 - Lennox Road Coal Depot	E(GNR)	G(All)	2420
01.04.1968	Heaths Jn - Congleton Brunswick Wharf	LM(NSR)	G(All)	2421
01.04.1968	Latchford - MSC lines Jn	LM(LNW)	G(All)	2422
01.04.1968	Llangollen Goods Jn - Llangollen Goods	LM(GWR)	G(All)	2423
01.04.1968	Pensnett Jn - Baggeridge Jn	LM(GWR)	G(All)	2424

Date	Line	Region (Company)	Type of Traffic	Reference Number
01.04.1968	Ruabon South - Llangollen Goods Jn	LM(GWR)	G(All)	2425
01.04.1968 [1]	Southampton Yard - Southampton Terminus	S(LSW)	G(All)	2426
01.04.1968	Kelso Jn - Kelso	Sc(NBR)	G(All)	2427
01.04.1968	Longniddry - Haddington	Sc(NBR)	G(All)	2428
17.04.1968	Llanbadarn Exchange Siding - Aberystwyth VOR alignment	LM(GWR)	P(All)	2429
22.04.1968	Cherry Tree Jn - Feniscowles	LM(LUJt)	G(All)	2430
26.04.1968	Glazebrook West Jn - Golborne New Spur Jn	LM(GCR)	G(All)	2431
26.04.1968 [1]	Hailsham - Heathfield	S(LBSC)	G(All)	2432
29.04.1968	Harpenden Jn - Claydale Light Weight Concrete Siding	LM(Mid)	G(All)	2433
29.04.1968	Burnhill - Weatherhill	E(NER)	G(All)	2434
30.04.1968 [3]	Six Pit Jn Imperial Smelting Siding - Ynyscedwyn	W(Mid)	G(All)	2435
06.05.1968	Newhaven Jn - Leith Walk West Goods	Sc(Cal)	G(All)	2436
27.05.1968	Weekday Cross Jn - Langwith Jn	LM/E(GC/GNR)	G(All)	2437
27.05.1968	Bulwell Common - Basford North	LM(GNR)	G(All)	2438
27.05.1968	Bagthorpe Jn - Stanton Jn	LM(GNR)	G(All)	2439
27.05.1968	Stanton Jn - Stanton Works	LM(GNR)	G(All)	2440
00.05.1968	Blackwall Bridge - Poplar Dock North	LM(LNW)	G(All)	2441 *
01.05.1968	Malvern & Tewkesbury Jn - Malvern (New Midland Sidings)	W(Mid)	G(All)	2442
04.05.1968	Royston Jn - Crigglestone East	E(Mid)	G(All)	2443
06.05.1968	Annesley GN Jn - Annesley Colliery	LM(GNR)	G(All)	2444
06.05.1968	Egglinton Jn - Hawkins Lane Sidings	LM(NSR)	G(All)	2445
06.05.1968	Egglinton Jn - Stanton Jn	LM(GNR)	G(All)	2446 *
06.05.1968	Kirkby South Jn - Kirkby Bentinck	LM(GCR)	G(All)	2447
06.05.1968	Kirkby Bentinck - Bentinck Colliery LWS	LM(GCR)	G(All)	2448
06.05.1968 [5]	Ormskirk Station - Ormskirk Branch Sidings	LM(L&Y)	G(All)	2449
06.05.1968	Skegby Jn - Teversall East GF	LM(GNR)	G(All)	2450
06.05.1968	Stratford upon Avon East Jn - Stratford upon Avon Goods	LM(GWR)	G(All)	2451
06.05.1968	Llandaff College Road Sidings - Roath Dock GF	W(Taff)	G(All)	2452
06.05.1968	PENARTH - CADOXTON [Jn]	W(Barry)	P	2453
06.05.1968	Penarth Cement Works - Cadoxton South	W(Taff)	P(All)	2454
06.05.1968	Meldon - Quarry Bere Alston	W(LSW)	G(All)	2455
06.05.1968	OKEHAMPTON - BERE ALSTON	W(LSW)	P	2456
06.05.1968	Trenance Jn GF - Boskell Siding	W(GWR)	G(All)	2457
06.05.1968	YEOVIL (Pen Mill) - YEOVIL JN	W(GWR)	P	2458
06.05.1968	Yeovil Pen Mill - Yeovil Town	W(GWR)	G(All)	2459
06.05.1968	South Lynn - East Rudham	E(MGN)	G(All)	2460
06.05.1968	ULCEBY - BROCKLESBY	E(GCR)	P	2461
06.05.1968	CAIRNIE JN - ELGIN East (via Buckie)	Sc(GNoSR)	P(All)	2462
06.05.1968	Grangemouth Jn - Fouldubs Jn	Sc(Cal)	G(All)	2463 *
06.05.1968	KEITH JN - ELGIN (via Dufftown)	Sc(GNoSR)	P	2464
06.05.1968	Leith Bath Street Jn - Leith Walk West Goods	Sc(Cal)	G(All)	2465
06.05.1968 [2]	Longcarse Jn - Throsk RNAD Siding	Sc(Cal)	G(All)	2466 *
06.05.1968	STEVENSTON [No 1] - ARDROSSAN (Montgomery Pier)	Sc(Cal)	P*(All)	2467
06.05.1968	TILLYNAUGHT - BANFF	Sc(GNoSR)	P(All)	2468
12.05.1968 [4]	Fazakerley West Jn - Fazakerley East Jn	LM(CLC)	G(All)	2469
15.05.1968	High Blantyre (Birdsfield Wagon Works) - C.W.Ireland's Siding	Sc(NBR)	G(All)	2470
16.05.1968	Perth Friarton - Perth Harbour	Sc(Cal)	G(All)	2471
18.05.1968	Elvington - Wheldrake	DVLR	G(All)	2472
25.05.1968	Gorgie Jn - Gorgie Mills Siding	Sc(NBR)	G(All)	2473
27.05.1968	Bulwell South Jn - Basford North	LM(GC&GNJt)	G(All)	2474
27.05.1968	Bestwood Jn - Bestwood Colliery	LM(GNR)	G(All)	2475
27.05.1968	Sutton in Ashfield (Metal Box's Siding) - Shirebrook North	LM(GNR)	G(All)	2476
27.05.1968	Weekday Cross Jn - Kirkby in Ashfield Summit SB	LM(GNR)	G(All)	2477 *
31.05.1968	Bowhill Branch Jn - Glencraig Colliery	Sc(NBR)	G(All)	2478
03.06.1968	Bagthorpe Jn - Ilkeston Derby Road Siding	LM(GNR)	G(All)	2479

►Robinson designed J11 64325 (40B) arrives at New Holland Pier with a local train from Cleethorpes on 22nd September 1956. The paddle boat service ceased after the opening of the Humber Bridge. Oxmarsh Jn to New Holland Pier closed to all traffic from 24th June 1981. (H.B.Priestley/ G.Hurst Collection)

▼The fireman is filling up the water tank of a L1 67790 whilst waiting to depart north with a down morning local from Nottingham Victoria, in July 1959. This fine station was closed on 4th September 1967 when the Rugby Central locals were terminated at Arkwright Street. (P.H.Groom)

▲Fairburn tank 42222 (16B) comes to a halt at Langwith with the 2.25 p.m. SO local from Mansfield Town to Worksop on 24th March 1962. The Nottingham Midland to Worksop service was withdrawn on 12th October 1964. This is to be restored through Derbyshire and Nottinghamshire County Council funding as well as half a dozen district councils. (H.B.Priestley/G.Hurst Collection)

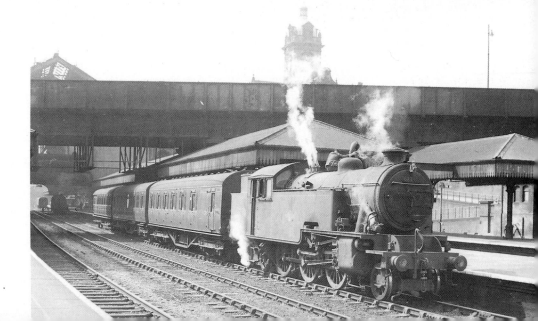

Date	Line	Region (Company)	Type of Traffic	Reference Number
03.06.1968	Beverley Road Jn - Hull Cannon Street Goods	E(H&B)	G(All)	2480
03.06.1968	Marfleet (Dawney's Siding) - Hedon	E(NER)	G(All)	2481
03.06.1968	Kings Cliffe - Nassington (Naylor Benzon Mining GF	LM(LNW)	G(All)	2482
25.06.1968 [2]	Pilning Jn - Green Lane Crossing GF	W(GWR)	G(All)	2483
01.07.1968	Denton Jn - Stalybridge Jn (via Hooley Hill)	LM(LNW)	G(All)	2484
01.07.1968	Par Bridge Crossing - Carne Point	W(GWR)	G(All)	2485
01.07.1968	Loop Line Jn - Poplar Dock South	LM(NLR)	G(All)	2486
01.07.1968	Nine Elms North - Viaduct Loco Jn	S(LSW)	G(All)	2487
01.07.1968	Nine Elms North - Viaduct Nine Elms A	S(LSW)	G(All)	2488
01.07.1968	Eastgate Cement Works Siding - Westgate in Weardale	E(NER)	G(All)	2489
01.07.1968	Queens Road (Battersea) - Nine Elms Goods	S(LSW)	G(All)	2490
01.07.1968	MATLOCK - CHINLEY [North Jn]	LM(Mid)	P	2491
01.07.1968	Peak Forest Jn - Mswlock	LM(Mid)	G(All)	2492
01.07.1968	Rowsley North Jn - Rowsley Goods	LM(Mid)	G(All)	2493
01.07.1968 [5]	Low Moor No.1 - Low Moor No.5	E(L&Y)	G(All)	2494
08.07.1968	Cardiff General - Curran's Siding	W(GWR)	G(All)	2495
15.07.1968	Marsh Jn - Midsomer Norton & Welton	W(GWR)	G(All)	2496
15.07.1968	Sheepford Mineral Depot - Coatdyke Goods	Sc(NBR)	G(All)	2497
15.07.1968	Kevinhaugh Jn - Stobcross Goods	Sc(Cal&NBJt)	G(All)	2498
22.07.1968	Padgate Jn - Sankey Jn (Warrington Avoider)	LM(CLC)	G(All)	2499
24.07.1968	Glebe Street Crossing - Port Dundas West (DCL Siding)	Sc(Cal)	G(All)	2500
28.07.1968	Nine Elms - Nine Elms Goods Depot	S(LSWR)	G(All)	2501
29.07.1968	Denby North - Marehay Crossing	LM(Mid)	G(All)	2502
29.07.1968	Long Eaton Jn - North Erewash Jn	LM(Mid)	G(All)	2503
29.07.1968	Thornhill Midland Jn - Crigglestone East	E(Mid)	G(All)	2504
04.08.1968	Carne Point - Fowey (Jetty No.7)	W(GWR)	G(All)	2505
05.08.1968	Duddingston Jn - St Leonards Goods	Sc(NBR)	G(All)	2506
05.08.1968	Pontypridd Jn East - Rhondda Cutting	W(Taff)	G(All)	2507
05.08.1968	Bishop Auckland (Tenters Street Oil Sid.) - Reilly Mill Jn	E(NER)	G(All)	2508
05.08.1968	Alton - Farringdon	S(LSW)	G(All)	2509
05.08.1968	Merton Abbey - Tooting Goods	S(LSW&LBSC)	G(All)	2510
05.08.1968	Red Doles Jn - Huddersfield Newtown Goods	E(LMS/Mid)	G(All)	2511
05.08.1968	Leith North - George Street Depot	Sc(Cal)	G(All)	2512
07.08.1968	CASTLEFORD (Cutsdyke) [Jn] - LEEDS [Methley Jn]	E(L&Y)	P	2513
12.08.1968	Netherfield & Colwick - Colwick North Jn	LM(GNR)	G(All)	2514
12.08.1968	Snydale Branch Jn - Sharlston Colliery Jn	E(Mid)	G(All)	2515
12.08.1968	Sharlston Colliery Jn - Ackton Hall Colliery	E(Mid)	G(All)	2516
19.08.1968	Tunnel Jn - Worcester Goods Yard	W(GWR)	G(All)	2517
12.08.1968	Swing Bridge Jn - Orchardhall (BA Co.Sid)	Sc(Cal/NBR)	G(All)	2518
19.08.1968 [3]	Larkhill Central - Auchlochan Colliery	Sc(Cal)	G(All)	2519
00.09.1968 [5]	Immingham East Jn East Points - Immingham East Jn West Points	E(GCR)	G(All)	2520
09.09.1968	CHESTER (Northgate) [Chester South Jn] - HAWARDEN BRIDGE [Dee Marsh Jn]	LM(CLC/GCR)	P	2521
09.09.1968	Crow Nest Jn - Hindley & Blackrod Branch Jn	LM(L&Y)	G(All)	2522
09.09.1968	Dobbs Brow Jn - Horwich Fork Jn	LM(L&Y)	G(All)	2523
09.09.1968	Old Hill - Halesowen Goods	LM(GWR)	G(All)	2524
09.09.1968	Polegate A - Hailsham	S(LBSC)	G(All)	2525
09.09.1968	DEREHAM [Central SB] - KINGS LYNN [Jn]	E(GER)	P(All)	2526
09.09.1968	Dereham Station Central - Middleton Towers	E(GER)	G(All)	2527
09.09.1968	MARCH [Whitemoor Jn] - KINGS LYNN [Magdalen Road]	E(GER)	P	2528
09.09.1968	Wisbech Goods Jn - Magdalen Road	E(GER)	G(All)	2529
16.09.1968	AYR [Alloway Jn] - HEADS of AYR	Sc(GSW)	P*(All)	2530
22.09.1968	Fazakerley South Jn - Aintree Central (Metal Box Co's Siding)	LM(CLC)	G(All)	2531
24.09.1968	Donnington - Newport (Salop)	LM(LNW)	G(All)	2532
29.09.1968	Cudworth Yard North - Monkton Empty Sidings	E(H&B)	G(All)	2533
30.09.1968	Rootes Siding - Ferguslie (Chain Road)	Sc(Cal)	G(All)	2534

Date	Line	Region (Company)	Type of Traffic	Reference Number
30.09.1968	Edge Hill No.4 - Top of Grid GF	LM(LNW)	G(All)	2535
00.10.1968	Grimsby Pasture Street Jn - Grimsby GN Goods Jn	E(GNR)	G(All)	2536
07.10.1968	Chester South Jn - Liverpool Road West Jn	LM(GCR)	G(All)	2537
07.10.1968	Dee Marsh Jn - Dee Marsh East Jn	LM(GCR)	G(All)	2538
07.10.1968 [3]	Hawkesbury Lane Sidings - Longford CEGB PS	LM(LNW)	G(All)	2539
07.10.1968	MANCHESTER (Exchange) - HUDDERSFIELD	LM(LNWR)	P(Locals)	2540
07.10.1968	Maesaraul Jn - Brofiscin	W(Taff/GWR)	G(All)	2541
07.10.1968	Alnmouth - Alnwick	E(NER)	G(All)	2542
07.10.1968	Shipley Jn - Shipley & Windhill	E(GNR)	G(All)	2543
07.10.1968	Shipley Leeds Jn - Idle	E(GNR)	G(All)	2544
07.10.1968 [2]	Lanark Jn West - Lanark Jn South	Sc(Cal)	G(All)	2545
07.10.1968	STIRLING - DUNFERMLINE (Lower)	Sc(NBR)	P	2546
21.10.1968 [4]	Embsay Jn - Embsay	LM(Mid)	G(All)	2547 *
28.10.1968	Halewood East Jn - Halewood North Jn	LM(CLC)	G(All)	2548
28.10.1968	Anlaby Road - Botanic Gardens	E(NER)	G(All)	2549
28.10.1968	Botanic Gardens - Wilmington (Earle's Siding)	E(NER)	G(All)	2550
02.11.1968	Bonnington East Jn - Chancelot Mill Siding	Sc(NBR)	G(All)	2551
02.11.1968	Bonnington South Jn - Bonnington Goods	Sc(NBR)	G(All)	2552
04.11.1968	Old Dalby - Nottingham London Road Jn	LM(Mid)	G(All)	2553 *
04.11.1968	Widnes No.4 Alumina Co. Sid. - Widnes Canal Bridge	LM(LNW)	G(All)	2554
04.11.1968	Aviemore North - Boat of Garten	Sc(High)	G(All)	2555
04.11.1968	Boat of Garten - Aberlour	Sc(GNoSR)	G(All)	2556 *
04.11.1968	Elgin East - Craigellachie	Sc(GNoSR)	G(All)	2557
04.11.1968	Haughhead Jn - Larkhill Central	Sc(Cal)	G(All)	2558
18.11.1968	Scotstoun West - Balmoral Street LC	Sc(Cal)	G(All)	2559
27.11.1968 [5]	Worthington - New Lount Colliery	LM(Mid)	G(All)	2560
29.11.1968	Lime Kiln Sidings - Cwmcarn Colliery	W(GWR)	G(All)	2561 *
30.11.1968	Sighthill East - Germiston Jn (Via Braby's Siding)	Sc(Cal)	G(All)	2562
09.12.1968	Brent Jn No.1 - Brent Jn No.2 (Engine Lines)	LM(Mid)	G(All)	2563
22.12.1968 [5]	Swanwick Sidings - Swanwick Colliery	LM(Mid)	G(All)	2564
23.12.1968	Swanwick Sidings - Crich Jn	LM(Mid)	G(All)	2565 *
23.12.1968	Riddings Jn - Ironville Jn	LM(Mid)	G(All)	2566
29.12.1968	Wilmington - Southcoates Lane GF	E(NER)	G(All)	2567
31.12.1968	Poulton No.1 - Poulton Goods	LM(P&WJt)	G(All)	2568
31.12.1968 [9]	Harworth Jn GF - Firbeck Main Colliery	E(SYJt)	G(All)	2569
01.01.1969	Hatfield No.3 - Butterwick Cold Store Siding	E(GNR)	G(All)	2570
01.01.1969	Pembroke Dock - Hobbs Point	W(GWR)	G(All)	2571
06.01.1969	NORTHAMPTON (Castle) - Blisworth	LM(LNW)	P(All)	2572
06.01.1969	Howe Bridge East - Hulton's Sidings	LM(LNW)	G(All)	2573
06.01.1969	Howe Bridge West - Tyldesley No.2	LM(LNW)	G(All)	2574
06.01.1969	Carlisle No.3 - Canal Jn	LM(Cal)	G(All)	2575
06.01.1969	ASHURST [Jn] - GROOMBRIDGE	S(LBSC)	P(All)	2576
06.01.1969	Bedenham Siding - Gosport	S(LSW)	G(All)	2577
06.01.1969	Broadstone - Blandford Forum (Bailey Gate Milk Depot)	S(S&DJt)	G(All)	2578
06.01.1969	Farncombe - Godalming Old	S(LSW)	G(All)	2579
06.01.1969	Polegate B - Stone Cross Jn	S(LBSC)	G(All)	2580 *
06.01.1969	Lewes C - Lewes East Yard	S(LBSC)	G(All)	2581
06.01.1969	Laisterdyke - Bowling Jn	E(L&Y)	P	2582
06.01.1969	LEUCHARS JN [South] - ST ANDREWS	Sc(NBR)	P(All)	2583
06.01.1969	EDINBURGH (Waverley) [Portobello East] - CARLISLE [No.3]	Sc/LM(NBR)	P	2584
06.01.1969	Hawick - Longtown	Sc(NBR)	G(All)	2585
17.01.1969	Kenilworth Jn - Berkswell Jn	LM(LNW)	G(All)	2586
20.01.1969	Polkemmet Jn - Whitrigg Colliery No.5	Sc(NBR)	G(All)	2587

►Ex North Eastern Railway 0-6-0T J71 68287 comes to stand at North Cave on the former Hull & Barnsley line in July 1949. The passenger service between Hull Paragon and South Howden survived another six years until 1st August 1955. The line remained open as a though route until 6th April 1959. *(T.J.Edgington)*

▼Leeds Central is a scene of activity with N2 69453 bringing an empty stock train into the station, whilst N7 69694 is simmering on a local train. This station was a victim of the one station policy and closed on 1st May 1967. *(H.B.Priestley/G.Hurst Collection)*

▲Class 2 Ivatt 41325 on a two coach train at Oxenhope on 11th September 1954. The Worth Valley lost its passenger service after a fight on 1st January 1962, its goods trains lasted a little longer until 18th June. The line has since been reopened as a preserved railway. *(Brian Hilton)*

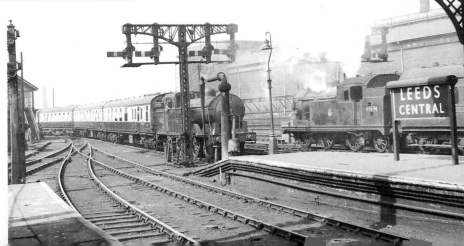

Date	Line	Region (Company)	Type of Traffic	Reference Number
27.01.1969	Ryde Pier Gates - Ryde Pierhead (tramway)	S(LBSC/LSW)	P(All)	2588
03.02.1969	Bewdley North - Alveley Sidings	LM(GWR)	G(All)	2589 *
03.02.1969	Bradwell Sidings - Parkhouse Colliery Sidings	LM(NSR)	G(All)	2590
03.02.1969	Drayton - Norwich City	E(MGN)	G(All)	2591
03.02.1969	Tuxford West - Tuxford North	E(GCR)	G(All)	2592
03.02.1969	Sprotborough Jn - Yorkshire Main Colliery	E(GC&HBJt)	G(All)	2593
06.02.1969 [1]	Bewdley - Alveley Sidings	LM(GWR)	G(All)	2594
07.02.1969	Gasswater Siding GF - Muirkirk	Sc(GSW)	G(All)	2595 *
10.02.1969	Aldridge Jn - BICC Siding	LM(Mid)	G(All)	2596
24.02.1969	UCKFIELD - LEWES [B]	S(LBSC)	P(All)	2597 *
28.02.1969	Burton on Trent Victoria Crescent LC - Horninglow Wharf	LM(Mid)	G(All)	2598
00.03.1969	Widnes No.4 - Widnes West Deviation Jn	LM(LNW)	G(All)	2599
02.03.1969	St Helens Jn No.1 - Sutton Oak Jn	LM(LNW)	G(All)	2600
03.03.1969	New Inn Yard - Worship Street Goods	LM(NLR)	G(All)	2601
03.03.1969	DARLINGTON [Eryholme Jn] - RICHMOND	E(NER)	P	2602
03.03.1969	Catterick Bridge - Richmond	E(NER)	G(All)	2603
03.03.1969	Southcoates - Drypool Goods	E(NER)	G(All)	2604
03.03.1969	Southcoates - Victoria Dock (Hedon Road)	E(NER)	G(All)	2605
03.03.1969	Wilmington - Sweet Dews (Scrap Siding)	E(NER)	G(All)	2606
03.03.1969	KILMARNOCK - AYR via Gatehead	Sc(GSWR)	P	2607 *
03.03.1969	Balmoral Street LC - Meadowside Granary Siding	Sc(Cal)	G(All)	2608
10.03.1969 [4]	Tamworth H.L. - Tamworth L.L.	LM(Mid)	G(All)	2609
11.03.1969 [4]	Nine Mile Point No.3 - Nine Mile Point Colliery	W(LNW)	G(All)	2610
24.03.1969 [1]	Blackfriars Jn - Farringdon Jn	S(SEC)	G(All)	2611 *
31.03.1969	Craighall Branch Jn - Craighall Depot	Sc(NBR)	G(All)	2612
31.03.1969	Pontrilas - Moss MOD Depot	W(GWR)	G(All)	2613
00.04.1969 [8]	Ripon - Melmerby Ordnance Depot	E(NER)	G(All)	2614
01.04.1969	Easton Lodge - Dunmow	E(GER)	G(All)	2615
01.04.1969	Cranmore - Cheddar	W(GWR)	G(All)	2616 *
02.04.1969	Humberstone Road Jn - 1964 Spur Jn	LM(BRB)	G(All)	2617
02.04.1969	1964 Spur Jn - Leicester Belgrave Road	LM(GNR)	G(All)	2618
07.04.1969	Trevethin Jn - Branches Fork Coal Yard	W(GWR)	G(All)	2619
28.04.1969	Bedford (Cold Store Siding) - Cardington	LM(Mid)	G(All)	2620
28.04.1969	Lady Victoria Pit - Hawick	Sc(NBR)	G(All)	2621
30.04.1969	Tredegar Jn Lower - Tredegar	W(LNW)	G(All)	2622
01.05.1969 [1]	Consett East - Burnhill WD Sidings	E(NER)	G(All)	2623
01.05.1969 [5]	Consett North - Hownes Gill Jn	E(NER)	G(All)	2624
05.05.1969	MANCHESTER (Exchange) [Eccles Jn] - LIVERPOOL (Lime Street)[Kenyon Jn]	LM(LNW)	P(All)	2625
05.05.1969	Derby North Jn - Derby South Jn	LM(Mid)	G(All)	2626
05.05.1969	NOTTINGHAM (Arkwright Street) - RUGBY (Central)	LM(GCR)	P	2627
05.05.1969	East Leake - Rugby Central	LM(GCR)	G(All)	2628 *
05.05.1969	MANCHESTER (Central) - CHINLEY [New Mills South Jn]	LM(CLC/Mid)	P	2629
05.05.1969	MANCHESTER (Central) - TRAFFORD PARK [Cornbrook West Jn]	LM(CLC)	P(All)	2630
05.05.1969	Throstle Nest East Jn - Chorlton Jn	LM(CLC)	G(All)	2631
05.05.1969	Chorlton Jn - Cheadle Heath North Jn	LM(Mid)	G(All)	2632
05.05.1969	Chaddesden (Loom's Siding) - Spondon	LM(Mid)	G(All)	2633
05.05.1969	Lifford West Jn - Lifford East Jn	LM(Mid)	P	2634
05.05.1969	ROMSEY - EASTLEIGH	S(LSWR)	P	2635
05.05.1969	Ardsley - Morley Top	E(GNR)	G(All)	2636
05.05.1969	KINGS LYNN [Jn] - HUNSTANTON	E(GER)	P(All)	2637
05.05.1969	DUNDEE (Tay Bridge)[Tay Bridge South] - NEWPORT ON TAY (East)	Sc(NBR)	P(All)	2638
12.05.1969 [4]	Southport South - St Lukes	LM(L&Y)	G(All)	2639
19.05.1969	Buxton No.2 - Buxton LNW Station	LM(LNW)	G(All)	2640
19.05.1969 [4]	Ince Moss Jn - Amberswood Jn West	LM(LNW)	G(All)	2641
19.05.1969 [4]	Fir Tree House Jn - Platt Bridge Jn	LM(LNW)	G(All)	2642

Date	Line	Region (Company)	Type of Traffic	Reference Number
21.05.1969 [4]	Shildon Tunnel North - Randolph Colliery GF	E(NER)	G(All)	*2643*
00.06.1969 [5]	Bidston Dee Jn - Birkenhead North No.2 Jn	LM(Wirral)	G(All)	*2644*
00.06.1969 [8]	Radstock West GF - Midsomer Norton & Welton	W(GWR)	G(All)	*2645*
01.06.1969	Bilston Glen Colliery Sidings - Roslin Colliery	Sc(NBR)	G(All)	*2646*
02.06.1969	Carlisle Canal Jn - Coop Coal Siding	LM(NBR)	G(All)	*2647*
02.06.1969 [4]	Fork Jn - Temple Mills East	E(GER)	G(All)	*2648*
16.06.1969 [4]	Burscough Bridge Jn - Burscough Jn North	LM(L&Y)	G(All)	*2649*
16.06.1969	Argyle Street - Newcastle Quayside	E(NER/RTA)	G(All)	*2650*
30.06.1969	Lancaster Freeman's Wood Siding - Lancaster Quay Sidings	LM(LNW)	G(All)	*2651*
30.06.1969	Limestone Branch GF - Cilrychen Lime Works	W(GWR)	G(All)	*2652*
06.07.1969	Ashton Moss Jn - Droylesdon Station Jn	LM(LNW)	G(All)	*2653*
08.07.1969 [5]	Wombwell Main Jn - Wombwell Main Colliery	E(GCR)	G(All)	*2654*
14.07.1969	PEMBERTON [Pemberton Jn] - HINDLEY [Hindley No.2 SB] (Westwood Park Loop)	LM(L&Y)	P	*2655*
14.07.1969	Allerton Main - Garforth	E(NER)	G(All)	*2656*
21.07.1969	Huskisson Goods - Sandon Dock Jn with MDHB	LM(Mid)	G(All)	*2657*
00.07.1969 [7]	South Shields (Mowbray Road) - Whitburn Colliery	SS&MR	G(All)	*2658* *
04.08.1969	Etruria - Waterloo Road (York Street Wharf)	LM(NSR)	G(All)	*2659*
04.08.1969	Lewes A - Lewes Friar Walk Goods	S(LBSC)	G(All)	*2660*
04.08.1969 [4]	Stainton Jn - Carlisle Canal Yard	LM(NBR)	G(All)	*2661*
04.08.1969 [4]	Kingmoor - Stainton Jn	LM(BRB)	G(All)	*2662*
11.08.1969	Swinden Lime Works Siding - Grassington & Thresfield	LM(Mid)	G(All)	*2663*
17.08.1969 [4]	Weddington Jn - Ashby Jn	LM(A&NJt)	G(All)	*2664*
17.08.1969	Cheadle Heath SB - Chorlton Jn	LM(Mid)	G(All)	*2665*
18.08.1969	Kings Sutton - Adderbury	W(GWR)	G(All)	*2666*
18.08.1969	Knockshinnoch Colliery - Bank Colliery Exchange Sidings	Sc(GSW)	G(All)	*2667*
18.08.1969 [3]	Ullcoats Branch Token Hut - Ullcoats No.1 Pit Reversing Siding	LM(WCEJt)	G(All)	*2668*
18.08.1969 [3]	Ullcoats No.1 Pit reversing siding - Ullcoats No.7 Pit	LM(WCEJt)	G(All)	*2669*
01.09.1969	MARYLEBONE [Neasden North Jn] - [Neasden North Jn] (via Wembley Stadium)	LM(LNE)	P*(All)	*2670*
08.09.1969 [5]	Langwith Colliery Jn - Langwith Colliery	E(GCR)	G(All)	*2671*
08.09.1969	Starbeck North - Ripon	E(NER)	G(All)	*2672*
09.09.1969	Dronfield - H.Boot Siding	E(Mid)	G(All)	*2673*
15.09.1969 [5]	Pembroke Dock - Dockyard RAF Siding	W(GWR)	G(All)	*2674*
29.09.1969	Wincobank North Jn - Wincobank West Jn	E(Mid)	G(All)	*2675*
29.09.1969 [2]	Gelli GF - Avon Colliery	W(GWR)	G(All)	*2676*
29.09.1969 [2]	Cymmer Afan - Gelli GF	W(GWR)	G(All)	*2677*
30.09.1969	Castlehill Jn - Parkhouse Jn	Sc(GSW)	G(All)	*2678*
01.10.1069	Old Hill Jn - Halesowen	LM(GWR)	G(All)	*2679*
01.10.1969	Halesowen Canal GF - Halesowen Canal Basin	LM(GWR)	G(All)	*2680*
01.10.1969	Amble Broomhill - Staithes	E(NER)	G(All)	*2681*
06.10.1969 [5]	Broak Oak Jn - Marsh's Sidings	LM(LNW)	G(All)	*2682*
06.10.1969	Mickle Trafford Jn - CHESTER Northgate	LM(CLC)	P(All)	*2683*
06.10.1969	Chester East Jn - Chester Northgate	LM(CLC)	G(All)	*2684*
06.10.1969	CREWE - PRESTON (via Earlestown)	LM(LNW)	P(Locals)	*2685*
06.10.1969	Golbourne Jn - Parkside No.2 SB	LM(LNW)	P	*2686*
06.10.1969	Holwell Sidings - Old Dalby	LM(Mid)	G(All)	*2687* *
06.10.1969 [5]	West London Carriage Sidings - North Pole Jn	W(GWR)	Ecs(All)	*2688*
06.10.1969	Amble Branch Jn - Amble	E(NER)	G(All)	*2689*
06.10.1969	Fareham - Gosport	S(LSW)	R(All)	*2690*
06.10.1969 [5]	Croft GF - Geneva	E(NER)	G(All)	*2691*
06.10.1969	NORWICH [Wymondham] - DEREHAM	E(GER)	P	*2692*
06.10.1969	THORNTON JN - LEVEN	Sc(NBR)	P	*2693*
06.10.1969	East Fife Central Jn - Leven	Sc(NBR)	G(All)	*2694*
09.10.1969	Dunstable London Road (APCM) - Dunstable North	LM(GNR)	G(All)	*2695*
09.10.1969 [1]	Starbeck North - Ripon Goods	E(NER)	G(All)	*2696*
13.10.1969	Penarth - Penarth Cement Works	W(Taff)	G(All)	*2697*

Date	Line	Region (Company)	Type of Traffic	Reference Number
20.10.1969	Leckethill Sidings New Spur Jn - Bedlay	Sc(NBR)	G(All)	2698
24.10.1969	Kettering Station Jn - Twywell	LM(Mid)	G(All)	2699
31.10.1969	Liss - Bordon	LMilR	M(All)	2700 *
31.10.1969	Whitehill - Longmoor Downs (via Hollywater Loop)	LMilR	M(All)	2701 *
02.11.1969 [5]	Manors North - Argyle Street	E(NER)	G(All)	2702
03.11.1969	Irchester Jn - Higham Ferrers	LM(Mid)	G(All)	2703
03.11.1969	Colbren Jn - Gwaunton Opencast Site	W(GWR)	G(All)	2704
23.11.1969	Pont Shon Norton - Albion Colliery	W(Taff)	G(All)	2705
01.12.1969	Ebbw Vale LL - Ebbw Vale LL Goods	W(GWR)	G(All)	2706
08.12.1969	Leighton Buzzard - Billington Road Crossing	LM(LNW)	G(All)	2707
00.01.1970 [8]	Warrington Dewsey - Dallam Forge	LM(CLC)	G(All)	2708
01.01.1970	Canal Branch GF - Glenalbyn Distillery Sid. Is. Canal Basin	Sc(High)	G(All)	2709
01.01.1970	Robertsbridge - Hodson's Sid.	S(KESR)	G(All)	2710 *
03.01.1970	Lawrence Hill GF - Mangotsfield North Jn	W(Mid)	G(All)	2711
05.01.1970	BANGOR [Menai Bridge Jn] - CAERNARVON	LM(LNW)	P(All)	2712 *
05.01.1970	KIDDERMINSTER - BEWDLEY	LM(GWR)	P	2713 *
05.01.1970	Bewdley - Stourport on Severn	LM(GWR)	G(All)	2714
05.01.1970	BEWDLEY - HARTLEBURY [Jn]	LM(GWR)	P	2715
05.01.1970	Foley Park British Sugar - Bewdley North	LM(GWR)	G(All)	2716
05.01.1970	MANCHESTER (Piccadilly) [New Mills Jn] - HAYFIELD	LM(GC&MidJ)	P(All)	2717
05.01.1970	Netherfield Jn - Trent Lane Jn	LM(GNR)	G(All)	2718
05.01.1970	Gotham Sidings - Gotham Company Siding	LM(GCR)	G(All)	2719
05.01.1970 [2]	North Mersey HL Yard - Langton Dock Goods	LM(Mid)	G(All)	2720
05.01.1970	ROSE HILL (Marple) - MACCLESFIELD	LM(GC&NSJt)	P(All)	2721
05.01.1970	MANCHESTER (Piccadilly) [Hadfield] - SHEFFIELD (Victoria) [Huddersfield Jn]	LM/E(GCR)	P	2723
05.01.1970	MANCHESTER (Piccadilly) [Huddersfield Jn] - CLEETHORPES [Barnsley Station Jn]	E(GCR)	P	2724
05.01.1970	MANCHESTER (Piccadilly) [Quarry Jn] - CLEETHORPES [Mexborough East Jn]	E(GCR)	P	2725
05.01.1970	YORK [Burton Salmon] - SOWERBY BRIDGE [Castleford Central]	E(NER)	P	2726
05.01.1970	YORK [Whitwood Jn] - SOWERBY BRIDGE [Altofts Jn]	E(NER)	P	2727
05.01.1970	YORK [Heaton Lodge Jn] - SOWERBY BRIDGE [Bradley Wood Jn]	E(L&Y)	P	2728
05.01.1970	YORK [Greetland Jn] - SOWERBY BRIDGE [Milner Royd Jn]	E(L&Y)	P	2729
05.01.1970	Victoria Dock - Sweet Dews (Scrap Siding)	E(NER)	G(All)	2730
05.01.1970	EDINBURGH (Waverley) - [Cowdenbeath North Jn] PERTH [Hilton Jn]	Sc(NBR)	P	2731
05.01.1970	Milnathort - Bridge of Earn	Sc(NBR)	G(All)	2732
05.01.1970	Touch North Jn - Touch South Jn	Sc(NBR)	G(All)	2733
19.01.1970 [5]	Beckermet Mines Jn - Sellafield	LM(WCEJt)	G(All)	2734
26.01.1970	Bolton West (West Jn) - Bolton West (North Jn) Johnson St. Fork	LM(L&Y)	G(All)	2735
02.02.1970	COLNE - SKIPTON [North Jn]	LM(Mid)	P(All)	2736
02.02.1970 [5]	Mold Jn No.3 - Hope Jn	LM(LNW)	G(All)	2737
09.02.1970	Eryholme - Catterick Bridge	E(NER)	G(All)	2738
23.02.1970	Kelty North Jn - Lochore Coup	Sc(NBR)	G(All)	2739
02.03.1970	Paisley West - Potterhill	Sc(GSW)	G(All)	2740
16.03.1970	Rawcliffe Bridge - Potters Grange (Via Oakhill)	E(L&Y/NER)	P(All)	2741
23.03.1970	Bristol East - Lawrence Hill GF	W(Mid)	G(All)	2742 *
31.03.1970	High Shields - South Shields Goods	E(NER)	G(All)	2743
06.04.1970	Royton Jn - Higginshaw Gas Siding	LM(L&Y)	G(All)	2744
13.04.1970	Rectory Jn - Colwick North Jn	LM(GNR)	G(All)	2745
22.04.1970	Camborne Holman's Sid. - North Parade Crossing	W(GWR)	G(All)	2746
27.04.1970	Felixstowe Town - Jn with new Felixstowe Beach line	E(GER)	G(All)	2747
30.04.1970 [5]	Paisley Abercorn - Paisley Greenlaw Goods	Sc(GSW)	G(All)	2748
04.05.1970	SKIPTON - CARLISLE	LM(Mid)	P(Locals)	2749
04.05.1970	Picton Road Jn - Top of Grid GF	LM(LNW)	G(All)	2750
04.05.1970	Rogerstone North - Penar Jn	W(GWR)	G(All)	2751

Date	Line	Region (Company)	Type of Traffic	Reference Number
04.05.1970	BOURNE END - HIGH WYCOMBE [South]	W(GWR)	P(All)	2752
04.05.1970	Heathfield Gulf Oil Siding - Bovey	W(GWR)	G(All)	2753 *
04.05.1970	Yarmouth North Quay Jn - White Swan Coal Yard	E(GER)	G(All)	2754
04.05.1970	LOWESTOFT (Central) - YARMOUTH (South Town)	E(N&SJt)	P(All)	2755
04.05.1970	NEWCASTLE UPON TYNE [Percy Main] - Percy Main North SB	E(NER)	P	2756
04.05.1970	Percy Main North SB - TYNE COMMISSION QUAY	E(NER)	P	2757
04.05.1970	Kelty North Jn - Milnathort	Sc(NBR)	P(All)	2758
04.05.1970	Exhibition Jn - Top of Grid GF	LM(LNW)	G(All)	2759
17.05.1970	Northallerton West Jn - Northallerton	E(NER)	G(All)	2760
18.05.1970 [5]	Longcarse Jn - Alloa West Jn	Sc(NBR)	G(All)	2761
30.05.1970	Devonport Kings Road - Stonehouse Pool	W(LSW)	G(All)	2762
00.06.1970	Warrington Dewsey - Whitecross Wireworks	LM(CLC)	G(All)	2763
01.06.1970	POULTON le FYLDE [Poulton No.3] - FLEETWOOD	LM(PWYJt)	P	2764
01.06.1970	Barnstaple Jn A SB - Barnstaple Victoria Road	W(GWR)	G(All)	2765
01.06.1970	Temple Mills East - Leyton LT Jn	E(GER)	G(All)	2766
01.06.1970	Norwood - Dunston East	E(NER)	G(All)	2767
20.06.1970 [2]	Braintree - Felsted	E(GER)	G(All)	2768
22.06.1970 [5]	Cransley - Loddington	LM(Mid)	G(All)	2769
06.07.1970	Leek Brook Jn - Leek	LM(NSR)	G(All)	2770
13.07.1970 [5]	Bletchley No.1 - Fletton's Siding	LM(LNW)	G(All)	2771
13.07.1970	Coaley Jn - Dursley	W(Mid)	G(All)	2772
15.07.1970	BRIDGEND - TREHERBERT	W(GWR/RSB)	P	2773 *
20.07.1970	Bristol East Depot - Marsh Jn	W(GWR)	G(All)	2774
26.07.1970 [5]	Slough West - Bath Road	W(GWR)	G(All)	2775
03.08.1970 [5]	South Pelaw - Stella Gill Flats	E(NER)	G(All)	2776
17.08.1970 [5]	Loco Jn - Barrow in Furness MPD Siding	LM(Furn)	G(All)	2777
24.08.1970 [5]	Caerau - Cymmer Afan	W(GWR)	G(All)	2778
24.08.1970 [5]	Cymmer Afan Duffyn - Rhondda West	W(RSB)	P(All)	2779
24.08.1970 [5]	Cymmer Tunnel GF - North Rhondda Colliery Sid. (Glyncorrwg)	W(SWMR)	G(All)	2780
26.08.1970	Laird's Siding - Irvine Harbour & Quay	Sc(GSW)	G(All)	2781
31.08.1970	Brunthill - Longtown	LM(NBR)	G(All)	2782
31.08.1970	Longtown - Smalmstown MOD Depot	LM(NBR)	G(All)	2783
31.08.1970	Paisley Abercorn - Pitt's Siding	Sc(GSW)	G(All)	2784
07.09.1970	Maud Jn - Peterhead	Sc(GNoSR)	G(All)	2785
07.09.1970	Bullcroft Jn - Bullcroft Main Colliery	E(GC&HBJt)	G(All)	2786
07.09.1970	Doncaster Jn - Thorpe Marsh CEGB Sidings	E(GC&HBJt)	G(All)	2787
07.09.1970	Skellow Jn - Bullcroft Jn	E(GC&HBJt)	G(All)	2788
20.09.1970 [5]	Devonport Albert Road East GF - Devonport GW Goods Engineers Sid.	W(GWR)	G(All)	2789
01.10.1970	Aberayon Jn - Pont Llanio	W(GWR)	G(All)	2790
05.10.1970	BOLTON (Trinity Street) - ROCHDALE [Castleton East Jn]	LM(L&Y)	P	2791
05.10.1970	Bolton East Jn - Bury West	LM(L&Y)	G(All)	2792
05.10.1970 [5]	Broughton Crossing - Brymbo	LM(GCR)	G(All)	2793
05.10.1970 [5]	Brymbo - Fishpond Sidings	LM(GCR)	G(All)	2794
05.10.1970	BARNSTAPLE JN - ILFRACOMBE	W(LSW)	P(All)	2795
05.10.1970	Finsbury Park No.7 - Park Jn (Highgate)	E(GNR)	G(All)	2796 *
05.10.1970	PETERBOROUGH (North) - [Werrington Jn] GRIMSBY (Town) [Garden Street Jn]	E(GNR)	P	2797
05.10.1970	Spalding No.3 BSc Siding - Boston Sleaford Jn	E(GNR)	G(All)	2798
05.10.1970	Firsby South Jn - Louth	E(GNR)	G(All)	2799
05.10.1970	FIRSBY - SKEGNESS [Firsby East Jn]	E(GNR)	P(All)	2800
05.10.1970	LINCOLN (Central) [Greetwell Jn] - FIRSBY [Bellwater Jn]	E(GNR)	P	2801
05.10.1970	Woodhall Jn - Bellwater Jn	E(GNR)	G(All)	2802
05.10.1970	WILLOUGHBY - MABLETHORPE	E(GNR)	P(All)	2803
12.10.1970	Annesley Colliery Jn - Kirkby in Ashfield Station Jn	LM(Mid)	G(All)	2804
00.11.1970 [5]	Wyre PS - Fleetwood	LM(PWYJt)	G(All)	2805
02.11.1970	Yarnton - Witney Goods	W(GWR)	G(All)	2806

►A desolate Oldham Clegg Street is host to an OAGB train, the 6.19 p.m to Guide Bridge hauled by C14 67450 on a wet 25th April 1959. This service was withdrawn from 4th May 1959. *(Brian Hilton)*

▼ Fowler tank 40061 has arrived at Delph on 2nd August 1954, deep in the Pennines with a local from Oldham Clegg Street. The local nickname for this service was 'The Delph Donkey' afters its humble origins. It lost its passenger service in 1st May 1955, however goods served the line until 4th November 1963. *(Brian Hilton)*

▲The service between Lancaster Castle and Heysham was electrified at 6.25Kv AC by the Midland Railway. A three car electric multiple unit leaves Lancaster Green Ayre on its final leg to Lancaster Castle station. This service was withdrawn on 3rd January 1966. The alternative route to Morecambe was via Bare Lane. *T.J.Edgington)*

Date	Line	Region (Company)	Type of Traffic	Reference Number
02.11.1970	Honeybourne Station South - Honeybourne East Loop	W(GWR)	G(All)	2807
08.11.1970 [5]	Langton Colliery LWS - Bentinck Colliery South Branch reversing Sid.	LM(Mid)	G(All)	2808
08.11.1970 [5]	Bentinck LWS Branch Jn - Langton Colliery EWS	LM(Mid)	G(All)	2809
28.11.1970 [5]	Mansfield South Jn - Kings Mill	LM(Mid)	G(All)	2810
07.12.1970 [5]	Sincil Bank - Bracebridge Gas Sidings	E(GNR)	G(All)	2811
12.12.1970	Bottesford West Jn - Redmile	E(GN&LNWJt)	G(All)	2812
14.12.1970 [5]	Saltney Dee Jn - Spencer's Scrapyard	LM(GWR)	G(All)	2813
14.12.1970 [3]	Cymmer Afan - Treherbert RSB Jn	W(RSB/GWR)	G(All)	2814
21.12.1970	Princes Dock Branch Points - Princes Dock Whitehead Yard	Sc(PDJt)	G(All)	2815
00.01.1971	Pallion - Hylton Quarry Siding (Ford Works)	E(NER)	G(All)	2816
04.01.1971	TAUNTON [Norton Fitzwarren] - MINEHEAD	W(GWR)	P(All)	2817 *
04.01.1971 [5]	Lawton Jn - Lawton	LM(NSR)	G(All)	2818
13.02.1971	Alma Jn (West) - Alma Jn (South)	LM(Mid)	G(All)	2819
13.02.1971	Avenue Sidings - Williamthorpe Colliery	LM(Mid)	G(All)	2820
14.02.1971	Hawthorn - Seabanks	E(NER)	G(All)	2821
01.03.1971	Waterloo Dock Riverside Branch Jn - Liverpool Riverside	MDHB	G(All)	2822
07.03.1971 [5]	Devonport Jn - Devonport Kings Road Goods	W(LSW)	G(All)	2823
29.03.1971	Loversall Carr - Black Carr Sidings East	E(DVR)	G(All)	2824
31.03.1971	Invergordon - Invergordon Harbour (Admiralty Fuelling	Sc(High)	G(All)	2825
31.03.1971	Bellfield Jn - Glenfield & Kennedy's Sid.	Sc(GSW)	G(All)	2826
04.04.1971 [5]	Highbridge East - Highbridge North	W(BRB)	G(All)	2827
05.04.1971	Bardney - Woodhall Jn	E(GNR)	G(All)	2828
05.04.1971	Abergavenny Jn GF - Abergavenny Brecon Road Goods	W(LNW)	G(All)	2829
05.04.1971	Severn Bridge Jn - Shropshire Union Yard	LM(LNW)	G(All)	2830
19.04.1971 [7]	Associated Octel Siding - Hayle Coal Wharves	W(GWR)	G(All)	2831
03.05.1971	Altrincham & Bowden - Bowden Electric Depot	LM(MSJA)	Ecs(All)	2832
03.05.1971	Miles Platting Tank Yard - New Allen Street	LM(L&Y)	G(All)	2833
03.05.1971	Keadby Canal Jn - Keadby Goods	E(GCR)	G(All)	2834
03.05.1971	Brunswick (Liverpool) - Toxteth Dock (Jn with MDHB Lines)	LM(CLC)	G(All)	2835
24.05.1971	ST IVES (New) - ST IVES (Old)	W(GWR)	P(All)	2836
31.05.1971	Yate South Jn - Bath Midland Bridge Road	W(Mid)	G(All)	2837 *
07.06.1971	Falkirk Wallace St. LC - Falkirk Dalderse Depot	Sc(NBR)	G(All)	2838
07.06.1971	West Street Jn - Glasgow West Street Goods	Sc(Cal)	G(All)	2839
21.06.1971 [5]	Reading HL GF - Reading Signal Works	W(GWR)	G(All)	2840
21.06.1971 [5]	Low Moor - Ellison's Sidings	E(L&Y)	G(All)	2841 *
28.06.1971	Kemp Town Jn - Kemp Town	S(LBSC)	G(All)	2842
00.07.1971 [8]	Cambois - Cambois Colliery	E(NER)	G(All)	2843
01.07.1971	Plymouth West - Millbay Docks	W(GWR)	G(All)	2844
05.07.1971	Lilliehall Jn - Gask Jn	Sc(NBR)	G(All)	2845
05.07.1971	Gask Jn - Lathalmond RNAD Siding	Sc(NBR)	G(All)	2846
19.07.1971	Fenny Compton - Burton Dassett	LM(SMJ)	G(All)	2847 *
19.07.1971 [5]	Poulton No.4 - Poulton No.5	LM(PWYJt)	G(All)	2848
19.07.1971 [5]	Abbey Jn (Judkins Siding) - Market Bosworth	LM(ANJt)	G(All)	2849
27.07.1971 [5]	Islip Sidings - Twywell	LM(Mid)	G(All)	2850
30.07.1971	Dunblane North Jn - Springbank Mill Siding	Sc(Cal)	G(All)	2851
00.08.1971	Marshgate Goods - Wheatley Park (International Harvesters)	E(LNE)	G(All)	2852
02.08.1971 [5]	Tynemouth South - Tynemouth B&T Depot	E(NER)	G(All)	2853
18.08.1971	Greenside Jn - Kipps Incline Foot	Sc(NBR)	G(All)	2854
18.08.1971	Kipps Jn - Sun Foundry	Sc(NBR)	G(All)	2855
06.09.1971	Newhailes Jn - Musselburgh	Sc(NBR)	G(All)	2856
01.10.1971	**Barton Street Jn - High Orchard**	W(Mid)	G(All)	2857
01.10.1971	**Knightswood South Jn - Baird's Siding**	Sc(NBR)	G(All)	2858
01.10.1971	**Possilpark - Sarcacen Goods**	Sc(NBR)	G(All)	2859

Date	Line	Region (Company)	Type of Traffic	Reference Number
04.10.1971	Ironville Jn - Swanwick Sidings	LM(Mid)	G(All)	*2860*
04.10.1971	Bonnybridge SSEB Sidings - Carrongrove Paper Mill	Sc(Cal)	G(All)	*2861*
04.10.1971	BUCKFASTLEIGH - ASHBURTON	DVR(GWR)	P*(All)	*2862*
04.10.1971	Springbank Coal Yard - Springhead Wagon Works	E(H&B)	G(All)	*2863*
12.10.1971 [5]	Bestwood Park Jn - Bestwood Park Colliery	LM(Mid)	G(All)	*2864*
18.10.1971 [1]	BARRY ISLAND - BARRY Pier	W(Barry)	P*(All)	*2865*
00.11.1971 [8]	Wisbech Road Maltings - King's Lynn Harbour Coal Yard	E(GER)	G(All)	*2866* *
01.11.1971	Newark South - Newark Cross Street Coal Depot	E(GNR)	G(All)	*2867*
01.11.1971	FAIRLIE [Pier Jn] - FAIRLIE (Pier)	Sc(GSW)	P(All)	*2868*
08.11.1971	Penwithers Jn - Truro Newham Goods	W(GWR)	G(All)	*2869*
12.11.1971 [5]	Measham - Market Bosworth	LM(ANJt)	G(All)	*2870* *
15.11.1971	Dufftown - Aberlour	Sc(GNoSR)	G(All)	*2871*
26.11.1971 [1]	Mickleover - Derby Friargate	DRC(GNR)	T(All)	*2872*
29.11.1971	Aberdare H.L. - Mountain Ash Cardiff Road	W(GWR)	G(All)	*2873*
00.12.1971 [8]	Boars Head Jn - Adlington Jn	LM(LUJt)	G(All)	*2874*
06.12.1971	Ashton Jn - Bristol West Depot	W(GWR)	G(All)	*2875*
08.12.1971 [5]	Marchweil - Pickhill Cadbury's Siding	LM(Cam)	G(All)	*2876*
12.12.1971 [5]	Kirkburton Jn - ICI Sidings	E(LNW)	G(All)	*2877*
20.12.1971	Newtongrange - Lady Victoria Pit	Sc(NBR)	G(All)	*2878*
20.12.1971 [5]	Finsbury Park No.5 - Finsbury Park No.7	E(GNR)	P(All)	*2879*
20.12.1971	Finsbury Park No.7 - Finsbury Park No.6	E(GNR)	P(All)	*2880*
31.12.1971	Kilbowie Branch Jn GF - Singer Works	Sc(NBR)	G(All)	*2881*
00.01.1972	Bargoed - McLaren Colliery	W(Rhy)	G(All)	*2882* *
01.01.1972	Arnside - Sandside	LM(Furn)	G(All)	*2883*
01.01.1972	Brymbo West - Minera	LM(GWR)	G(All)	*2884*
03.01.1972	Pains Siding - Buckminster Siding	LM(Mid)	G(All)	*2885* *
03.01.1972	WAREHAM [Jn] - SWANAGE	S(LSW)	P	*2886*
03.01.1972	Furzebrook Sidings - Swanage	S(LSW)	G(All)	*2887* *
24.01.1972 [5]	Dock Storage North - Roath Goods	W(Taff)	G(All)	*2888*
31.01.1972	Menai Bridge Jn - Caernarvon	LM(LNW)	G(All)	*2889* *
07.02.1972	REDDITCH (New) - REDDITCH (Old)	LM(Mid)	P(All)	*2890*
17.02.1972	Bishops Stortford - Easton Lodge	E(GER)	G(All)	*2891* *
06.03.1972	Blencow (Flusco Siding) - Keswick	LM(C&KP)	G(All)	*2892*
06.03.1972	WOLVERHAMPTON L.L.-BIRMINGHAM (Snow Hill)	LM(GWR)	P	*2893*
06.03.1972	SMETHWICK (West)-BIRMINGHAM (Snow Hill)	LM(GWR)	P	*2894*
06.03.1972	Handsworth Jn - Birmingham (Snow Hill)	LM(GWR)	G(All)	*2895*
06.03.1972	Handsworth Jn - Swan Village North	LM(GWR)	G(All)	*2896*
03.04.1972	Larbert Jn - Bonnybridge SSEB Sidings	Sc(Cal)	G(All)	*2897*
03.04.1972	Kirkby North Sidings New Spur Jn - Bentinck Colliery SB New spur Jn	LM(Mid)	G(All)	*2898* *
10.04.1972 [5]	Immingham West Jn (North) - Immingham West Jn (East)	E(GCR)	G(All)	*2899*
17.04.1972	Brunswick Goods - LIVERPOOL (Central HL)	LM(CLC)	P(All)	*2900*
17.04.1972	Bo'ness Jn - Stein's Brickworks	Sc(NBR)	G(All)	*2901*
01.05.1972	Moss Lane Jn - Lostock Hall Engine Shed	LM(L&Y)	G(All)	*2902*
01.05.1972	Christchurch - Christchurch Goods	S(LSW)	G(All)	*2903*
01.05.1972 [5]	Barkston North Jn - Barkston East Jn	E(GNR)	G(All)	*2904*
01.05.1972	Batley - Shaw Cross Colliery	E(GNR)	G(All)	*2905*
01.05.1972	Hammerton Street - Bradford Aldolphus Street Goods	E(GNR)	G(All)	*2906*
01.05.1972	Southcoates Lane GF - Marfleet	E(NER)	G(All)	*2907*
01.05.1972	Ibrox Jn - Govan Shafting Co.'s Siding	Sc(G&PJt)	G(All)	*2908*
01.05.1972	London Road Jn - Leith Central	Sc(NBR)	G(All)	*2909*
01.05.1972	Lochend Jn - Lochend North Jn	Sc(NBR)	G(All)	*2910*
15.05.1972	Wapping Bank Head - Liverpool (Crown Street)	LM(LNW)	G(All)	*2911*
02.06.1972	BOLTON (Bolton Street) - RAWTENSTALL	LM(L&Y)	P	*2912* *

▶Birkenhead Woodside was the Birkenhead Joint Railways terminus in the Wirral. A Fairburn tank 42086 awaits its departure on a midday parcels train on 29th October 1966. This station was closed on 5th November 1967 when services were terminated at Rock Ferry. (T.J.Edgington)

◀41226 awaits its depart from Amlwch with the 1405 to Bangor on 27th August 1963. This busy rural terminus would, if had survived be no more than a bus shelter. This service succumbed on 4th December 1964 and luckerly an oil terminal ensures all but the Amlwch station end is still used today. (T.J.Edgington)

▶ Blaenau Ffestinog was served by three railways, the last line to retain its passenger service was the Conwy Valley line to Llandudno Jn. The ex LNW terminus is host to Stanier Class 2 tank 40208 awaited to depart with the 5.39 p.m. local on 1st October 1955. This site was vacated when a new station was opened on the old spur line to Bala Jn in 1984. (T.J.Edgington)

Date	Line	Region (Company)	Type of Traffic	Reference Number
19.06.1972	Penrith No.1 - Blencow (Flusco Quarry)	LM(CK&P)	G(All)	2913
03.07.1972	Cart Jn - Kilbirnie	Sc(GSW)	G(All)	2914
12.07.1972 [5]	Cowdenbeath North Jn - Kelty Coup	Sc(NBR)	G(All)	2915
17.07.1972	Manchester (Ashton Road) - Ancoats Goods	LM(Mid)	G(All)	2916
00.08.1972 [8]	Bishop Auckland North - Bishop Auckland East	E(NER)	G(All)	2917
00.08.1972 [5]	Hedon Road Bridge - Victoria Dock Goods	E(NER)	G(All)	2918
00.08.1972 [2]	Luton 1965 Spur Jn - Vauxhall South GF	LM(GNR)	G(All)	2919
08.08.1972 [5]	Deal Jn - Kearsney Loop Jn	S(SEC)	G(All)	2920
28.08.1972 [5]	St Dunstans West Jn - St Dunstans North Jn	E(GNR)	G(All)	2921
28.08.1972	St Dunstans East - Bradford City Road Goods	E(GNR)	G(All)	2922
31.08.1972	Aberpergwm Jn - Glyn Neath	W(GWR)	G(All)	2923
04.09.1972	Preston No.4 - Preston East Lancs	LM(L&Y)	P(All)	2924
04.09.1972	Abenbury Sidings - Marchweil	LM(Cam)	G(All)	2925
25.09.1972	Dentonholme Goods Yard South - Carlisle No.11 (Rome Street Jn)	LM(DJC)	G(All)	2926
30.09.1972	Dunnington - Elvington	DVLR	G(All)	2927
02.10.1972	Hindley No.2 - De Trafford Jn	LM(LNW)	G(All)	2928
02.10.1972	Platt Bridge Jn - Standish Jn (via Whelley)	LM(LNW)	G(All)	2929
02.10.1972	Highbridge Crossing - Bason Bridge United Dairies Sidings	W(S&DJt)	G(All)	2930 *
19.10.1972	Skillington Road Jn - Stainby Sidings	E(GNR)	G(All)	2931 *
30.10.1972	PAIGNTON - KINGSWEAR	W(GWR)	P(All)	2932
06.11.1972	Fletton Jn - Oundle	E(LNW)	G(All)	2933
08.11.1972 [2]	Ryhope - Silksworth Colliery	E(NER)	G(All)	2934
15.11.1972	Killamarsh West - Norwood Tar Distillers Siding	E(Mid)	G(All)	2935
18.12.1972	Plymouth Commercial Road Crossing - Bayly's Wharf	W(GWR)	G(All)	2936
28.12.1972 [5]	Richmond (LMR) - Richmond (SR)	S(LSW)	G(All)	2937
01.01.1973	Sutton Harbour - North Quay (Turner Siding)	W(GWR)	G(All)	2938
01.01.1973	Sutton Harbour - North Quay (Pearse's Siding)	W(GWR)	G(All)	2939
01.01.1973	Raglan OCS - Wern Tarw West GF	W(GWR)	G(All)	2940
15.01.1973	BRADFORD (Exchange) Old - BRADFORD (Exchange) New	E(L&Y)	P(All)	2941
31.01.1973 [2]	Hindlow - Harpur Hill	LM(LNW)	G(All)	2942
31.01.1973 [2]	Harpur Hill - Hillhead Quarry	LM(LNW)	G(All)	2943
05.02.1973	ALTON - WINCHESTER [Jn]	S(LSW)	G(All)	2944
05.02.1973	Broadstone - Doulton's Siding	S(LSW)	G(All)	2945
05.02.1973 [5]	Tunnel Jn - Chapel Crossing	S(LSW)	G(All)	2946
00.03.1973 [5]	Todmorden East Jn - Stansfield Hall	LM(L&Y)	G(All)	2947
05.03.1973	Goods & Mineral Jn - Kings Cross Goods	E(GNR)	G(All)	2948
12.03.1973 [5]	Stratford Southern Jn - Stratford Eastern Jn	E(GER)	G(All)	2949
00.04.1973 [5]	Horninglow Bridge - Allsopp's Siding	LM(Mid)	G(All)	2950
02.04.1973 [5]	Whitwood - Aire & Calder Chemical Works	E(NER)	G(All)	2951
02.04.1973 [5]	Wadebridge - Wadebridge Quay	W(LSW)	G(All)	2952
02.04.1973	Duckmanton North Jn - Arkwright Town Jn	E(GCR)	G(All)	2953
02.04.1973	Arkwright Town Jn - Arkwright Colliery	E(GCR)	G(All)	2954
08.04.1973 [5]	Exhibition Jn - Waterloo Tunnel Mouth	LM(LNW)	G(All)	2955
16.04.1973	BOTLEY [Knowle Jn] - FAREHAM (via Deviation)	S(LSW)	P(All)	2956
00.05.1973 [2]	Woodend Jn - Woodend Colliery	Sc(NBR)	G(All)	2957
23.05.1973	Parton Jn - Parton No.4 Pit Siding	LM(WCEJt)	G(All)	2958
23.05.1973	Moss Bay Sidings - Rosehill Jn	LM(C&W)BSC	G(All)	2959
23.05.1973	Rosehill Jn - Lowca	BSC(H&LL)	G(All)	2960
23.05.1973	Moss Bay Sidings - Moss Bay Sidings Ironworks	LM(C&WJt)	G(All)	2961
23.05.1973 [3]	Moss Bay Sidings - Harrington Harbour	LM(C&WJt)	G(All)	2962
23.05.1973	Wolverhampton L.L. - South Priestfield	LM(GWR)	G(All)	2963
23.06.1973	Langside Jn - Gorbals Jn	Sc(GB&K)	G(All)	2964
23.06.1973	Thornton West Jn - Thornton Central Jn	Sc(NBR)	G(All)	2965

Date	Line	Region (Company)	Type of Traffic	Reference Number
25.06.1973	Alloa - Dollar	Sc(NBR)	G(All)	2966
02.07.1973	Holme - Ramsey North	E(GNR)	G(All)	2967
30.07.1973	Lower Duffryn L.L. New Spur Jn - Aberdare H.L. New Spur Jn	W(Taff)	G(All)	2968
06.08.1973	High Dyke - Sproxton	E(GNR)	G(All)	2969 *
00.09.1973 [8]	Immingham West Jn (West) - Immingham Dock	E(GCR)	G(All)	2970
00.09.1973 [8]	Choppington - Netherton Colliery	E(NER)	G(All)	2971
00.09.1973 [8]	Goonbarrow (Rock Dries Sidings) - New Caudledown South GF	W(GWR)	G(All)	2972
00.09.1973 [8]	Hednesford No.1 - Cannock Wood Colliery	LM(LNW)	G(All)	2973
00.09.1973 [5]	Holderness Drain South - King George Dock Jn	E(HB/NERJt)	G(All)	2974
03.09.1973	Bathgate Upper - Easton Colliery	Sc(NBR)	G(All)	2975
08.09.1973	Prestatyn - Dyserth	LM(LNW)	G(All)	2976
01.10.1973	Carmarthen Goods - Felin Fach [Green Grove Siding]	W(GWR)	G(All)	2977 *
01.10.1973	Pencader Jn - Newcastle Emlyn	W(GWR)	G(All)	2978
08.10.1973	Annfield East - Morrison (Busty) Colliery Exchange Sidings	E(NER)	G(All)	2979
14.10.1973 [5]	Newark Castle - Newark Northgate Exchange Siding	E(GN&MidJt)	G(All)	2980
15.10.1973	Wolverton South GF - Triangle GF	LM(LNW)	G(All)	2981
17.10.1973 [5]	Birkenhead (Brook Street Jn) - Morpeth Dock Goods	LM(LNW)	G(All)	2982
22.10.1973	DALRY [No.3 SB] - KILMARNOCK [No.2 SB]	Sc(GSW)	P(All)	2983
29.10.1973	Wilton New Spur Jn - Tinkerpit A.M.Siding	S(GWR)	G(All)	2984
29.10.1973 [5]	Beynon Colliery - Coalbrookvale	W(GWR)	G(All)	2985
29.10.1973 [5]	Port Meadow New Spur Jn - Rewley Road Exchange Sidings	W(LNW)	G(All)	2986
29.10.1973 [5]	Oxford 1940 Spur Jn - Oxford North Jn	W(LNW)	G(All)	2987
05.11.1973	Newbury West - Welford Park USNS Depot	W(GWR)	G(All)	2988 *
19.11.1973	Radstock West GF - Writhington Colliery Sidings	W(GWR)	G(All)	2989
19.11.1973	Cefn Jn - Pyle	W(GWR)	G(All)	2990
19.11.1973	Radstock West (Marcroft Wagon Works) - Radstock West GF	W(GWR)	G(All)	2991
24.11.1973	Watford No.3 - Jn with new spur at MP 0¼ (St Albans line)	LM(LNW)	P(All)	2992
26.11.1973	Prestwick (Texaco Siding) - Auchincruive Colliery	Sc(GSW)	G(All)	2993
00.12.1973	Heap Bridge Jn - Heap Bridge Duxbury's Siding	LM(L&Y)	G(All)	2994
02.12.1973	Ashwell Sidings - Cottesmore	LM(Mid)	G(All)	2995
03.12.1973	Barassie Jn - Barassie Harbour	Sc(GSW)	G(All)	2996
31.12.1973	Portobello Kings Road - Leith South Meadows	Sc(NBR)	G(All)	2997
31.12.1973	Meadows Yard - Leith East Goods	Sc(BRB/Cal)	G(All)	2998
31.12.1973 [5]	Texaco Sidings - Ayr Goods	Sc(GSW)	G(All)	2999
31.12.1973 [5]	Chellaston Jn - Sinfin Rolls Royce Siding	LM(Mid)	G(All)	3000
31.12.1973 [5]	Cartsdyke Jn - Greenock Victoria Harbour	Sc(Cal)	G(All)	3001
31.12.1973 [5]	Sutton Harbour GF - Sutton Harbour Goods	W(GWR)	G(All)	3002
15.02.1974	Bevoir Jn - Denton Siding	E(GNR)	G(All)	3003 *
04.03.1974	Geldard Jn - Leeds Wellington Street L.L. Goods	E(NER)	G(All)	3004
24.03.1974 [5]	Edge Hill - Rathbone Road Sidings (Wapping Goods Lines)	LM(LNW)	G(All)	3005
01.04.1974	Halifax Goods Yard - Halifax North Bridge Goods	E(HOJt)	G(All)	3006
08.04.1974	Trent Lane Jn - Weekday Cross Jn	LM(GNR)	G(All)	3007
08.04.1974	Weekday Cross Jn - Ruddington MOD Depot	LM(GCR)	G(All)	3008
00.06.1974 [2]	Maesmawr - Treforest Trading Estate	W(BRB)	G(All)	3009
01.07.1974	Grange Park - Enfield Chase Goods	E(GNR)	G(All)	3010
15.07.1974	Morningside Stirling Road GF - Kingsmill Coll.(BRB boundary Castlehill Jn	Sc(Cal/NCB)	G(All)	3011
22.07.1974	Wimborne - West Moors MOD Siding	S(LSW)	G(All)	3012
00.08.1974	Bickershaw Jn - Howe Bridge West	LM(LNW)	G(All)	3013
00.08.1974	Howe Bridge West - Parsonage Colliery	NCB	G(All)	3014
16.09.1974	Pontardulais - Brynlliw New Spur Jn	W(LNW)	G(All)	3015
11.11.1974	Norwood 1967 Spur Jn - Warsop Sidings 1974 Spur Jn	E(BRB/GCR)	G(All)	3016
09.12.1974	Stockton FLT - Billingham Beck ICI Sidings	E(NER)	G(All)	3017
09.12.1974	Haverton Hill South Jn - Haverton Hill East Jn	E(NER)	G(All)	3018

Date	Line	Region (Company)	Type of Traffic	Reference Number
11.02.1975 [5]	Bickershaw Jn - Howe Bridge West	LM(LNW)	G(All)	3019
05.05.1975	MAIDEN NEWTON - BRIDPORT	W(GWR)	P(All)	3020
05.05.1975	Merton Park - Merton Abbey	S(LBSC/LSWR)	G(All)	3021
05.05.1975	Blackhouse Jn - Hawkhill Jn	Sc(GSW)	P(All)	3022
05.05.1975	Mauchline No.1 - Blackhouse Jn	Sc(GSW)	P	3023
02.06.1975	FORT WILLIAM (New station) - FORT WILLIAM (Old Station)	Sc(NBR)	P(All)	3024
28.07.1975	JAMES STREET - LIVERPOOL (Central L.L.)	LM(Mersey)	P(All)	3025
28.07.1975	Llantrisant - Llanharry	W(Taff)	G(All)	3026
07.09.1975	OLD STREET - MOORGATE	LT(GNC)	P	3027 *
08.09.1975	Ordsall Lane No.1 - Manchester Liverpool Road	LM(LNW)	G(All)	3028
04.10.1975 [1]	CARDIFF (Central) [Dr Days Jn] - PORTSMOUTH (Harbour) [North Somerset Jn]	W(GWR)	P*	3029
06.10.1975	MORECAMBE [Station Jn] - HEYSHAM HARBOUR	LM(Mid)	P	3030
06.10.1975	GLOUCESTER (Eastgate) - Tuffley Jn	W(Mid)	P	3031
05.10.1975	Old Street - Moorgate	LT(GN&C)	ECS(All)	3032
05.10.1975	DRAYTON PARK - OLD STREET	LT(GN&C)	P(All)	3033 *
31.10.1975	Grimsby Royal Dock Lines Jn - Grimsby Docks BRB/BTDB Boundary	E(GCR)	G(All)	3034
03.11.1975	Warcop - Merrygill Quarry	LM(NER)	G(All)	3035
03.11.1975	Wombwell Main Jn - New Oaks Jn	E(GCR)	G(All)	3036
31.12.1975 [5]	Swindon Rushey Platt Jn - Swindon Rushey Platt Lower Jn	W(MSWJ)	G(All)	3037
31.12.1975 [5]	Rushey Platt Lower Jn - Moredon CEGB	W(MSWJ)	G(All)	3038
01.01.1976	Yarmouth Vauxhall - Yarmouth South Quay	E(GER)	G(All)	3039
05.01.1976	Wilmington (Hornsea PDS) - Wilmington New Jn	E(NER)	G(All)	3040
19.01.1976	Kidsgrove Liverpool Road Jn - Park Farm Opencast Site	LM(NSR)	G(All)	3041
24.01.1976 [5]	Heath's Jn - Chatterley Whitfields Coll. Sid. GF	LM(NSR)	G(All)	3042
26.01.1976	Fawkham Jn - Southfleet APCM	S(SEC)	G(All)	3043
17.03.1976 [5]	Lancaster Green Ayre CEGB - Lancaster Castle	LM(Mid)	G(All)	3044
05.04.1976	Falkirk Roughcastle Jn - Roughcastle end of branch	Sc(NBR)	G(All)	3045
16.04.1976	Ford Green LC - Chatterley Whitfield	LM(NSR)	G(All)	3046
03.05.1976	HALTWHISTLE - ALSTON	E(NER)	P(All)	3047
03.05.1976	Benton Jn - Benton North Jn	E(NER)	P	3048
10.05.1976 [5]	Beighton Jn - Brookhouse Colliery	E(Mid)	G(All)	3049
07.05.1976	Lydney Jn - Parkend	W(SWJt)	G(All)	3050 *
24.05.1976 [5]	Rectory South Jn - Rectory East Jn	LM(BRB)	G(All)	3051
01.06.1976	Auchinleck - Hillhouse Colliery	Sc(GSW)	G(All)	3052
05.07.1976 [3]	BARRY ISLAND - BARRY PIER	W(Barry)	P(All)	3053
05.07.1976	Rose Heyworth - Blaina	W(GWR)	G(All)	3054
14.07.1976 [5]	Stalybridge - Staley & Millbrook	LM(LNW)	G(All)	3055
19.07.1976 [5]	Maesteg Llynfi Jn - Caerau	W(GWR)	G(All)	3056
31.07.1976	Hull Burleigh Street North Jn - Stoneferry Crossing	E(LNE/NER)	G(All)	3057
31.07.1976 [5]	Warsop Jn - Warsop Colliery Sidings	E(GCR)	G(All)	3058
31.08.1976 [5]	Hunts Cross West Jn - Huskinson Goods	E(CLC)	G(All)	3059
11.10.1976	Kilbowie BRB connection - Yoker Ferry	Sc(BRB/Cal)	G(All)	3060
00.11.1976	Margate Station - Margate Goods	S(SR)	G(All)	3061
08.11.1976	BROAD STREET [Canonbury Jn] - FINSBURY PARK [Jn]	LM(NLR/GNR)	P	3062
20.11.1976 [5]	Pallion - Hylton Quarry	E(NER)	G(All)	3063
20.11.1976 [5]	Wellfield Jn - Thornley Washery	E(NER)	G(All)	3064
00.04.1977	Belvoir Jn - Casthorpe Jn	E(GNR)	G(All)	3065
01.06.1977	Westfield OCS - Lurgi SGB end of line	Sc(NBR)	G(All)	3066
08.08.1977 [5]	Bishop Auckland North Jn - Shell Mex PS	E(NER)	G(All)	3067

Date	Line	Region (Company)	Type of Traffic	Reference Number
29.08.1977	Bentinck Colliery - Bentinck Colliery EWS	LM(Mid)	G(All)	3068
17.09.1977 [1]	Royal Oak East Jn - FILEY HOLIDAY CAMP	E(LNE)	P*(All)	3069
17.09.1977 [1]	Royal Oak East Jn - Royal Oak North Jn	E(LNE)	P*(All)	3070
10.10.1977	West London Jn - Acton Jn	LM(NSWJt)	P*	3071
31.10.1977	Maidstone East - Tovil Goods	S(SEC)	G(All)	3072
03.11.1977 [3]	Lansdown Jn - Honeybourne West Loop Jn	W(GWR)	G(All)	3073 *
30.11.1977 [3]	Todd Lane Jn - Lostock Hall Gas Works	LM(L&Y)	G(All)	3074
05.12.1977	Portsmouth High Level Jn - Portsmouth Dockyard North	S(LSW/LSBC)	G(All)	3075
19.12.1977	Brownhill Jn - Kilbirnie	Sc(GSW)	G(All)	3076
19.12.1977	Kilbirnie Jn - Glengarnock Steel Works	Sc(Cal)	G(All)	3077
08.01.1978	Benton No.2 - Benton North Jn	E(NER)	G(All)	3078
23.01.1978	NEWCASTLE [Manors Jn] - WEST MONKSEATON (via Benton)	E(NER)	P(All)	3079 *
31.01.1978	Common Branch Jn - Creigiau Quarry	W(Taff)	G(All)	3080
05.03.1978 [2]	Cresswell Jn - Cheadle	LM(NS/LMS)	G(All)	3081
20.03.1978	Kettering Jn - Twywell	LM(Mid)	G(All)	3082
01.04.1978	Larbert Alloa Jn - Throsk (RNAD Bandeath)	Sc(Cal)	G(All)	3083
10.04.1978	Manors Jn - Gosforth East Jn	E(NER)	G(All)	3084
10.04.1978	South Gosforth Jn - Gosforth West Jn	E(NER)	G(All)	3085
08.05.1978	LIVERPOOL (Lime Street) [Bootle Branch Jn] - SOUTHPORT [Bootle Jn]	LM(LNW)	P	3086
14.05.1978	Dearne Valley South Jn - Hickleton Coll.Sid.SB	E(Dearne)	G(All)	3087
31.05.1978 [5]	Percy Main West Jn - Point Pleasant	E(NER)	G(All)	3088
05.06.1978 [3]	Alloa Station Jn - Alloa East Goods	Sc(NBR)	G(All)	3089
05.06.1978	Renfrew Porterfield Road - Renfrew Wharf (Buchanan PS)	Sc(GSW)	G(All)	3090
19.06.1978	Tod Point Jn (Old) - Redcar	E(NER)	P(All)	3091
00.08.1978	Dovecliffe - Rockingham Colliery	E(GCR)	G(All)	3092
07.08.1978	Masborough South Jn - Holmes Jn (Holmes Curve)	E(Mid)	G(All)	3093
19.08.1978 [1]	Bradford South Jn - Thingley Jn	W(GWR)	P*	3094
04.09.1978	Raglan East - Tondu Ynysawdre Jn	W(GWR)	G(All)	3095
04.09.1978 [2]	Boscarne Jn - Wadebridge	W(LSW)	G(All)	3096
02.10.1978 [1]	Bidston West Jn - Bidston North Jn	LM(Wirral)	P	3097
23.10.1978	Partick Central Jn - Meadowside Granary Sid.	Sc(Cal/BRB)	G(All)	3098
31.10.1978 [5]	Bolsover - Glapwell Colliery	E(Mid)	G(All)	3099
03.12.1978	Wheal Henry - New Cauldown	W(GWR)	G(All)	3100
11.12.1978	Kempston Road Jn - Bedford Jn (old alignment)	LM(LNW)	P(All)	3101
04.03.1979 [5]	Milton Jn - Ford Green	LM(NSR)	G(All)	3102
17.03.1979	Penmanshiel Tunnel South - Penmanshiel Tunnel North	E/Sc(NBR)	P(All)	3103
??.04.1979	Codnor Park Jn Adamson–Butterley Siding - Swanwick	LM(Mid)	G(All)	3104
09.04.1979	Panteg & Coedygric Jn - Hafodrynys Colliery (Glyntillery)	W(GWR	G(All)	3105
14.05.1979	Stainforth Jn - Adwick Jn	E(WRJt)	P	3106
00.07.1979	Southwick Goods - Hylton Colliery	E(NER)	G(All)	3107
16.07.1979 [5]	Bo'ness Jn - Kinneil Colliery	Sc(NBR)	G(All)	3108 *
06.08.1979	Laisterdyke East - Phoenix Works Sid	E(GNR)	G(All)	3109
06.08.1979	Laisterdyke West Jn - Dudley Hill Yard	E(GNR)	G(All)	3110
06.08.1979	Kincardine Jn - Bogside Noble Explosives Sid.	Sc(NBR)	G(All)	3111
03.09.1979 [5]	Maesglas Jn - East Mendalgief Jn	W(ANSW)	G(All)	3112
03.09.1979	Layerthorpe - Dunnington	DVLR	P*	3113
10.09.1979	WEST MONKSEATON - TYNEMOUTH	E(NER)	P(All)	3114 *
10.09.1979	Tynemouth South Box - Tynemouth Old Goods	E(NER)	G(All)	3115
03.10.1979	Trench Crossing (Government Sid.) - Donnington Walker's Sid.	LM(LNW)	G(All)	3116
08.10.1979	Dyce Jn - Fraserburgh	Sc(GNoSR)	G(All)	3117
29.10.1979	Newport Dock Street Depot - Newport Town Dock Sid.	W(GWR)	G(All)	3118

Coniston station is dwarfed by the mountains
the background. 41217 sits beneath the canopy
ch covers part of the platform on 3rd Sep-
ber 1954. The passenger service survived until
October 1958, and the line closed after 30th
ril 1962. *(T.J.Edgington)*

The magnificent steel viaduct at Belah, high
the Pennines is being crossed by Ivatt Class 2
472 on a Penrith to Darlington train during Au-
st 1951. The line from Merrygill Quarry to Bar-
rd Castle closed with the withdrawal of pas-
nger services on 1st January 1962. *(T.J.Ed-
gton)*

06 63439 shunts in Consett station goods yard
8th September 1963, the station is well kept
though it lost its last passenger service on
May 1955. With the demise of the steelworks
branch to Ouston Jn lost its last source of
ic and closed in the early 1980's. *(T.J.Ed-
ton)*

Date	Line	Region (Company)	Type of Traffic	Reference Number
31.10.1979	Burton on Trent - Shobnall Maltings Branch	LM(Mid)	G(All)	3120
05.11.1979	GLASGOW (High St.) [High Street West Jn] - BRIDGETON	Sc(NBR)	P	3121
24.12.1979	Bathgate - Woodend Washery	Sc(NBR)	G(All)	3122
31.12.1979 [5]	Oakdale Colliery - Markham Colliery	W(GWR)	G(All)	3123
14.01.1980	Kincardine Jn - Bogside Nobel Explosives Siding	Sc(NBR)	G(All)	3124
18.02.1980	Deepdale Jn - Preston Courtaulds Red Scar Siding	LM(P&LJt)	G(All)	3125
21.02.1980 [1]	High Marnham SB - Pyewipe Jn	E(GCR)	G(All)	312ɛ
29.02.1980 [1?]	Newstead Colliery - Annesley Colliery	LM(Mid)	G(All)	3127
01.03.1980	Castleford - Hickson & Welsh Ltd Siding	E(NER)	G(All)	3128
17.03.1980	Bury Loco Jn - BURY (Bolton Street)	LM(L&Y)	P(All)	3129
22.03.1980	Yoker Yard - Partick Meadowside Wharf	Sc(Cal)	G(All)	3130
24.03.1980	Dumbarton East Goods Jn - Hiram Walker's PS	Sc(Cal)	G(All)	3131
01.04.1980 [3]	Hamilton West - Birdsfield C.W.Ireland's Sid.	Sc(Cal)	G(All)	3132
03.04.1980	Ryburgh - Fakenham East	E(GER)	G(All)	3133
21.04.1980 [5]	Souterhouse GF - BSC British Works Souterhouse	Sc(NBR)	G(All)	3134
28.04.1980	Laira Jn - Mount Gould Jn	W(GWR)	G(All)	3135
30.04.1980 [5]	Narborough Station - Enderby	LM(LNW/MidJt)	G(All)	3136
03.05.1980 [3]	Llantarnam Jn - Blaenavon Furnace Sid.	W(GW/LNW)	G(All)	3137
05.05.1980	Aston Windsor Street Jn - Aston Goods (Windsor Street Wharf)	LM(LNW)	G(All)	3138
12.05.1980	Ryecroft Jn - Birchills PS	LM(Mid)	G(All)	3139
12.05.1980	Percy Main - Percy Main North	E(NER)	G(All)	3140
21.05.1980	Worthington - Worthington Jn	LM(Mid)	G(All)	3141
26.05.1980	Norwood Yard - Dunstan Staithes	E(NER)	G(All)	3142
31.05.1980	Northampton No.2 - Market Harborough Jn	LM(LNW)	G(All)	3143
00.05.1980 [5?]	Portwood - Cheadle Jn	LM(CLC)	G(All)	3144
29.06.1980 [8]	Dalmeny Jn - Royal Elizabeth RNAD	Sc(NBR)	G(All)	3145
25.07.1980 [9]	Butcherwood Sidings - Teversall Colliery EWS	LM(Mid)	G(All)	3146
11.08.1980	HEATON [East] - TYNEMOUTH	E(NER)	P(All)	3147 *
30.08.1980	Holwell Jn - Holwell BSC Sidings	LM(Mid)	G(All)	3148
30.08.1980	Northallerton High Jn - Eaglescliffe South Jn	E(NER)	P*	3149
13.09.1980	LEEDS [Adwick Jn] - CLEETHORPES [Stainforth Jn]	E(WRGJt)	P	3150
20.09.1980 [1]	Wensum Jn - Swing Bridge Jn	E(GER)	P*	3151
29.09.1980	Kettering - Cransley G.Cohen Sid.	LM(Mid)	G(All)	3152
29.09.1980?	South Pelaw - Washington	E(NER)	G(All)	3153
01.10.1980	Hartlebury - Stourport on Severn Station	LM(GWR)	G(All)	3154
01.10.1980	Stourport Station - Stourport CEGB PS	LM(GWR)	G(All)	3155
03.10.1980	Grimsby Garden Street Jn - Louth	E(GNR)	G(All)	3156
06.10.1980	Whitehaven Corkickle No.1 - Beckermet Mines	LM(WCEJt)	G(All)	3157
14.10.1980 [5]	Knightswood South Jn - Maryhill Central Jn	Sc(NBR)	G(All)	3158
24.11.1980 [5]	Cargo Fleet Old Station LC - Normanby	E(NER)	G(All)	3159
04.01.1981	Lightmoor Jn - Horsehay Adamson–Butterley Sid.	LM(GWR)	G(All)	3160
05.01.1981	KENTISH TOWN [Mortimer Street Jn] - UPPER HOLLOWAY [Engine Shed Jn]	LM(Mid)	P	3161 *
05.01.1981 [5]	Swing Bridge Jn - Wensum Jn	E(GER)	G(All)	3162
05.01.1981	Faslane Jn - Faslane MOD Navy Sids.	Sc(LNE)	G(All)	3163
07.01.1981	Butcherwood Sidings GF - Pleasley Colliery	LM(Mid)	G(All)	3164
11.01.1981 [5]	Kentish Town Mortimer Street Jn - Engine Shed Jn	LM(Mid)	G(All)	3165
12.01.1981	Stourport - Hartlebury	LM(GWR)	G(All)	3166
27.01.1981	Colnebrook - Staines West New Spur Jn	W(GWR)	G(All)	3167
23.02.1981 [2]	Methley Lofthouse Jn - Charlesworth Newmarket Colliery	E(MJt)	G(All)	3168
23.02.1981 [5]	Methley North Jn - Castleford Cutsdyke Jn	E(NER)	G(All)	3169
28.02.1981	New Hucknall GF - New Hucknall Colliery	LM(Mid)	G(All)	3170

Date	Line	Region (Company)	Type of Traffic	Reference Number
00.03.1981 [2?]	St Dennis Jn - Meledor Mill	W(GWR)	G(All)	3171
01.04.1981	Dysart - Francis Colliery	Sc(NBR)	G(All)	3172
06.04.1981	Wednesbury Bagnall's Siding - Bloomfield Jn	LM(LNW)	G(All)	3173
06.04.1981 [8]	Tipton Curve Jn - Tipton Station Jn	LM(LNW)	G(All)	3174
06.04.1981 [5]	Bedford St Johns - Goldington PS	LM(LNW)	G(All)	3175
06.04.1981	Alloa East Jn - Kincardine	Sc(NBR)	G(All)	3176
08.04.1981	Heywood Standard Wagon Co.Sid. - Rawtenstall	LM(L&Y)	G(All)	3177
04.05.1981	Kinnaber Jn - Brechin	Sc(Cal)	G(All)	3178
04.05.1981	Wrexham Central - Abenbury	LM(Cam)	G(All)	3179
09.05.1981 [1]	Nuneaton Midland Jn - Nuneaton Abbey Jn	LM(Mid)	P	3180
28.05.1981	Cholsey & Moulsford - Wallingford ABM Sid.	W(GWR)	G(All)	3181
00.06.1981	Uphall GF - Pumpherston	Sc(NBR)	G(All)	3182
01.06.1981 [3]	Bidston West Jn - Bidston North Jn	LM(Wirral)	P	3183
01.06.1981	NEWCASTLE (Central) [Pelaw North Jn] - SOUTH SHIELDS	E(NER)	P	3184 *
01.06.1981	Harton Jn - South Shields	E(NER)	P(All)	3185
05.06.1981	Cortonwood Jn - Elsecar Main Colliery	E(GCR)	G(All)	3186
01.06.1981	NEW HOLLAND (Pier) [Town] - BARTON ON HUMBER [Barton Jn]	E(GCR)	P(All)	3187
20.06.1981	Measham & Overseal Colliery - Overseal	LM(Mid)	G(All)	3188
22.06.1981	North Kent West Jn - North Kent East Jn	S(SEC)	R(All)	3189
24.06.1981	CLEETHORPES [Oxmarsh Jn] - NEW HOLLAND (Pier)	E(GCR)	P(All)	3190 *
26.06.1981 [2]	Newdigates Siding SB - Newdigate Colliery	LM(LNW)	G(All)	3191
20.07.1981	Hadfield - Huddersfield Jn	LM/E(GCR)	G(All)	3192
20.07.1981	Wombwell Main Jn - Penistone Huddersfield Jn	E(GCR)	G(All)	3193
20.07.1981	Hyde Jn - Hadfield	LM(GCR)	G	3194
20.07.1981	Godley Jn - Apelthorne Jn	LM(GCR)	G(All)	3195
20.07.1981	Dodworth SB - West Silkstone Jn	E(GCR)	G(All)	3196
00.08.1981?	Three Spires Jn - Gosford Green	LM(LNW)	G(All)	3197
03.08.1981	Astley Bridge Jn - Halliwell Goods	LM(L&Y)	G(All)	3198
10.08.1981	Haghill Jn - Parkhead North Jn	Sc(NBR)	G(All)	3199
29.08.1981 [1]	Dore West Jn - Dore South Jn	E(Mid)	P*	3200
29.08.1981 [1]	Philips Park No.1 - Ashburys West Jn	LM(L&Y)	P*	3201
05.09.1981 [1]	Pyewipe Jn - Greetwell Jn (via Boultham Jn)	E(GN&GEJt)	P*	3202
28.09.1981	Colwyn Bay SB - Colwyn Bay Goods	LM(LNW)	G(All)	3203
11.09.1981?	Chelsea & Fulham SB - Chelsea Basin	LM(WLEJt)	G(All)	3205
01.10.1981	Layerthorpe - Dunnington	DVLR	G(All)	3206
06.10.1981	Norwood Fork Jn - Gloryhole Jn	S(LBSC)	P(All)	3207
16.11.1981 [5]	Welwyn Garden City - GKN Siding	E(GNR)	G(All)	3208
18.11.1981 [5]	Barrow Hill Station - Hall Lane Jn	E(Mid)	G(All)	3209
30.11.1981	Wellingborough Jn - Wellingborough London Rd (Whitworth B.Sd)	LM(Mid)	G(All)	3210
10.12.1981 [9]	Garnqueen South Jn - Bedlay Colliery	Sc(NBR/BRB)	G(All)	3211
12.12.1981 [5]	Wednesbury Central - Swan Village	LM(GWR)	G(All)	3212
01.02.1982	Plains Springbank Sid. - Bathgate	Sc(NBR)	G(All)	3213
28.03.1982	St.Bedes Jn - Harton	E(NER)	G(All)	3214
31.03.1982	Caerphilly - Caerphilly NCB Tar Plant	W(Rhy)	G(All)	3215
00.04.1982	Bridgend - Bridgend & Coity Goods	W(Barry)	G(All)	3216
00.04.1982 [2]	Kidderminster Jn - Foley Park (British Sugar)	W(GWR)	G(All)	3217 *
01.04.1982 [5]	Easter Road Jn - Granton Texaco Siding	Sc(NBR)	G(All)	3218
03.04.1982 [3]	St Dennis Jn - Meledor Mill	W(GWR)	G(All)	3219
14.04.1982 [1]	Dunston West Yard - Redheugh Iron & Steel	E(NER)	G(All)	3220
18.04.1982 [5]	Widnes No.7 - Farnworth & Bold	LM(LNW)	G(All)	3221
00.05.1982 [5]	Oakley - Bogside	Sc(NBR)	G(All)	3222
17.05.1982 [2]	Finsbury Park - Ashburton Grove Depot	E(GNR)	G(All)	3223
04.06.1982?	Hayle - Hayle Wharf	W(GWR)	G(All)	3224

Date	Line	Region (Company)	Type of Traffic	Reference Number
21.06.1982 [5]	Aber Jn - Walnut Tree Jn	W(Rhy)	G(All)	3225
05.06.1982	Stanley Jn - Forfar	Sc(Cal)	G(All)	3226
27.06.1982	Burscough Bridge - Burscough Jn MOD Depot	M(L&Y)	G(All)	3227
03.08.1982 [5]	Partington Jn - Glazebrook East Jn	LM(CLC)	G(All)	3228
15.08.1982	Blackwell East Jn - New Hucknall LC	LM(Mid)	G(All)	3229
15.08.1982	New Hucknall LC - New Hucknall Tip	LM(GC)	G(All)	3230
15.08.1982 [4]	Dairycoates (Tilcon Siding) - Hull Neptune Street	E(NER)	G(All)	3231
23.08.1982 [5]	Beighton Station Jn - Staveley Central new spur Jn	E(GCR)	G(All)	3232
04.09.1982	Atlantic Dock Jn - Bootle Canada Dock	LM(LNW)	G(All)	3233
03.10.1982	Winsford Jn - Over & Wharton	LM(LNW)	G(All)	3234
25.09.1982 [5]	Moor Row - Beckermet	LM(WCEJt)	G(All)	3235
02.10.1982 [5]	Dysart - Francis Colliery	Sc(NBR)	G(All)	3236
04.10.1982?	Croes Newydd - Brymbo Steelworks	W(GWR)	G(All)	3237
04.10.1982	NEWCASTLE (Central) [Scotswood] - CARLISLE [Blaydon Jn]	E(NER)	P(All)	3238
04.10.1982	SHEFFIELD [Wath Road Jn] - LEEDS [Goose Hill Jn]	E(Mid)	P	3239
04.10.1982	Oakenshaw South Jn - Oakenshaw Jn	E(L&Y)	P	3240
04.10.1982	Oakenshaw Jn - Wakefield Kirkgate Jn	E(L&Y)	P	3241
04.10.1982	Altofts Jn - Whitwood Jn	E(NER)	P	3242
04.10.1982	CASTLEFORD (Central) - Burton Salmon Jn	E(NER)	P	3243
06.11.1982 [7]	Bristol East Jn - Bristol NCL	W(GWR)	G(All)	3244
06.11.1982 [1]	Barnstaple Jn - Torrington	W(LSW/SR)	G(All)	3245
28.11.1982 [5]	Hessle Haven Jn - Hessle Yard	E(NER)	G(All)	3246
28.11.1982	MARCH - SPALDING [No.1]	E(GE&GNJt)	P	3247
28.11.1982	Grassmoor - Spalding No.1	E(GE&GNJt)	G(All)	3248
28.11.1982 [3]	Sleaford South Jn - Sleaford North Jn	E(GN&GEJt)	P	3249
28.11.1982 [3]	Greetwell Jn - Pyewipe Jn	E(GN&GEJt)	P*	3250
28.11.1982 [3]	Boultham Jn - West Holmes Jn	E(GN&GEJt)	P*	3251
03.01.1983	GLASGOW (Central) [Shields Jn] - KILMACOLM [Elderslie No.1]	Sc(GSW)	P	3252 *
03.01.1983	GLASGOW (Central) [Elderslie No.2] - KILMACOLM	Sc(GSW)	P(All)	3253
08.01.1983 [3]	Denver Jn - Abbey	E(GER)	G(All)	3254
20.01.1983 [5]	Croxley Carriage Shed Jn - Croxley Mills	LM(LNW)	G(All)	3255
24.01.1983	HUDDERSFIELD [Clayton West Jn] - CLAYTON WEST	E(L&Y)	P	3256
05.03.1983 [3]	Barnstaple Jn - Meeth ECC Siding	W(LSW/SR)	G(All)	3257
15.03.1983 [5]	Consett Carr House SB - Blackhill Coal Yard	E(NER)	G(All)	3258
16.03.1983 [5]	Castleford East Branch Jn - Hickson & Welch Siding	E(NER)	G(All)	3259
25.04.1983	Orgreaves Colliery SB - Orgreave BSC Coking Plant	E(GCR)	G(All)	3260
07.05.1983	Wednesbury Central - Wolverhampton Steel Terminal Walsall St.	LM(GWR)	G(All)	3261
16.05.1983	Guide Bridge - Crowthorne Jn	LM(GCR)	G(All)	3262
16.05.1983	Fairfield Jn - Hyde Jn	LM(GCR)	G(All)	3263
16.05.1983	WOODSIDE [Jn] - SANDERSTEAD [Selsdon Jn]	S(W&SCJt)	P(All)	3264
16.05.1983	Selhurst Jn - St.James Jn (Emergency Spur)	S(LBSC)	P	3265
16.05.1983	SHEFFIELD [Nunnery Jn] - PENISTONE [Huddersfield Jn]	E(GCR)	P	3266
16.05.1983	Deepcar - Penistone Huddersfield Jn	E(GCR)	G(All)	3267
16.05.1983	Gascoigne Wood Jn - Sherburn South Jn	E(NER)	P	3268
21.05.1983 [4]	Swansea Eastern Depot - Upper Bank	W(Mid)	G(All)	3269
30.05.1983	Carmyle Jn - Westburn Steel Works	Sc(Cal)	G(All)	3270
06.06.1983 [2]	Dunston & Barlow North Jn - Sheepbridge Whittington Rd PDS	E(Mid)	G(All)	3271
15.06.1983	Wroxham - Lenwade	E(GE/BR/MGN)	G(All)	3272
27.06.1983	Firbeck East Jn - Firbeck South Jn	E(SYJt)	G(All)	3273
00.07.1983 [9]	Raisby Hill - East Hetton Colliery	E(NER)	G(All)	3274
01.07.1983	Rhondda Cutting Jn - Rhondda Cutting GF (Tymawr Colliery)	W(Taff)	G(All)	3275
15.07.1983 [1]	Lincoln Street Jn - Babbington Colliery	LM(Mid)	G(All)	3276
05.08.1983 [1]	Linby Station LC - Newstead Colliery	LM(Mid)	G(All)	3277

Date	Line	Region (Company)	Type of Traffic	Reference Number
09.08.1983	Bushbury Jn - Cannock Road Jn	LM(GWR)	G(All)	3278
09.08.1983	Cannock Road Jn - Stafford Road Jn	LM(GWR)	G(All)	3279
26.08.1983	Greetwell Jn - Bardney (British Sugar)	E(GNR)	G(All)	3280
00.09.1983 [9]	Ogmore Valley Washery - Wyndham Colliery	W(GWR)	G(All)	3281
03.09.1983	Coulsdon North Jn - COULSDON (North)	S(LBSC)	P(All)	3282
17.09.1983 [1]	Torrington - Meeth ECC Siding	W(LSW/SR)	G(All)	3283
17.09.1983	Pembrey East Jn - Kidwelly Branch Jn	W(BPGV)	G(All)	3284
24.09.1983 [1]	SELBY [Barlby Jn] - YORK [Chaloners Whin Jn]	E(NER)	P(All)	3285
02.10.1983	Gloucester Road Jn - Windmill Bridge Jn (Slow Lines)	S(LBSC)	P(All)	3286
03.10.1983 [5]	Victoria Park Jn - Poplar Docks	LM(NLR)	G(All)	3287
03.10.1983 [5]	Cwmbargoed - Dowlais Furnace Top	W(TBJt)	G(All)	3288
00.10.1983 [9]	Lynemouth Colliery - Ellington Colliery	NCB	G(All)	3289
07.10.1983	Bricklayers Arms Jn - Bricklayers Arms (Crane Depot)	S(SEC)	D(All)	3290
08.10.1983 [5]	Carmarthen - Carmarthen Goods	W(GWR)	G(All)	3291
15.10.1983 [3]	Tondu Ogmore Jn - Wern Tawr	W(GWR)	G(All)	3292
23.10.1983 [9]	Bargoed - Bargoed Colliery	W(Rhy)	G(All)	3293
19.11.1983 [4]	Heath Town Jn - Wednesbury	LM(Mid)	G(All)	3294
05.12.1983	Southcote Jn - Reading Central Goods (Coley Branch)	W(GWR)	G(All)	3295
05.12.1983 [5]	Ashton Jn - Portishead	W(GWR)	G(All)	3296
12.12.1983	Mansfield South Jn - Rufford Colliery	LM(Mid)	G(All)	3297
00.01.1984	Sheepford Branch Jn - Sheepford CCD	Sc(NBR)	G(All)	3298
10.01.1984 [1]	Amoco Sidings - Herbrandston Esso Oil Sidings	W(BRB)	G(All)	3299
29.01.1984??	Niddrie West Jn - Wanton Wells Jn	Sc(NBR)	G(All)	3300
10.02.1984 [9]	Beighton Jn - Westhorpe Colliery	E(GCR)	G(All)	3301
19.03.1984	Ryecroft Jn - Anglesea Sidings	LM(LNW)	G(All)	3302
25.03.1984 [3]	Stratford Western Jn - Stratford Southern Jn	E(GER)	G(All)	3303
01.04.1984 [5]	Attenborough Jn - Chilwell ROF	LM(LMS)	G(All)	3304
07.04.1984	Selhurst Jn - St.James Emergency Spur	S(LBSC)	P(All)	3305
00.05.1984??	Colnebrook LC - Staines West New Spur Jn	W(GWR)	G(All)	3306
07.05.1984 [2]?	Falsgrave SB - Scarborough Coal Depot	E(NER)	G(All)	3307
14.05.1984	Bedford Jn - BEDFORD (St Johns)	LM(LNW)	P	3308
14.05.1984	Streatham North Jn - Streatham South Jn Reversible Spur	S(LBSC)	P	3309
14.05.1984 [1]	Wortley South Jn - Wortley West Jn	E(GNR)	P(All)	3310
21.05.1984 [5]	Mickle Trafford Jn - Dee Marsh Jn	LM(CLC/GCR)	G(All)	3311
04.06.1984 [5]	Cudworth Station Jn - Stairfoot	E(Mid/BR/GCR)	G(All)	3312
09.06.1984 [1]?	Hotchley Hill - Ruddington MOD Depot	LM(GCR)	G(All)	3313
09.06.1984 [5]	Coxhoe Jn - Coxhoe Quarry	E(NER)	G(All)	3314
13.06.1984 [5]	Abbey Mills Jn - Plaistow & West Ham Coal Depot	E(GER)	G(All)	3315
29.07.1984 [5]	Elliot Jn - Metal Box Siding	Sc(D&AJt)	G(All)	3316
00.09.1984?	Clayton West Jn - Clayton West	E(L&Y)	G(All)	3317
09.09.1984	Penyffordd - Mold Synthite Sid.	LM(LNW)	G(All)	3318
23.09.1984	Blackwell South Jn - Blackwell East Jn	LM(Mid)	G(All)	3319
23.09.1984	Blackwell East Jn - Tibshelf & Blackwell Branch Jn	LM(Mid)	G(All)	3320
00.10.1984 [4]	Kirkcaldy - Kirkcaldy Harbour	Sc(NBR)	G(All)	3321
01.10.1984	Basford Hall Sorting Sidings - North Staffs Jn	LM(NSR)	G(All)	3322
21.10.1984 [5]	Paisley St.James - Linwood	Sc(Cal)	G(All)	3323
00.11.1984 [5]?	Scunthorpe West Jn - Dawes Lane SB	E(LNE)	G(All)	3324
10.11.1984	Hawkhead Shell OT - Elderslie No.1	Sc(GSW)	G(All)	3325
24.11.1984 [5]	Alloa West - Alloa Coop Siding	Sc(NBR)	G(All)	3326
27.11.1984	Hendon - Pallion Yard	E(NER)	G(All)	3327
27.11.1984	Pallion Yard - Deptford Johnson Siding	E(NER)	G(All)	3328
00.12.1984	Shell Jn - Teesport Refinery Reception Sids.	E(BRB)	G(All)	3329
17.12.1984	Denton Jn - OA&GB Jn	LM(LNW)	P	3330

Date	Line	Region (Company)	Type of Traffic	Reference Number
01.04.1985	Annbank Jn-Mauchline Jn	Sc(GSW)	G(All)	3331
12.05.1985	Boultham Crossing-Durham Ox Jn	E(Mid/GCR)	P	3332
12.05.1985	Boultham Crossing-Lincoln East Goods	E(Mid/GCR)	G(All)	3333
13.05.1985	St.Mary Cray Jn-Chislehurst Jn (Up Chatham Loop)	S(SEC)	P	3334
19.05.1985	Stafford Common-Stafford	LM(GNR)	G(All)	3335
00.06.1985 [9]	Wath Yard - Barrow Colliery	E(GCR)	G(All)	3336
22.06.1985	Langley Mill Sidings-Moor Green Colliery	LM(Mid)	G(All)	3337
08.07.1985	Skelton Jn-Latchford	LM(CLC/LNW)	G(All)	3338
08.07.1985	TUNBRIDGE WELLS [Grove Jn]-ERIDGE [Birchden Jn]	S(LBSC)	P(All)	3339
01.08.1985	Marton Jn-Southam & Long Itchington	LM(LNW)	G(All)	3340
01.08.1985	New Bilton-Marton Jn	LM(LNW)	G(All)	3341
12.08.1985	Tunbridge Wells West-Eridge Birchden Jn	S(LBSC)	Ecs(All)	3342
28.06.1985 [1]	Bowesfield - South Stockton Goods	E(NER)	G(All)	3343
08.07.1985	STRATFORD L.L. [Channelsea N.Jn] - TOTTENHAM HALE [Copper Mill Jn]	E(GER)	P	3344 *
00.00.1985 [9]	Machen Quarry?? - Bedwas Colliery	W(B&M)	G(All)	3345
31.08.1985 [1]	SHEFFIELD [Wath Road Jn] - YORK [Goose Hill Jn]	E(Mid)	P*	3346
01.09.1985 [5]	Metropolitian Jn - Southwark Depot	S(SEC)	Ecs(All)	3347
00.09.1985	Merehead Quarry Loop West Jn - Cranmore	W(GWR)	G(All)	3348
30.09.1985 [2]	Weymouth Jn - Weymouth Quay	S(W&PJt)	P*(All)	3349
00.10.1985 [9]	Killingworth Exchange Sidings - Brenkley Drift	E/BC	G(All)	3350
21.10.1985 [9]	Wath Central - Cortonwood Colliery	E(GCR)	G(All)	3351
21.10.1985 [9]	St Catherines Jn - Yorkshire Main Colliery	E(DVR)	P(All)	3352
00.11.1985 [9]	Llynfi Jn - St Johns Colliery	W(GWR)	G(All)	3353
00.12.1985 [9]	Tondu SB - Garw Colliery	W(GWR)	G(All)	3354
00.01.1986 [9]	Hickleton Main SB - Hickleton Main Colliery	E(S&KJt)	G(All)	3355
11.01.1986	Airdrie - Inverhouse Distillery Siding	Sc(NBR)	G(All)	3356
15.01.1986	Forks Jn - Rome Street Jn	LM(M&C)	G(All)	3357
15.01.1986	Rome Street Jn (Metal Box Sid.) - Caldew Jn	LM(CGCJt)	G(All)	3358
10.02.1986	Terminus Jn - General Terminus	Sc(Cal)	G(All)	3359
01.03.1986 [7]	Nottingham East Jn - Sneinton Jn (Goods Lines)	LM(Mid)	G(All)	3360
27.04.1986 [5]	Toton East Jn SF - Toton High Level Goods	LM(Mid)	G(All)	3361
10.05.1986	Cardonald North Jn - Shieldhall	Sc(G&PJt)	G(All)	3362
12.05.1986	Filton Jn - NORTH FILTON Platform	W(GWR)	W(Un)	3363
12.05.1986 [3]	Cresswell Jn - Cheadle	LM(NSR)	G(All)	3364
12.05.1986 [3]	Wath Road Jn - Goose Hill Jn	E(Mid)	P*	3365
25.05.1986 [5]	Auchinleck - Barony Colliery	Sc(GSW)	G(All)	3366
09.06.1986 [5]	Radley Jn - Abingdon	W(GWR)	G(All)	3367
18.06.1986	Porth SB - Maerdy Colliery	W(Taff)	G(All)	3368
20.06.1986	Easter Road Jn - Granton Gas Works	Sc(NBR)	G(All)	3369 *
21.06.1986	Abbeyhill Jn - Craigentinny Jn (via Lochend Jn)	Sc(NBR)	P	3370
28.06.1986	Cowlairs Jn - Port Dundas	Sc(NBR)	G(All)	3371
30.06.1986	Dalston Western Jn - BROAD STREET	LM(NLR)	P(All)	3372
17.07.1986 [9]	Benhar Jn - Polkemmet Colliery	Sc(Cal)	G(All)	3373
01.08.1986 [5?]	Thornhill Jn - Liversedge Oil terminal	E(L&Y/BRB)	G(All)	3374
03.08.1986	ARDROSSAN Harbour (New) - ARDROSSAN Harbour (Winton Pier) (Old)	Sc(GSW)	P(All)	3375
27.08.1986 [1]	Crigglestone Jn - Horbury Station Jn	E(L&Y)	P*	3376
30.08.1986	Greetland Jn - Milner Royd Jn	E(L&Y)	P*	3377
30.08.1986	Hare Park Jn - Wakefield Kirkgate Jn	E(WRJ/L&Y)	P*	3378
26.09.1986 [7?]	Bredbury Tilcon - Portwood Tilcon	LM(CLC)	G(All)	3379
27.09.1986 [1]	ROTHERHAM (Masborough) - CHESTERFIELD [Tapton Jn]	E(Mid)	P*	3380
27.09.1986 [1]	Bradley Wood Jn - Bradley Jn	E(L&Y)	P*	3381

Date	Line	Region (Company)	Type of Traffic	Reference Number
27.09.1986 [1]	Greetland Jn - Dryclough Jn	E(L&Y)	P*	3382
27.09.1986 [1]	Foxhall Jn - Didcot North Jn	W(GWR)	P*	3383
29.09.1986 [5]	Trowse Upper Jn - Norwich Victoria CCD	A(GER)	G(All)	3384
29.09.1986	BALLOCH (Central) - BALLOCH (Pier)	Sc(D&BJt)	P(All)	3385
00.10.1986 [9]	Cadeby Colliery Jn - Cadeby Colliery	E(GCR)	G(All)	3386
03.11.1986	Corkickle No.1 Siding - Corkickle Brake Incline Top	LM(Furn)	G(All)	3387
03.11.1986	Corkickle Brake Incline Top - Albright & Wilson	NCB	G(All)	3388
01.12.1986 [5]	Scotswood - Newburn	E(NER)	G(All)	3389
00.04.1987 [8]	St Peters (Shepherds Scrap Siding) - Carville (Swan Hunter Siding)	E(NER)	G(All)	3390
04.04.1987 [8]	Cardonald North Jn - Shieldhall King George Vth Dock	Sc(G&PJt)	G(All)	3391
11.04.1987 [1]	Walnut Tree Jn - Nantgarw Colliery	W(BRB)	G(All)	3392
16.04.1987 [1] ?	Bottesford West Jn - Newark South Jn	E(GNR)	G(All)	3393
09.05.1987	PENDLETON [Brindle Heath Jn] - CLIFTON [Agecroft Jn]	LM(L&Y)	P(All)	3394
01.06.1987	Wath Road Jn - Houghton Main Colliery	E(Mid)	G(All)	3395
01.06.1987	Oakenshaw South Jn - Goose Hill Jn	E(Mid)	G(All)	3396
01.06.1987 [8]	High Street Jn - Bridgeton Central Carriage Depot	Sc(NBR)	Ecs(All)	3397
23.06.1987 [8]	Hyndland Jn - Hyndland Depot	Sc(NBR)	Ecs(All)	3398
00.07.1987	Loughton Branch Jn - Temple Mills Yard (old alignment)	E(GER)	G(All)	3399
17.07.1987 [9]	Polmaise SB - Polmaise Colliery	Sc(Cal)	G(All)	3400
31.07.1987 [3]	Ashton Gate - Bristol Wapping Wharf	W(GWR)	G(All)	3401
26.09.1987	Moor Street - BIRMINGHAM (Moor Street)	LM(GWR)	P(All)	3402 *
03.10.1987 [5]	Whitehaven Bransty - Whitehaven Dock	LM(LNW)	G(All)	3403
07.10.1987 [9]	Neath & Brecon Jn - Aberpergwm Colliery	W(GWR)	G(All)	3404
10.10.1987	Sutton Oak Jn - Sutton Manor Colliery	LM(LNW)	G(All)	3405
11.10.1987 [5]	Gelderd Road Jn - Leeds West Jn	E(BRB/LNW)	P(All)	3406 *
31.12.1987 [3]	Shepherd's Well Siding - Tilmanstone Colliery	S(EKLt)	G(All)	3407
08.02.1988 [3]	Woodburn Jn - Sheffield Parkway Market	E(BRB)	G(All)	3408
13.03.1988 [3]	Bidston Dee Jn - Seacombe Jn	LM(Wirral)	G(All)	3409
13.03.1988	Seacombe Jn - Slopes Jn	LM(Wirral/MDH)	G(All)	3410
20.03.1988	Abbeyhill Jn - Craigentinny via Lochend Jn	Sc(NBR)	P	3411
21.03.1988 [10]	Bestwood Park Jn - Linby Station SB	LM(Mid)	G(All)	3412 *
26.03.1988 [3]	Shoreham by Sea - Beeding	S(LBSC)	G(All)	3413
31.03.1988 [8]	Riverside Jn - St Peters Shepherds Scrap Siding	E(NER)	G(All)	3414
25.04.1988	BALLOCH [New Station] - BALLOCH (Central) [Old Station]	Sc(D&BJt)	P(All)	3415
09.05.1988 [10]	Bradley Wood Jn - Bradley Jn	E(L&Y)	G(All)	3416
09.05.1988 [10]	Greetland Jn - Dryclough Jn	E(L&Y)	G(All)	3417
15.05.1988	Primrose Tunnel ML - Primrose Hill Station	LM(LNW)	P	3418
15.05.1988	Channelsea South Jn - Stratford ML Station	E(GER)	P	3419
16.05.1988	Wortley South Jn - Wortley West Jn	E(GNR)	P(All)	3420
05.06.1988 [5]	Dudley SB - Dudley FLT	LM(GWR)	G(All)	3421
29.06.1988 [1]	Hapsford GF - Radstock West	W(GWR)	G(All)	3422
09.07.1988	YORK (Burton Lane) - ROWNTREES HALT	E(NER)	W(Und)	3423
15.07.1988	Sutton Bridge (Severn Valley) Jn - Severn Valley Headshunt	LM(GWR)	G(All)	3424
15.07.1988	Severn Valley Headshunt - Shrewsbury Abbey (Bates & Hunts) Esso Sd	LM(BRB/S&M)	G(All)	3425
18.07.1988 [5]	Mexborough East Jn - Wath Central Jn	E(GCR)	G(All)	3426
18.07.1988 [5]	Wath Central Station Jn - Manvers Exchange Sidings	E(GCR)	G(All)	3427
24.07.1988 [5]	Arkwright Branch Jn - Arkwright Colliery	E(BRB/GCR)	G(All)	3428
00.08.1988 [9]	Silverdale Colliery - Holditch Colliery	LM(NSR)	G(All)	3429
19.08.1988 [5]	Far Cotton - Brackmills (Hammer Steel Siding)	LM(Mid)	G(All)	3430
30.08.1988	Leek Brook Jn - Oakamoor Sidings (BIS Sidings)	LM(NSR)	G(All)	3431
05.09.1988	Rochester Station - Rochester Common Headshunt	S(SEC)	G(All)	3432

Date	Line	Region (Company)	Type of Traffic	Reference Number
05.09.1988	Rochester Common Headshunt - Rochester Freight Depot (Furrells Rd. Whf	S(SEC)	G(All)	3433
09.09.1988 [5]	Sykes Jn - Torksey Shell OT	E(GCR)	G(All)	3434
01.10.1988	Trent East Jn - Toton Centre	LM(Mid)	P*	3435
15.10.1988 [1]	Trafford Park Jn - Gorton Jn	LM(CLC/GCR)	G(All)	3436
28.10.1988 [10]	Gobowen South GF - Blodwell Quarry	LM(GWR/Cam)	G(All)	3437
04.11.1988	Chessington South - Chessington Charringtons CD	S(SR)	G(All)	3438
31.12.1988	York Burton Lane SB - Layerthorpe (Wayahead Fuels Sid.)	E(NER/DVLR)	G(All)	3439
15.01.1989 [5]	Durham Ox Jn - Lincoln East Coal Concentration Depot	E(GCR)	G(All)	3440
20.01.1989	Dereham - North Elmham	A(GER)	G(All)	3441
27.01.1989	St Helens Junction - Leather's GF	LM(LNW)	G(All)	3442
03.02.1989 [8]	Wye Valley Jn - Tintern Quarry	W(GWR)	G(All)	3443
03.02.1989 [5]	Attercliffe Jn - Darnall West Jn	E(GCR)	G(All)	3444
09.02.1989 [1]	Stoke Jn - Leek Brook Jn	LM(NSR)	G(All)	3445
09.02.1989 [1]	Leek Brook Jn - Caldon Low Derbyshire Stone Quarry Sid	LM(N&S)	G(All)	3446
10.02.1989 [8]	Turnchapel Branch Jn - Plymstock Blue Circle Siding	W(LSW)	G(All)	3447
14.02.1989	EPSOM DOWNS (New) - EPSOM DOWNS (Old)	S(LSW)	P(All)	3448
19.02.1989	Springs Branch Jn - CWS Glassworks GF	LM(LNW)	G(All)	3449
19.02.1989	CWS Glassworks GF - CWS Glassworks	LM(LNW)	G(All)	3450
23.02.1989 [3]	Burton Lane SB - Foss Island	E(NER)	G(All)	3451
24.03.1989 [9]	Rufford Coal Stocking Site Jn - Blidworth Colliery	E(Mid)	G(All)	3452
24.03.1989 [9]	Rufford Jn - Mansfield Colliery	E(GCR)	G(All)	3453
27.03.1989 [10]	Llanelli West Jn - Cynheidre Colliery	W(L&MM)	G(All)	3454
31.03.1989	ABERYSTWYTH - RHEIDOL FALLS	LM(VOR)	P*(All)	3455 *
31.03.1989	Appleby Jn - Appleby North Headshunt	LM(Mid)	G(All)	3456
31.03.1989	Appleby North - Headshunt Warcop	LM(NER)	G(All)	3457
00.04.1989 [9]	Renishaw Park Jn - Renishaw Park Colliery	E(Mid)	G(All)	3458
24.04.1989	CREWE - CREWE WORKS Halt	LM(LNW)	W(Und)	3459
30.04.1989 [10]	Luton Midland Road South - Luton Bute St. Reversing Sid.	LM(BRB)	G(All)	3460
30.04.1989 [10]	Luton Bute St. Reversing Sid. - Dunstable	LM(GNR)	G(All)	3461
00.05.1989 [2]	Kingsbury Jn GF - Baddesley Colliery	LM(Mid)	G(All)	3462
00.05.1989 [10]	Millerhill Yard - Monktonhall Colliery	Sc(BRB)	G(All)	3463
05.06.1989 [10]	Millerhill Jn - Bilston Glen Colliery	Sc(NBR)	G(All)	3464
30.06.1989	Wymondham Jn - Dereham	A(GER)	G(All)	3465
25.08.1989 [1]	Goonbarrow Jn - Carbis Wharf	W(GWR)	G(All)	3466
25.08.1989 [9]	Sutton Colliery - Sutton Colliery	LM(Mid)	G(All)	3467
25.08.1989 [9]	Shirebrook MPD - Warsop Colliery	LM(Mid)	G(All)	3468
00.10.1989 [5]	Llantrisant - Cwm Llantwit	W(GWR/Taff)	G(All)	3469
01.11.1989	Black Lion Crossing - Merthyr Vale Colliery	W(Taff)	G(All)	3470
00.12.1989	Wednesbury SB - Ocker Hill PS	LM(LMS?)	G(All)	3471
00.12.1989 [5]	Rufford Coal Stocking Site Jn - Blidworth Colliery	E(Mid)	G(All)	3472
20.12.1989 [1]	Princes Risboro - Chinnor Cement Works	W(GWR)	G(All)	3473
31.12.1989 [3]	Goonbarrow Jn - Carbis Wharf	W(GWR)	G(All)	3474
00.01.1990 [5]	Nuneaton Abbey Jn - Judkins Siding	LM(A&NJt)	G(All)	3475
29.01.1990	Ludgate Hill Jn - HOLBORN VIADUCT	S(SEC)	P(All)	3476
00.03.1990	Wye Valley Jn GF - Tintern Quarry	W(GWR)	G(All)	3477
00.03.1990	Inverkeithing South Jn - Rosyth Dockyard	Sc(NBR)	G(All)	3478
00.03.1990 [5]	Bradford upon Avon North - Bradford upon Avon West	W(GWR)	G(All)	3479
17.03.1990	Aldwarke South Jn (GC) - Mexborough East Jn	E(GCR)	P	3480
17.03.1990	Aldwarke South Jn (Mid) - Aldwarke North Jn (GCR)	E(GCR)	P(All)	3481
00.04.1990 [7]	Benhar Jn - Polkemmet Colliery	Sc(Cal)	G(All)	3482
00.04.1990 [5]	Ladyburn Jn - James Watt Dock	Sc(Cal)	G(All)	3483

Date	Line	Region (Company)	Type of Traffic	Reference Number
12.04.1990 [3]	Wortley South Jn - Wortley West Jn	E(GNR)	P(All)	3484
00.05.1990	Rosehill Jn - BSC Imperial Tube Works	Sc(NBR)	G(All)	3485
28.05.1990	KETTERING [North Jn] - CORBY	LM(Mid)	P	3486
00.06.1990	Pantyfynnon - Wernos Washery	W(GWR)	G(All)	3487
00.07.1990 [5]	Low Fell Sidings - Bensham Jn	E(BR)	G(All)	3488
00.07.1990 [5]	Rufford Jn - Mansfield Colliery	E(GCR)	G(All)	3489
09.07.1990 [1]	Egglinton Jn - Mickleover	DRC(GNR)	T(All)	3490
00.09.1990 [9]	Castle Hills North Jn - Brodsworth Colliery	E(WRJt)	G(All)	3491
00.09.1990 [9]	Castle Hills South Jn - Castle Hills West Jn	E(BRB)	G(All)	3492
01.10.1990	NORMANTON [Altofts Jn] - WOODLESFORD [Methley Jn]	E(Mid)	P	3493
01.10.1990	NORTHALLERTON [High Jn] - EAGLESCLIFFE [South Jn]	E(NER)	P	3494
29.10.1990	North Pole Jn - Old Oak Common East Jn	W(GWR)	P(All)	3495
26.01.1991	Courtybella Jn - Newport Dock Street (Gwent CCD)	W(ASW)	G(All)	3496
04.02.1991 [5]	Crigglestone Jn - Horbury Station Jn	E(L&Y)	G(All)	3497
01.02.1991	Barrow Hill South Jn - Barrow Hill Loco Stabling Point	E(Mid)	L(All)	3498
25.02.1991	Fletton Jn - Fletton CEGB Fly Ash Disposal Point	E(BRB)	G(All)	3499
15.03.1991	Fishbourne Crossing - Lavant	S(LBSC)	G(All)	3500
01.04.1991	KEITH JN - DUFFTOWN	Sc(GNoSR)	P*(All)	3501
17.04.1991 [1]	Princes Risboro - Thame BP Oil Depot	W(GWR)	G(All)	3502
00.05.1991	MP29¾ - Westfield	Sc(BRB)	G(All)	3503
00.05.1991	UCKFIELD (New) - UCKFIELD (Old)	S(LBSC)	P(All)	3504
20.05.1991	Tursdale Jn - Wardley	E(NER)	G(All)	3505
25.06.1991 [1]	Clydebank Central Jn - Dalmuir Riverside (Chivas Regal Siding)	Sc(Cal)	G(All)	3506
15.07.1991	MANCHESTER (Victoria) - CRUMPSALL	LM(L&Y)	P(All)	3507 *
17.08.1991	CRUMPSALL - BURY Interchange	LM(L&Y)	P(All)	3508 *
14.09.1991 [5]	Helsby West Cheshire Jn - Mouldsworth Jn	LM(CLC)	G(All)	3509
31.09.1991 [1]	West Parade North Jn - Hessle Road Jn	E(BRB)	P(All)	3510
31.09.1991 [1]	Gascoigne Wood Jn - Milford Jn	E(NER)	P	3511
00.11.1991 [9]	Ryhope Grange Jn - Murton Colliery	E(NER)	G(All)	3512
15.11.1991 [1]	Netherfield East Jn - Gedling Colliery	LM(GNR)	G(All)	3513
06.12.1991 [2]	Dinnington Colliery SB - Thurcroft Colliery	E(GC&MidJt)	G(All)	3514
24.12.1991 [1]	MANCHESTER (Oxford Road) [Cornbrook Jn] - ALTRINCHAM [Deansgate Jn]	LM(MSAJ)	P	3515 *
24.12.1991	Cornbrook Jn - Deansgate Jn	LM(MSJA)	G(All)	3516

Ref. No.	Notes	Ref. No.	Notes
0104	Closed by flooding.	0236	Wartime spur last used 28.11.1946 reopened 23.02.1953 because of flooding.
0115	Line severed by flooding on 12.08.1948.	0256	A wartime spur not used for sometime.
0127	Line used by railtour 28.06.1952.	0258	Closed by flooding.
0149	Officially closed on 01.07.1951.	0264	Laymoor Jn - Drybrook Road used by military traffic until 16.06.1953.
0171	Down line restored on 11.11.1974 to serve W.Davis Wagon Works,Langwith.	0271	Part of line reinstated to serve CEGB Siding.
0181	Line used for filming of ⅝The Titfield Thunderbolt" in 1952.	0272	Traffic suspended since 08.08.1949.
0184	Officially closed on 01.07.1951.	0293	Line closed on opening of BR spur from Taff Wells to Nantgarw.
0185	Line used by railtour on 23.03.1957.	0300	Traffic ceased on 21.08.1948.
0192	Last train was a railtour.	0321	Blantyre to Peacock Cross served by BR spur from Cadzow (Cal).
0203	Part of line reopened to serve Shell and BP Oil refinery.	0314	Used by railtour 26.04.1958.
0210	Closed by flooding on 06.09.1950.	0323	Line only used by offical opening train of Calverton branch.
0216	Last train ran on 02.09.1939.	0332	Line reopened because of coastal flooding.

0346 Line closed after North Kent line reopened after flooding.
0349 Line closed by coastal flooding.
0351 Clifton Tunnel collapsed on 28.04.1953, during maintainence.
0353 Used by railtour on 12.09.1954.
0358 Only used by Military Traffic until closure.
0369 Most of line traversed by railtour on 05.01.1958.
0376 Used by engines turning on triangle for some years.
0411 Line reopened on 31.12.1956.
0422 Access to Bridgwater North retained over GWR Docks branch.
0442 Reopened to Themelthorpe on 12.09.1960 to gain acess to MGN.
0458 Last train on 28.05.1955 due to ASLEF dispute. Used by railtour 12.10.1957.
0459 Last train on 28.05.1955 due to ASLEF dispute.
0461 Last train on 28.05.1955 due to ASLEF dispute. Closure illegal due to a
       clause in Act of Parliament and reopened 07.08.1956.
0462 Last train on 28.08.1955 due to ASLEF dispute. Closure illegal due to a
       clause in Act of Parliament and reopened 07.08.1956.
0466 Line passed to MOD(Army) control. Closed by MOD on 31.07.1963.
0471 Bridge rebuilt to north of old alignment.
0478 Newbridge Jn(Bathgate Jn)-Bathgate reopened to passengers on 12.05.1986.
0482 Lydbrook Jn to Upper Lydbrook reopened on this day.
0507 Railtour used the line on 09.09.1956.
0519 Line reopened in sections by W&LLR Preservation Society.
0522 Line taken over by MOD(Navy) and closed by them on 16.04.1965.
0546 Last train ran 31.08.1957.
0552 Line moved onto new alignment and bridge to north of old line.
0561 Line previously illegally closed on 13.06.1955 and reopened on 07.08.1956.
0562 Line previously illegally closed on 13.06.1955 and reopened on 07.08.1956.
0565 Rose Bridge Jn GF to Kirklees Hall Jn reopened upon this closure.
0572 Alphington Road GF to Marsh Barton reopened on 07.07.1958.
0581 Reopened on 01.03.1965.
0591 Reopened to Passenger and goods traffic on 01.06.1966.
0612 Bullcroft Jn to near Thorpe Marsh Power Station reopened.
0653 Hensall Jn to Carlton reopened to serve Drax PS 28.02.1972.
0679 Reopened to passengers on 16.05.1983 when Nunnery Jn to Penistone closed.
0686 Line closed upon opening of BR spur from LNW line at Hemel Hempstead.
0714 Retained for Sugar Beet traffic and closed later.
0715 Sykes Jn to Torksey reopened to aircraft fuel trains on 31.01.1966.
       Clarborough Jn to Cottam PS reopened to coal trains in 1968.
0735 Ex MOD line. Used by SLS railtour 20.03.1960.
0745 Ex MOD line. Used by SLS railtour 20.03.1960.
0746 Ex MOD line. Used by SLS Railtour 20.03.1960.
0747 Ex MOD line. Used by SLS Railtour 20.03.1960.
0756 Line closed upon opening of BR spur to Abbey.
0759 Bus service substituted because of bad condition of Mapperley Tunnel.
0817 Severn Bridge hit by Ship and never reopened.
0824 Last train ran on 10.05.1960.
0827 Used by railtour 13.05.1961.
0828 Used by railtour 13.05.1961.
0829 Used by railtour 13.05.1961.
0830 Reopened in Second World War.
0839 Trawsfynydd to Blaenau Ffestinog reopened to goods on 24.04.1964.
0844 Part of line reopened 07.06.1971 to serve Container depot.
0853 Line severed by flood on 30.09.1960.
0865 Reopened in 1974 to connect to Nene Valley Railway. Used by a
       special passenger service fron Peterborough North.
0866 Partially reopened as part of Kent & East Sussex Rly Preservation Society.
0897 Part of line used as access to Shelton Steelworks.
0932 Part used by railtour on 05.05.1962.
0933 Part used by railtour on 05.05.1962.
0953 Reopened by Keighley and Worth Valley Railway on 29.06.1968.
0982 Reopened by Dart Valley Railway.
0990 Engineer declared track unfit, bus substituted for trains.

0991 BR Goods trains withdrawn, and line passed totally under LT control.
1000 Sennybridge to Brecon used by Military special 18.10.1962.
1023 Reopened on 07.09.1964.
1043 Line served by BR spur opened on 15.09.1952.
1054 Closed when Tynycaeau North SB burntdown.
1055 Closed when Tynycaeau North SB burntdown.
1066 Used by railtour on 18.05.1968.
1103 Used by railtour on 20.06.1964.
1143 Reopened on 07.01.1964.
1154 Used for stock transfer to Bluebell Railway
1180 Regular traffic ceased on 06.07.1959.
1190 The line between Brackley and Buckingham used on 16.02.1966.
1195 Bridgnorth to Alveley reopened by Severn Valley Railway.
1206 Line flooded on 05.12.1960.
1209 Used by Brakevan Special on 01.05.1965.
1232 West Drayton to Middlesex Chemical Works reopened 23.05.1966.
1252 Abercynon to Aberdare L.L. reopened on 02.10.1987.
1259 Reopened in March 1966 by Stewerts & Lloyds.
1298 BR goods ceased, and line taken totally under LT control.
1318 BR goods ceased on 04.05.1964, line taken totally under LT control.
1329 Penar Jn to Pontllanfraith reopened 20.11.1967.
1341 Used by special on 15.08.1964.
1377 The Lochty terminus end used by Lochty Private Railway.
1387 Taken over by NCB.
1396 Leicester to Burton on Trent to be reopened as the 'IVANHOE' line.
1412 Traffic diverted to GWR line and connecting spur.
1414 Using MSWJ and 1933 GWR spur.
1429 Partially used in a new route from Cudworth to Stairfoot opened 03.06.1967.
1443 Reopened by Welshpool & Llanfair Light Railway 15.07.1972.
1454 The 1961 spur from LNW retained access to Tanhouse Lane sidings.
1468 Strathclyde PTE have plans to reopen Coatbridge to Rutherglen to passengers.
1469 Rutherglen to Partick (NBR) reopened on 12.05.1980.
1482 Nottingham to Newstead to reopen in October 1993 and later onto Mansfield.
1484 Old Harecastle tunnel unable to be electrified so new line was built to west.
1498 Last train was a railtour on 04.03.1967.
1544 Retained for Mainline diversions until 1966?.
1547 Line flooded and offically should have closed on 22.02.1965.
1548 Line flooded and offically should have closed on 18.01.1965.
1559 Line between Sheringham and Holt has been reopened by North Norfolk Railway.
1565 Last train railtour on 23.01.1965. BR connection ceased on 14.06.1965.
1566 Line worked by BR but property of Dover Harbour Board.
1569 Bankfield retained and served over MDHB lines via Canada Dock.
1581 Leamington to Coventry reopened to passengers on 02.05.1977. Nuneaton
       to Coventry reopened to passengers on 11.05.1987.
1583 Lichfield City to Lichfield T.V. reopened to passenger services on 28.10.1988.
1584 Walsall to Hednesford reopened to passengers on 07.04.1989.
1589 Official closure date, line severed by flood on 14.12.1964.
1589 Reopened by Llangollen Steam Railway between Llangollen and Deeside.
1590 Official closure date, line severed by flood on 14.12.1964.
1592 Official closure date, line severed by flood on 14.12.1964.
1608 Dewsbury Railway Street Goods retained by new conection to ex L&Y line.
1611 Official date, line flooded on 14.12.1965.
1612 Official date, line flooded on 14.12.1965.
1622 Used by railtour to Burton Dassett on 24.04.1965.
1626 Last used by Railtour on 27.03.1965.
1630 The line between Swinton and Mexborough reopened on 17.03.1990.
1633 Reopened by North Yorkshire Moors Railway to Pickering.
1654 Reopened to all traffic 06.09.1965.
1655 This line to be relaid for diverted Newquay passenger service.
1656 New east facing curve in Tavistock Yard opened same day.
1677 The MOD(Navy) closed the line.
1708 Retained by engineers department until 06.02.1967.

1738 The Metro have plans to reinstate Bradford to Huddersfield local services.
1752 Keighley to site of Great Northern Jn reopened by KWVR on 29.06.1968.
1757 Goods line ran parallel to passenger line.
1761 Part of line relaid by Yorkshire Dales Railway betweem Embsay and Skibeden.
1765 Line transfered to NCB control.
1792 Reopened on 29.11.1965.
1807 Reopened on 24.01.1966.
1838 Last train ran on 27.05.1955 due to ASLEF dispute. Used by railtour 03.01.1965.
1866 Southern part used as part of Heaton Lodge flyunder.
1892 Reopened on 18.04.1966.
1918 Reopened as 07.09.1964.
1942 Reopened as part of diversion of trains from Leeds Central to Leeds City.
1948 Used by railtour on 30.04.1966.
1963 Wyre Dock Station renamed Fleetwood upon closure of original station.
1964 Thingley Jn to Bradford Jn South reopened to passengers on 12.05.1986.
2007 A passenger service Kettering to Corby was reinstated on 13.04.1987.
2059 Reopened and leased to Stewarts & Lloyds 02.10.1967.
2067 Duckmanton North Jn to Arkwright Colliery reopened on 02.03.1974.
2072 Rotherham Cent. to Aldwarke N.Jns reopened to passengers on 11.05.1987.
2076 Reopened on 07.06.1971 to serve Greenock Container Port.
2139 Reopened with spur off GN at Gelderd Road to Leeds City West 01.05.1967.
2156 Relaid rails over road to transfer stock into North Norfolk Railway.
2199 Used after DP2 accident at Thirsk on 01.08.1967.
2214 First 62 chains reopened to Coalfields Farm Opencast on 07.03.1976.
2216 Used by railtour on 02.09.1967.
2308 Yate to Thornbury reopened 03.07.1972.
2311 Headshunt at westend moved onto old formation.
2313 Water traffic to Hartington ceased 05.09.1967.
2315 Aberpergwm to Glyn Neath retained for runround until 31.08.1972.
2345 Reopened on 04.05.1970.
2364 New Mills S.Jn to Hazel Grove reopened to passenger trains from 11.05.1987.
2366 Reopened as far as Linacre Branch GF during 00.03.1968. Access to Langton
     Dock through North Mersey Dock.
2372 Reopened on 13.07.1974.
2378 Oxford and Bicester (London Road) reopened to passengers on 09.05.1987.
2380 The line reopened to express passenger services from 06.05.1974.
2385 It is planned to reinstate passenger services from Stirling to Alloa.
2399 The Gloucestershire Warwickshire Railway have reopened the line from
     Toddington to Winchcombe
2404 Passenger services were reinstated to Birmingham Snow Hill on 04.10.1987.
2411 Stafford Road Jn to Cannock Road Jn reopened on 06.10.1969.
2441 Depot retained by access by new spur from Poplar Central SB.
2446 Line retained to Derby Friargate by Derby Research Centre.
2463 Reopened on 12.08.1968.
2466 Line retained to Forth Bridge until bridge fixed open on 18.05.1970.
2477 Access to Metal Box Siding through Kirkby Colliery until 03.04.1972.
2547 Partially reopened by Yorkshire Dales Railway.
2553 Melton Jn to Edwalton retained as test track by Derby Research Centre.
2556 Aviemore to Boat of Garten reopened by Strathspey Railway.
2561 Lime Kiln Sidings to Penar Jn reopened on 04.05.1970.
2565 Hammersmith to Ironville Jn reopened by Midland Railway Trust.
2580 Used by engineers trains, until severed at Polegate on 08.09.1974.
2589 Highley to Alveley reopened by Severn Valley Railway on 12.04.1974.
2595 Line used by railtour on 10.05.1969.
2597 Lavender Line have reopened a section north of Isfield.
2607 Used by diverted Euston - Stranraer trains after 05.05.1975.
2611 Reopened to passenger trains on 13.05.1985 as part of Thameslink scheme.
2616 Cranmore to Mendip Vale taken over by East Somerset Railway.
2628 Braunstone Gate Goods retained and served by spur off Coalville Line.
2628 Nottingham to Ruddington closed when spur opened at Loughborough on
     08.04.1974. MLST have reopened Loughborough Central to Birstall.
2658 Colliery closed 08.06.1968, but used by railtour 07.09.1968.
2687 Line retained for use by Derby Research Centre.

2700 Official closing down ceremony.
2701 Official closing down ceremony.
2710 Premature closure on 27.12.1969 due to landslide.
2712 Line reopened to goods because of Britannia Bridge fire.
2713 Line taken over by Severn Valley Railway and reopened.
2742 Avonside Wharf served from GW at Lawrence Hill and opened on 02.02.1970.
2753 Used by special train on 05.07.1970.
2773 Blaengwynfy Tunnel shut on 26.02.1968, emergency bus service from Cymmer
     Afan to Treherbert. Bridgend to Maesteg to reopen in October 1992.
2796 Line used by LT to transfer stock from 04.05.1964.
2817 Bishops Lydeard and Minehead by reopened by West Somerset Railway.
     Access to BR through Taunton Cider Siding.
2837 Yate South Jn to Westerleigh reopened.
2841 Line closed by contruction of M62 motorway. Reopened 01.04.1974.
2847 Line transferred to MOD(Army).
2866 Line closed by building of Ashburton by-pass.
2870 Shackerstone to Market Bosworth reopened as Battlefield Line.
2882 Line used as far as site of New Tredegar Colliery on 14.10.1972.
2885 Used by BSC?.
2887 Line reopened from Swanage to Corfe Castle by Swanage Railway.
2889 Line closed when Britannia Bridge across Menai reopened.
2891 Used by special train on 22.07.1972.
2898 Line closed and 2 LC's eliminated in Kirkby in Ashfield. Two new spurs
     built and part GN line from Kirkby Summit reopened.
2912 Bury Bolton St to Rawtenstall reopened by East Lancashire Railway.
2930 Northern end of line reopened for M5 flyash trains.
2931 Used by BSC to move engines to Market Overton.
2966 Partially reopened to Alloa Coop Coal Siding.
2969 Line to Skillington Road Jn used by BSC.
2977 Line reopened by Gwilli Railway from Bronwydd Arms to Llwyfan Cerrig.
2988 Last special passenger train ran 03.11.1973.
3003 Reopened from Belvoir Jn to Casthorpe Jn on 17.05.1976.
3027 Line taken over by BR. Reopened 16.08.1976.
3033 Line taken over by BR. Reopened 16.08.1976.
3050 Line taken over by Dean Forest Railway.
3073 Line closed by accident.
3079 Closed for conversion to Tyne & Wear Metro. Parts retained for BR goods.
3108 Line taken over by Bo'ness Railway.
3114 Closed for conversion to Tyne & Wear Metro.
3147 Closed for conversion to Tyne & Wear Metro.
3161 Diverted to Gospel Oak and reopened line to passenger trains.
3184 Closed for conversion to Tyne & Wear Metro. Single BR goods line retained.
3190 Closure of Humber Ferry service diverted trains to Barton on Humber.
3217 Reopened by Severn Valley Railway.
3243 Still retained with limited Summer service.
3252 Reopened between Shields Jn and new Paisley Canal terminus on 30.07.1990.
3344 Line reopened to passengers from 11.05.1987.
3354 Line reopened to Pontycymmer on 23.09.1991.
3369 Reopened to goods traffic from Piershill Jn to Powderhall on 29.10.1990.
3402 Passenger trains diverted into reopened Birmingham Snow Hill.
3406 Line closed to passengers without proper legal sanction.
3412 To reopen in October 1993 as Stage 1 of 'ROBIN HOOD' line project.
3455 Line sold to Brecon Mountain Railway.
3494 InterCity commenced running one train in October 1991.
3495 All traffic diverted via West London Jn and Acton Wells Jn.
3507 Line closed to be converted for Metrolink trams.
3508 Line closed to be converted for Metrolink trams.
3515 Line closed to be converted for Metrolink trams.

◄ 55207 on two coach Connel Ferry to Ballachulish on 25th June 1960, having just crossed the unique road rail Connel Ferry Bridge. The line succumbed to closure on 29th March 1966. (*J.L.Stevenson*)

◄▼ 45389 63A belchs smoke and steam into the eves of Edinburgh Princes Street Station having just backed onto Stirling train on 20th February 1960. The last trains were diverted to Waverley station on 6th September 1965(*J.L.Stevenson*)

▼A Y9 saddle tank 68123 trundles along the ex NBR Langloan branch with a single wagon on 18.06.1959. (*J.L.Stevenson*)